Academic Cultures

ACADEMIC CULTURES

Professional Preparation and the Teaching Life

EDITED BY SEAN P. MURPHY

The Modern Language Association of America
New York   2008

For information about obtaining permission to reprint material from
MLA book publications, send your request by mail (see address below),
e-mail (permissions@mla.org), or fax (646 458-0030).

LIBRARY OF CONGRESS CATALOGING-IN-PUBLICATION DATA
Academic cultures : professional preparation and the teaching life /
edited by Sean P. Murphy.
p. cm.
Includes bibliographical references and index.
ISBN 978-1-60329-000-5 (hardcover : alk. paper)
ISBN 978-1-60329-001-2 (pbk. : alk. paper)
1. College teachers—United States.   2. College teaching—Vocational
guidance—United States.   3. Corporate culture—United States.
I. Murphy, Sean P., 1970–
LB2331.72.A246 2008
378.1'25—dc22   2008022969

Published by The Modern Language Association of America
26 Broadway, New York, New York 10004-1789
www.mla.org

for Sandria Rodriguez
teacher, scholar, friend

Contents

II. Reflections on Careers at Teaching-Intensive Colleges

III. Preparing Future Faculty Members

Sean P. Murphy

INTRODUCTION

For better or for worse, the goal of securing tenure-track assistant professorships frames the graduate school experience for most students. When this goal meets with the realities of the well-documented job crisis, many job seekers wisely adopt a multisector application strategy, learning more about the academic cultures of the more than four thousand American institutions of higher learning. Even when PhDs apply widely for assistant professorships, with or without foreknowledge of institutions' particular cultures, only some candidates get on the tenure track. Since the profession defines *success* as an assistant professorship, often at a certain type of college, job seekers off the tenure track (the majority) learn coping skills, while their successful peers (the minority) learn unwritten codes of the professoriat. Both scenarios cultivate humility in new PhDs.

Aspirants to and members of the profession, however, can eschew some measure of humility when it comes to the processes of learning, given their tremendous investments in the life of the mind. I and others know learning often involves loss, at least initially. No exception to this phenomenon, new foreign language and English PhDs in tenure-track positions must learn to practice the role of assistant professor, often at institutions whose cultures do not mirror those of PhD-granting universities. While candidates who are off the tenure track persist in the wake of one type of loss, some of those now on the tenure track feel another sort of professional loss. Assistant professors may see their place in the profession as standing in contradistinction to an idealized version of professorships with which they approached a career in academe. Once the elation of securing a tenure-track appointment gives way to moderation, the same fortunate minority who emerge from a hostile labor situation with success becomes unfortunate. New assistant professors now cope with a second job crisis, one involving cross-sector transitions from research-intensive universities to teaching-intensive colleges.

My move from a research university to a community college, the resulting struggle with our profession's narrow definition of success, and my subsequent work with graduate students who visit my college all inspired *Academic Cultures: Professional Preparation and the Teaching Life*. The contributors to this book disclose to readers the details and outcomes of their cross-sector transitions. As active teacher-scholars, they consider it their good fortune to have traveled between and among diverse academic cultures, from graduate school to tenure-track positions, despite challenges associated with linking their individual college ethos to the broad imagined community of academe.

The essays in this volume aim to further professional dialogue on the subject of diversity in American higher education. Graduate students, administrators, and faculty members from research universities—the places primarily responsible for preparing future academics—will discover ways faculty members from a range of institutions build rewarding professional lives rooted in traditional components of the professoriat—teaching, service, and scholarship. Other audiences who engage this text will see a picture of contemporary higher education that documents the system's complexity. They might also note a fundamental paradox of academe: no discipline can adequately theorize or clarify the intricate structure of American higher education, even as all disciplines operate in it.

"DIVERSITY WITH DIGNITY"

Discussions of future English and foreign language faculties should consider the academic cultures in which professors establish satisfying careers. As such, this volume relies on practitioners in those cultures to provide rich but informal ethnographies of their academic settings for those of us inhabiting different academic cultures (tribal colleges; community colleges of all sorts—public, private, urban, rural, suburban, proprietary, with some four-year degrees—art schools; baccalaureate colleges; master's colleges and universities; and research institutions). If faculty members and administrators from all sectors of higher education communicated more systematically across academic borders to express distinctive features of their institutions, we might progress toward Ernest Boyer's goal of *"diversity with dignity* in American higher education" (64). Despite the established hierarchy of institutions composing the "diversity" Boyer mentions, humanists carry their varied professional identities to departments and classrooms, working to ensure, in the process, the centrality of student-faculty interaction to the collegiate experience.

Inquiry into humanists' professional identities is not new, of course, and organizations representing the entire profession initiate and sustain productive exchanges on the subject. My colleagues on the MLA Ad Hoc Committee on the Professionalization of PhDs have unequivocally advocated a shift from exclusive to inclusive language in discourses about careers inside and outside higher education, asserting that "many PhDs begin to explore the full range of employment opportunities available to them only after they have been unable to find a suitable academic position. As a consequence, that decision is usually experienced as one of defeat and personal failure" (191). Later in the report, readers learn that this sense of defeat and failure is not restricted to PhDs who decide to leave the academy to work in the business, government, or not-for-profit (BGN) sector: "A number of recently hired people spoke to committee members about the sense of failure they were made to feel by their dissertation supervisors (from PhD-granting institutions) when they accepted a position at another type of school" (196). Dissertation directors know the research-university culture well, so we must avoid blaming them for lacking comprehensive (experiential, preferably) knowledge of all types of colleges and instead explore notions of success and failure in the light of our profession's devaluation of what I'll call higher education cosmopolitanism. Foreign language and English graduate programs generally foster academic provincialism.

If we shift assigning the origin of career failure from dissertation directors to the academic culture at large, as the graduate career counselors Megan Pincus Kajitani and Rebecca Bryant do, the destructive effects of institutional isolation prompts academics in multiple sectors of academe to share the responsibility of preparing future faculty members:

> Failure, says academic culture, is anything other than achieving the ultimate goal of a tenure-track professorship. More specifically, the epitome of success is a tenure-track job at a major research university. You're still successful, albeit to a lesser degree, if that job is at a liberal-arts college, and even less so if it's at a community college. But a nonacademic career, well, that's just unacceptable.   (par. 4)

Why not broaden notions of success to include considerations of the social impact of an institution or the extent to which a work life fulfills professors or the nature of a match between the talents of PhDs and the needs of certain colleges or universities? If foreign language or English doctoral candidates aspire to teach at colleges that demonstrably affect the fabric of a community through strong undergraduate teaching and advising, they should receive encouragement from advisers. In short, what the graduate experience boasts in scholarly training it often lacks in institutional training—that is, in guiding future faculty members to see and experience positively the wide variety of professional identities rooted in assorted academic cultures. If it did so guide graduate students, we would enable them to form their career aspiration only after being educated about the places advertising their assistant professorships each year in the MLA's *Job Information List*.

While many graduate students regard life at anything other than Carnegie-classified research institutions as a mark of intellectual inferiority or occupational failure, the faculty members who contribute to this collection, and many outside of it (see, e.g., Hall, "Professional Life" and *Professions*; Lindenberger, "Must We" and "Utopian and Realist"; Zimmerman), specify the positive rewards of careers at teaching-intensive colleges. Most of them would agree that narrow definitions of career success limit professors' self-definitions and their potential as public intellectuals, that is, as societal forces. Humanists may have devoted too little attention to the relations among the profession, higher education, and society. As Vladimir Lenin notes, "One cannot live in society and be free from society" (48). Demands from external stakeholders for accountability in the professoriat make active teacher-scholars a necessity for the future of the humanities. In this regard, junior faculty members can take solace in knowing that the life of the mind finds nourishment across higher education in teaching, service, research, and public outreach; they must live in society.

Perceptions of failure combined with misconceptions about teaching-intensive colleges might prevent new assistant professors from growing where they're planted, to borrow from the title of Lynnell Edwards's contribution to this volume. The most common mistaken belief new faculty members import from graduate school to teaching-intensive positions relates to the claim that heavy teaching and service responsibilities foreclose anyone from conducting research. Although effective teaching demands both time and effort, which can crowd the intellectual space needed for reflection, fear of a dearth of research possibilities for the teaching-college professoriat seems, in part, a problem of definition. Boyer's *Scholarship Reconsidered: Priorities of the Professoriate* broadens definitions of *research* and *scholarship* to include classroom-based study, thus paving the way for similar redefinitions of *service* and *teaching* (see Marek). Evidence of the impact of Boyer's proposition consists in the success of academic journals devoted to college teaching such as *Pedagogy* and the *Journal of Excellence in College Teaching*, as well as of popular MLA book series such as Approaches to Teaching World Literature, Options for Teaching, and Teaching Languages, Literatures, and Cultures. Regional and national conferences about pedagogy also invigorate the scholarship of teaching (the annual Lilly Conference on College Teaching has been meeting since 1980). The concerted efforts of publishers, national initiatives such as the Pew Charitable Trust's Preparing Future Faculty program, and amended graduate curricula have contributed to a richer understanding of the day-to-day business of all foreign language and English departments, irrespective of level.

Opportunities to conduct classroom-based research abound in teaching-intensive colleges, and creative professors can explore the intersections of theory from graduate school and practice as instructors. They can teach in ways that both improve undergraduate learning and concretize modes of humanist analysis. In 1990 Boyer found that "more than 60 percent of today's faculty feel that teaching effectiveness, not publication, should be the *primary* criterion for promotion" (29). Somewhat surprisingly, Boyer's sixty percent includes professors from research institutions who seek to raise the status of teaching excellence in promotion guidelines: "While professors at two-year colleges feel most strongly about this, we found that 21 percent of those at *research* universities also support the proposition" (31). With faculty members from across higher education focusing attention on teaching effectiveness, logic dictates a need for research pertaining to it. Since the publication of Boyer's work there has been increased cross-cultural and cross-institutional conversation with regard to best practices in undergraduate teaching, dialogue that legitimizes the relationships between professing and learning or instructors and students as rich areas of study. In the process of articulating their investments in pedagogy, academicians from all Carnegie classifications may also explore connections between professional identity and their particular academic culture, even if teaching effectiveness is not the primary criterion for promotion or tenure in that culture.

Discussions of faculty roles as teachers and scholars are far from complete, though, if they do not entertain the role of service to colleges or universities through committee work, advising, peer evaluation, hiring, and the like. Service has assumed greater value for all ranks since it affirms the principle and practice of shared governance in higher education. Even so, Kelly Ward observes in *Faculty Service Roles and the Scholarship of Engagement* a persistent negativity about service duties: "Too often, service, in its myriad forms, is viewed as mindless activity unrelated to the real work of the university" (111). If newer faculty members shirk service obligations at their teaching-intensive colleges—if they hold fast to the view that service degrades rather than enhances teaching, scholarship, and the faculty voice in decisions affecting the direction of their college—they will likely experience their assistant professor years as burdens instead of as opportunities. Teaching-intensive colleges, especially smaller ones, depend on professors who willingly serve departments and colleges by striving to be well-rounded academic citizens.

Senior professors from teaching-intensive schools name service as a core academic principle. Since pedagogical decisions should remain the prerogative of faculty members, service work local to one college can be viewed as service to the profession, in that committees related to curriculum and instruction stay in faculty hands. Donald E. Hall advises assistant professors to "[r]emember that careers are always local even if they have national implications or aspects" ("Professional Life" 198). From the outset of their careers, novice instructors assess the national importance of teaching, research, and service relative to their local practice with students and colleagues.

The Teaching Life

A contributor to this volume, Ginny Carney is an academician who tirelessly serves her community and its students while articulating to national audiences the tribal college movement history and its future prospects. The interdisciplinary nature of American Indian epistemologies contrasts the discipline-based intellectual architecture of most colleges. Noting the change from disciplinarity to interdisciplinarity in graduate school (a change, I might add, that tribal colleges can aid), Chris M. Golde and Timothy M. Dore explain in their report *At Cross Purposes* that 61.2% of respondents to *The Survey on Doctoral Education and Career Preparation* "reported a strong interest in collaborating across disciplinary lines" (13). Community colleges, like tribal colleges, often encourage and reward interdisciplinary team teaching and learning communities. While most graduate students hope to conduct interdisciplinary work, "only 3.9% [has] a preference for a community college position" (10). Thus most covet interdisciplinary opportunities and avoid the teaching-intensive colleges where these opportunities await. The essays by Ellen Cohen, Deborah Gill, and Jo Ann Buck and MacGregor Frank will help academicians understand the work available to teacher-scholars in two-year colleges. Other authors speak to the valuable contributions teacher-scholars make to colleges and universities (and in one case a high school) from all the Carnegie classifications.

Academic Cultures: Professional Preparation and the Teaching Life gives voice to diversity in postsecondary education, a strength of the system rather than a problem to redress. Whether working at a private high school or a public comprehensive university, an open-access institution or a religiously affiliated college, contributors collectively reveal the ironic multiplicity of careers that grows from the standardization of graduate school. From one degree comes many exciting job possibilities, even if the market remains unsettled for English and foreign language professors.

Indeed, the available data concerning job placement for foreign language and English PhDs confirm two patterns, one troubling, the other encouraging: the job crisis continues, as too few PhDs find full-time tenure-track positions after their doctoral course of study, and the placement of PhDs who secure tenure-track professorships occurs at research institutions in large numbers relative to their share of higher education institutions overall. Of the 4,382 schools counted in the Carnegie Foundation for the Advancement of Teaching classification system, only 278 fall under the research universities category, leaving professional opportunities for candidates at 4,104 associate's colleges, master's colleges and universities, baccalaureate colleges, special focus institutions, tribal colleges, and other institutions.

As employment trends since 1980 attest, the landscape of higher education has changed, giving rise to the questions that frame this volume's essays:

1. How can PhD programs in English and foreign languages help prepare some graduate students for careers in teaching-intensive institutions?
2. What is the cultural work of the humanities faculty?
3. Indeed, what is culture, and how do we practice its definitions in the microcultures of, and micronarratives about, academe?
4. Given the vast body of theory concerning the postmodern condition, should academics rely on master narratives of the professoriat for professional identity or craft more diverse, contingent, culturally relevant narratives of their work as intellectuals?

Whether readers attend graduate school, teach graduate students, administer graduate programs, labor on the job market, or work in a tenure-track position, this volume will inform them about practitioners in sectors of higher education whose professional lives are often narrated, defined, and judged by people outside those sectors. In *Academic Cultures*, insiders encourage positive professional identity formation by writing narratives of their work lives. If we read closely, I am sure we will find in these essays reflections of our own commitments to the academy's deepest values.

WORKS CITED

Boyer, Ernest L. *Scholarship Reconsidered: Priorities of the Professoriate.* 1990. San Francisco: Jossey-Bass, 1997.

"The Carnegie Classification of Institutions of Higher Education." *Carnegie Foundation for the Advancement of Teaching.* 2005. 11 June 2007 <http://www.carnegiefoundation.org/classifications/>.

Golde, Chris M., and Timothy M. Dore. *At Cross Purposes: What the Experiences of Today's Doctoral Students Reveal about Doctoral Education.* Philadelphia: Pew Charitable Trusts, 2001.

Hall, Donald E. "Professional Life (and Death) under a Four-Four Teaching Load." *Profession 1999.* New York: MLA, 1999. 193–203.

———, ed. *Professions: Conversations on the Future of Literary and Cultural Studies.* Urbana: U of Illinois P, 2001.

Kajitani, Megan Pincus, and Rebecca A. Bryant. "A Ph.D. and a Failure." *Chronicle of Higher Education* 24 Mar. 2005. 11 June 2007 <http://chronicle.com/jobs/2005/03/2005032401c.htm>.

Lenin, Vladimir Ilich. "Party Organisation and Party Literature." 1905. *Collected Works, Volume 10: November 1905–June 1906.* Trans. Clemens Dutt. Moscow: Foreign Lang., 1962. 44–49.

Lindenberger, Herbert. "Must We Always Be in Crisis?" *ADFL Bulletin* 29.2 (1998): 5–9.

———. "Utopian or Realist: Some Ways of Responding to the Report of the Committee on Professional Employment." *ADE Bulletin* 121 (1998): 5–8.

Marek, Jayne E. "Scholarship Reconsidered: Ten Years After and the Small College." *Profession 2003.* New York: MLA, 2003. 44–54.

MLA Ad Hoc Committee on the Professionalization of PhDs. "Professionalization in Perspective." *Profession 2002.* New York: MLA, 2002. 187–210.

Ward, Kelly. *Faculty Service Roles and the Scholarship of Engagement.* ASHE-ERIC Higher Education Report 29.5 (2003).

Zimmerman, Bonnie. "The Past in Our Present: Theorizing the Activist Project of Women's Studies." *Women's Studies on Its Own: A Next Wave Reader in Institutional Change.* Ed. Robyn Wiegman. Durham: Duke UP, 2002. 183–90.

Part I

ACADEMIC CAREER OPTIONS

GINNY CARNEY

TRIBAL COLLEGE TEACHING
A Covert Option for Graduate Students

*Intellectuals have an obligation to be as smart as we can
possibly be, but we have an even greater obligation to be
good with the smarts we possess.*
— *Michael Eric Dyson* —

Sunbeams play across a table where four Anishinaabekwe (Ojibwe women) sit reading Winona LaDuke's historical novel *Last Standing Woman.* The women, ranging from nineteen to sixty-four, have arrived early for their class in contemporary American Indian literature at the Leech Lake Tribal College, in northern Minnesota. Outside, the temperature is thirty-five below, and already I have received calls from several students who report that they will be late to class (or absent) because of frozen water pipes, broken furnaces, or transportation problems. As class time approaches, other students begin to trickle in, including a young man who hopes to become a conservation officer, an eighty-three-year-old grandmother who has returned to school after raising fourteen children and numerous grandchildren, a middle-aged man who began his college education after a near-death experience with alcohol, a teenage mother with an infant in her arms and a toddler in tow, and a single father who is preparing for a career as a high school football coach. All are Anishinaabe, and each of them is a sterling blend of resilience, vision, and perseverance.

As I greet my students, I am impressed, as always, by their enthusiasm for learning and by the respect they show one another as well as their professors. Because my own cultural heritage (Cherokee and Appalachian) is, in many respects, similar to that of my Ojibwe students, I am at ease in a tribal college setting. Yet when I reflect back on my doctoral studies at a state university, I cannot recall a single mention of tribal colleges in any of my classes, and I am concerned about the dearth of PhDs applying for positions at these institutions today.

The paucity of PhD holders among tribal college teachers, however, can hardly be blamed on university professors who may be only vaguely familiar with the relatively new phenomenon known as the tribal college movement.[1] In addition, most of the thirty-five tribally chartered colleges in the United States are located west of the Mississippi River—and in only a dozen or so states—so it is not surprising that many American professors and graduate students know little about the opportunities available at such institutions. Hence my purpose here is to provide a brief overview of American Indian tribal colleges, explore some of the advantages and disadvantages of becoming a tribal college employee, and suggest ways of preparing graduate students who wish to teach or become administrators in these schools.

What Is a Tribal College?

Tribal colleges directly respond to the need for higher education among American Indians, especially in geographically isolated regions that make it difficult for students to attend mainstream colleges. Emphasizing both academic excellence and the infusion of cultural teachings and practices in all their classes, most tribal colleges are located on Indian reservations, where high unemployment rates, low per-capita income levels, and appalling educational attrition rates persist. On the 603,000-acre Leech Lake Reservation where I teach, the tribe owns only 2.1% of the land, almost one-third of the resident 3,800 Anishinaabe people are unemployed, the per-capita income is less than $5,000 annually, just 74% of the Native population are high school graduates, and a mere 4.1% hold a bachelor's degree or higher (United States Census Bureau).

Chartered and controlled by their tribes and locally managed, most tribal colleges enjoy full accreditation by regional accrediting agencies, and most are two-year institutions, offering associate's degrees or certification in a variety of professions. Several tribal colleges, however, offer bachelor's degrees, and two offer master's degrees. According to a recent American Indian Higher Education Consortium (AIHEC) report, tribal colleges share basic commonalities: most are less than twenty-five years old; most have relatively small, predominantly American Indian student bodies; most are located on remote reservations, all have open-admissions policies; and all began as two-year institutions (A-3).

The Joys and Sorrows of Working in a Tribal College

Academics keep alive a common misconception that those who choose to work in community colleges and tribal colleges must have been unable to secure positions at "real" colleges. I, for one, dreamed of teaching at a tribal college long before enrolling in a PhD program at fifty-two, yet I find that the mention of my affiliation at conferences and workshops often elicits sympathetic looks and words from my colleagues who teach in four-year institutions. One of my former graduate school professors, on learning of my affiliation with Leech Lake Tribal College, went so far as to deduce that I must have failed to complete my PhD requirements.

Having held teaching positions in several state universities—all deeply fulfilling and enjoyable assignments—I am keenly aware of the need for dedicated professors at both two-year and four-year colleges. On the other hand, I agree with Michael Eric Dyson:

> [Scholars must] look beyond a comfortable career, a safe niche behind academe's protective walls, and a serene existence removed from cultural and political battles that shape the nation's fate. . . . [I]ntellectuals must at some point get our hands dirty as we help our world become more just.

While I am not suggesting that everyone on the job market should consider teaching at a tribal college, I do believe that many new graduates would find such a career both educational and richly rewarding. I would further argue that any PhD—Native or non-Native—who hopes to teach American Indian studies should spend at least one year teaching in the tribal college setting before launching his or her career in a mainstream college or university. Before moving to a reservation or applying for a tribal college position, however, one should be prepared for the possibility of culture shock and temporary outsider status; geographic isolation from family and friends; housing shortages; comparatively low salaries; harsh climates; inadequate classroom space and poorly structured buildings; high attrition rates among students; limited library resources and research materials; and high rates of suicide, alcoholism, and domestic abuse in the community. As noted in a recent *Tribal College Journal* editorial:

> Outsiders looking at such negative aspects usually feel the situation is hopeless. The poverty rate in reservation areas is 60.3%, three times the national average. Onlookers may know that poverty goes hand in hand with self-destructive behavior, and they may know something about the historic trauma suffered by Indian people. Understanding such causes, however, does not ease the feelings of despair. They might believe that the students would be better off if they left their family, community, and culture, and assimilated into the mainstream.   (Ambler 8)

Negative perceptions of reservation life, a reliance on unquestioned stereotypes and hasty generalizations about American Indians, as well as a simplistic view of systemic problems endemic to reservations conspire to dissuade those just entering the teaching profession from even considering tribal college teaching positions, but elitist attitudes about teaching play a significant role, too. Kathleen McCormick, professor of literature and pedagogy at Purchase College, in New York, contends that the reluctance of many university professors to teach lower-division courses, for instance, sends a clear message to graduate students "that the more work teaching takes, the less valuable it is" (122).

Although teaching at a tribal college requires hard work, it provides the most exciting and gratifying challenges a teacher can experience. In my Native literature classes, for example, I relish the pleasure of teaching students who not only read assigned novels, poems, short stories, and nonfiction works themselves but also share this literature with others in the community: their children, grandparents, relatives in prison or detention centers, or neighbors who just love to read. It is not unusual either for one of the elders to visit a class or for preschool children to sit quietly through a ninety-minute class, listening intently to a lively discussion. Films based on American Indian novels—such as *House Made of Dawn*, *Grand Avenue*, or *Smoke Signals*—often attract friends and family members of tribal college students, providing a perfect forum for discussing community strengths and weaknesses and for strategizing solutions to persistent troubles.

American Indian students rarely have the benefit of such learning experiences in any other academic setting, and their enthusiasm is palpable. Equally exhilarating for a tribal college teacher, though, is the experience of watching the non-Native students—most of whom have never before found themselves a minority in the classroom—develop an understanding of and appreciation for Native people. Bryan, a young man who completed the law enforcement program at Leech Lake Tribal College, grew up in an all-white border town, where stereotypes of drunken, violent Indians were instilled in him at an early age.[2] Those negative images were quickly dispelled when Bryan came in contact with intelligent, sober, hardworking Native students at our college, and today he uses the knowledge he gained in a tribal college to combat negative attitudes and bigotry among his fellow police officers.

Students like Bryan move through traditional academic programs such as criminal justice by accumulating college credits, but they also encounter a unique worldview absent from traditional college settings. According to the Anishinaabe worldview, human beings did not weave the web of life but are merely strands in it. Whatever we do to the web, we do to ourselves. Therefore, kinship among all creation, not the mastery of our relatives (other human beings, animals, plants, and so on), is vital to harmonious living. Anishinaabe philosophy and culture, of course, permeate every aspect of the daily operation of Leech Lake Tribal College and infuse our classrooms in numerous ways. Our students are encouraged to express their ideas, ask questions, and listen respectfully to both their fellow students and their instructors; Ojibwe materials, including books, films, treaty documents, maps, arts and crafts, song and dance, and oral histories, are used in class; local elders and other speakers share their life stories, cultural skills, and wisdom with students; and the Ojibwe language is used both as a language of instruction for faculty and staff members and students and as a supplement to discourses in each of our classes.

Paramount, then, on my personal list of tribal college teaching rewards is the opportunity to learn from my students as well as from the community at large. Other bonuses include working with a team of administrators and faculty and staff members who share a common vision; teaching small classes and the ability to provide personalized attention to students; enjoying an opportunity to learn a new culture by immersion; securing faculty development grants and travel to conferences and workshops; and receiving the love and support of the Anishinaabe community. Since I am currently living almost twelve hundred miles from my nearest blood relative, the love and support of the Anishinaabe community play an especially important role in my job satisfaction at Leech Lake Tribal College. "Family" status, however, must be earned in a Native community—a topic I address more explicitly later in this essay.

Preparing Graduate Students to Teach in a Tribal College

Graduate school professors play a crucial role in shaping their students' perceptions of the teaching profession. It is both unrealistic and unfair, therefore, to imply that lucrative, tenure-track positions in prestigious universities are the profession; yet, as James Knapp points out, "For many graduate students and new faculty members, the entitlements of the most privileged members of the profession have become a part of their imaginary" (qtd. in McCormick 122). As demoralizing as it may be for those who fail to obtain such an appointment, many bright young scholars stridently resist settling for "second best," which is how they see teaching in two-year colleges (McCormick 120).

Those who do consider tribal college teaching deserve an opportunity to learn about tribal schools during their graduate courses of study, and I suggest focusing on three key groups of future faculty members: students who aspire to teach in "Indian country"; non-Native students who express a special interest in American Indian literature or Native studies programs; and American Indian or Alaska Native students.

Let us consider first those graduate students who hope to teach in a college or university located in western states populated by American Indians—states such as Arizona, Montana, New Mexico, or South Dakota, to name a few. Many new faculty members have interacted throughout their college careers with international students as well as with students representing virtually every ethnic group residing in the United States, yet few have had any opportunities to become acquainted with an American Indian student. Has graduate school prepared the average PhD to teach students whose entire worldview may contrast significantly with his or her own? Do the average graduate students feel competent in selecting textbooks that do not disparage American Indians or perpetuate stereotypical images of them? Will new faculty members' own preconceptions of Indians lead to frequent misunderstandings and personal offenses in the classroom?[3] Educators—Native as well as non-Native—often approach Indian communities with a messianic complex (a compulsion to save or heal the community) that only alienates them from their students. Consequently, they may experience chronic loneliness, feel unappreciated and misunderstood, or, worse, develop a superior attitude toward their colleagues who are accepted in the community. While it may not be the duty of graduate school professors to teach students the art of fitting in or the complexities of collegiality, refusing to augment any budding sense of elitism in them will prove invaluable should they choose to teach in a tribal college.

Daniel Wildcat contends:

> After all, most of what we know is *not* a result of explicit pedagogy or teaching; it is learned through living. Many human beings seem so caught up in their machines and technology that they have forgotten or lost the very real sense of what it means to live: to make choices that enrich life, as opposed to making existence more comfortable. (13)

Teaching in a tribal college, even for one year, could prove tremendously beneficial to any student planning to teach in states populated by Indians, and graduate school professors can play a vital role in encouraging their students to seize the opportunity, if appropriate.

Graduate students who plan to teach Native literature or other Native studies would also profit from the tribal college experience. Not all American Indians live on reservations; in fact, more than half live in urban areas and may have little or no contact with "the rez." Native literature, of course, reflects the diverse experiences of a broad spectrum of American Indians, representing hundreds of sovereign nations, and it can seldom be accurately interpreted through a Western lens. Moreover, even though most Indians share a common worldview, tribal cultures vary greatly; hence graduate students cannot assume that because they have studied, visited, or lived among the Diné (Navajo) people, they will automatically understand the Crow or the Seminole or the Haudenosaunee people.

Recently, several of my Leech Lake Tribal College students attended a conference where many seasoned professors as well as several graduate students presented papers on works by Ojibwe authors. My students were stunned by the lack of insight, the biased interpretations, and the patronizing attitudes reflected in some of these presentations;

yet, when two young Ojibwe students questioned the views of these non-Native academics, they were essentially told that they, the Ojibwe students, were interpreting the cultural meanings incorrectly. As Native people continue to insist, they themselves are the best source of information about the culture, history, and literature of American Indians—and what better way to immerse oneself in the culture than by living in an Indian community and teaching at a tribal college?

Finally, I am concerned about the teaching options American Indian students are given during their tenure in graduate school. According to AIHEC's latest report, American Indians earn fewer than one percent of all college degrees, including associate's, bachelor's, and advanced degrees (A-2). Of the Native students who pursue doctorates in English, few return to their own communities to teach. Numerous factors account for this brain drain; sometimes consciously, other times unwittingly, graduate school professors play a significant role in steering outstanding Native students into research university careers and away from their own people.

I do not mean to imply that Native teachers should teach only in Native schools; in fact, American Indians may choose not to teach at tribal colleges for the same reasons many non-Natives do not seek employment in their community colleges: a scarcity of full-time positions, inadequate wages, insufficient family support, lack of quality educational facilities for their children, and so forth. In addition, Native scholars who study at large urban universities often find it too difficult to make the social adjustment necessary for returning to their Indian community-based cultures. For many, Western values have replaced the personal and group values they once embraced. As the Lakota scholar Vine Deloria, Jr., explains:

> Too often [Native academics] model themselves after the professionals in their academic field or their institutional situation. This adjustment then forces them outside their Indian circle and greatly inhibits their ability to draw from their own tribal traditions the lessons that could be profitably learned. (81)

Unless Native scholars maintain strong connections with their own people, they are not likely to use their education to strengthen and assist other Indians. In the words of Allison Hedge Coke, "The more rooted people are in their own community, the more likely their work will lead there" (114).

For the sake of their Native students, then, as well as for non-Natives who might appreciate such an employment option, graduate school professors can become familiar with and value the dual mission of tribal colleges: to rebuild, reinforce, and explore traditional tribal cultures by using specifically designed curricula and institutional settings and to address Western models of learning by providing traditional disciplinary courses fully transferable to four-year institutions (AIHEC Report A3–4).

American Indian scholars who maintain a sense of pride and dignity in their culture and who take seriously their responsibility to their communities usually function most confidently in mainstream America. Unfortunately for all of us, however, some new Indian graduates will enter the teaching profession with a PhD and an internalized sense of shame and frustration over the "plight of Indian people." They may feel that assimilation is the only path to success yet yearn for a sense of belonging to an Indian community. Teaching for a year or two in a tribal college could help them both regain their sense of cultural identity and enhance the pedagogical skills needed for a career as a mainstream university professor.

Making graduate students aware of the teaching and administrative opportunities available at tribal colleges is only the first step in a program that could facilitate better communication between Indian communities and mainstream universities, attract more Native American students to graduate programs, and broaden current perceptions of the teaching profession among educators in general. Professors in graduate programs located within driving distance of tribal colleges, for example, might consider scheduling occasional field trips during which soon-to-be professors could observe classes in session or interact with faculty members and students. Alternatively, graduate students could be assigned various research projects pertaining to tribal colleges, or professors could invite one or more university students from reservation communities to participate in a class discussion of tribal colleges. Research universities could provide funding for a tribal college administrator or faculty member to travel to campus for a series of class lectures, workshops, or one-on-one consultations with graduate school faculty members and prospective teachers. Internships at tribal colleges might be funded with grants for those graduate students who are most serious about teaching in these schools.

Although I am not at all interested in romanticizing tribal colleges or in recruiting teachers who are merely intrigued with American Indian culture, I am concerned with the growth and continuity of these schools. Many graduate students, I repeat, would profit considerably from spending time on a reservation and teaching at a tribal college. And imagine how exciting Native studies programs would be if every professor in the program could begin his or her career by teaching at a tribal college.

While serving on a search committee at a large university several years ago, I was astounded by the number of applications we received for one tenure-track position in the Department of English (more than six hundred). I have listened to the pained stories of new English PhDs who have applied for scores of advertised teaching positions, hoping at least for an interview but more often than not failing to receive even the courtesy of a response. It is time that we begin preparing our graduate students for professional careers in a variety of academic settings, and as my current students and colleagues will attest, one of the most rewarding options available is that of teaching at an American Indian tribal college.

NOTES

1. The Navajo Nation established the first tribally controlled college—now known as Diné College—in 1968.

2. Border towns, as the name suggests, border Indian reservations and are often notorious for racism and maltreatment of Natives.

3. Numerous textbooks (and college instructors) continue to refer to American Indians in the past tense, to present nineteenth-century or Hollywood images of indigenous peoples, and to assume that all "real" Indians have been exterminated, assimilated, or hopelessly conquered by Euro-American settlers.

WORKS CITED

Ambler, Marjane. "Putting a Name to Cultural Resilience." Editorial. *Tribal College Journal* 14.4 (2003): 8–9.

American Indian Higher Education Consortium. *Tribal Colleges: An Introduction.* Alexandria: Amer. Indian Higher Educ. Consortium, 1999. <http://www.aihec.org/documents/Research/intro.pdf>.

Coke, Allison Hedge. "Seeds." *Speaking for the Generations: Native Writers on Writing.* Ed. Simon J. Ortiz. Tucson: U of Arizona P, 1998. 92–116.

Deloria, Vine, Jr. "Transitional Education." Deloria and Wildcat 79–86.

Deloria, Vine, Jr., and Daniel R. Wildcat. *Power and Place: Indian Education in America*. Golden: Fulcrum Resources, 2001.

Dyson, Michael Eric. "The Public Obligations of Intellectuals." *Chronicle of Higher Education* 5 Dec. 2003: B11.

McCormick, Kathleen. "Pedagogical Possibilities: Working at Teaching-Oriented Institutions." *Profession 2003*. New York: MLA, 2003. 120–31.

United States Census Bureau. *United States Census 2000*. 25 Jan. 2002. 12 June 2007 <http://www.census.gov/main/www/cen2000.html>.

Wildcat, Daniel R. "Indigenizing Education: Playing to Our Strengths." Deloria and Wildcat 7–19.

JAMES W. JONES

SINCE YOU DIDN'T ASK
Reflections on Foreign Language Teaching

On my first day of class as the sole teacher and teaching assistant of first-semester German, I faced forty-five students and wondered how in the world I would ever get them all to speak in the fifty-minute period, much less teach them to conjugate verbs and differentiate between the nominative, accusative, dative, and genitive cases. I continually struggled with these questions as I led my two sections, totaling almost ninety students, through daily activities designed to bring them to some level of mastery of the language, however minimal. The year was 1974, and the place was the University of Wisconsin, Milwaukee (UWM). There were six TAs in the German department, all pursuing master's degrees (the highest degree offered), and our supervisor was a talented, highly energetic native speaker, Johanna Moore. As was often the case at the university level, lecturers or junior faculty members assumed responsibility for the teaching aspect of the profession. An untenured lecturer, Johanna served as our mentor throughout our teaching careers at UWM and expertly taught us how to create lesson plans with a variety of activities aimed at achieving concrete goals, how to design quizzes and exams, and how to work with diverse students and learning styles.

In my first year of graduate studies, at the same time that I clung to Johanna's teaching advice, I took a course on East German literature taught by Jack Zipes. As an undergraduate German major, I had hated, even feared, writing papers in my literature classes, for it seemed that the critics had already said all that needed to be uttered or written about the books on our syllabi. When the products of my struggle to approach the methods of these masters were returned, I found perhaps a few sentences written by my professors, describing in general terms why my paper was not quite as good as it should be. In stark contrast, when Jack returned my paper to me, I found that he had written more than a page of comments, praising what I had written and encouraging me to believe in myself and in the validity of my ideas. That was a turning point for me. I became more confident and, through other courses, found an interest in the relatively undiscovered gay literature of the 1920s. A year and a half later, I completed my master's thesis, which became the foundation of my doctoral dissertation.

What does an almost thirty-year-old story have to do with this volume? Teachers in foreign languages might be thinking, "We teach classes at least half the size of that German 101 from 1974. TAs are even more closely supervised and more professionally trained today. The graduate faculty works closely with PhD students, motivating and mentoring them. Foreign language teaching has changed significantly." Certainly our focus has shifted to communicative competence, and the field has broadened beyond the traditional canon of literary texts. But I would like to investigate whether the training to become a successful member of the academic community has truly changed. I use my own story to illustrate several general points about the present situation of graduate education in the foreign languages.

After a period as a high school teacher of German and English, I entered the PhD program in German at the University of Wisconsin, Madison, in 1980. This time, the classes I taught as a TA were smaller (about twenty-five students) and the TAs more numerous. The camaraderie among the TAs facilitated easy sharing of ideas about pedagogy. From the variety of backgrounds and styles of my fellow student-teachers, I learned that talking about teaching—honestly discussing what failed and what succeeded in the classroom—improved my teaching. Yes, that observation seems simple, even painfully obvious, to current college and university faculty members, but we were not born with this insight. And, more important, these honest conversations about pedagogy become much more difficult to sustain on entering the profession, given the fears new faculty members have of losing their jobs and the anxieties of self-doubt that attend first faculty appointments. ("What if they think I haven't a clue what I'm doing in class? I have to play the role of the expert. That's the identity my training conferred on me").

In the collective of graduate students and TAs, I grew most as a teacher. Likewise, from a variety of professors I learned valuable lessons about how to be a professor. Several were, of course, my German literature professors, but I also discovered much about teaching and writing from professors in other departments, especially from the historians George Mosse and Harvey Goldberg. Members of my dissertation committee came from the German and history departments, and each of them warned me that my topic, a history of gay and lesbian literature in Germany from 1870 to 1933, might make me unemployable. In 1985–86, when I finished and defended the dissertation, the field of gay and lesbian studies was still generally ostracized in the academy. In that respect, the profession has certainly changed since then.

Perhaps they were right. Probably homophobia did play a role in my failure to get more job interviews or offers during the years I was on the market. It certainly did in one interview I had at the MLA Annual Convention with the chair of a German department at a major research university. She told me the members of her department were all married to the same person each had started out with (i.e., no divorces among this subgroup of heterosexuality). In fact, they and their families also socialized with one another. She then asked me bluntly, "So, what should I tell my colleagues when they ask me how you will fit in?" I was more than taken aback, I was angered at this line of questioning. Not wanting to appear equally rude, I told her she should inform her colleagues that I have always gotten along quite well in social situations and they need not fear any inappropriate behavior. Even with the MLA's stricter recommendations for today's interviewers, it is impossible, or at best very difficult, for a job candidate to protest this kind of treatment.

Somehow, I did find a tenure-track position in 1987 at Central Michigan University (CMU). Now classified as a doctoral research university, for most of my tenure CMU had been a regional comprehensive university, and, in terms of my department, it remains so.[1] We offer bachelor's degrees in French, German, and Spanish, along with a master's degree in Spanish. Our multilanguage department, with its chiefly undergraduate focus, presents a different professional reality from the one in which PhD candidates learn "how to be professors." But most members of the profession share these realities.

How then did someone who hated writing seminar papers become a rather active scholar? How did an outsider (American gay man in

German studies) become an insider (full-time tenured professor and department chair)? The value of individual mentoring and the importance of learning in a supportive collective are, I think, crucial. But in trying to gain entry into the profession, future faculty members might see these concerns as irrelevant or at the least difficult to articulate within the confines of a cover letter or curriculum vitae. Yet succeeding as a junior professor depends to a great extent on the mentoring of one's professors and the support of one's fellow graduate students, as well as on the development of one's identity as a scholar, teacher, and colleague.

To clarify my point, I focus on the job application and interview process from my perspective as a department chair. During my nine years as chair I was involved in at least a dozen searches. These were for tenure-track positions in Spanish or French, not in German. Several of these searches failed, and from those experiences we learned more about both our department's needs and our departmental culture. With a different perspective as a chair and a Germanist, I also learned something about the preparation of PhD students for positions in institutions where research is not the primary goal. Most of my discussion of the hiring process and the newly hired person's first year or so concerns the three categories used for reappointment, tenure, and promotion: teaching, scholarship, and service.

When I became involved in departmental searches as the external member of the search committee, I assiduously read the MLA guidelines on conducting searches and scoured past issues of the MLA's *Job Information List* to learn how other institutions phrased their advertisements. Although my department had conducted searches before, I thought it might help our planning to see what academic areas (and subspecialties) were in demand and how a university or department described itself to potential candidates. I also read recent issues of the *ADFL Bulletin*, paying particular attention to articles that dealt with the job search and hiring process, from the perspectives of the department chair and the candidate. These articles informed me of the current state of affairs in job searches and sensitized me to issues on both sides of the interview table.

In general, this process inspired specific job listings that described the areas we wanted and gave a sense of our institution (faculty duties, workload, and even geographic location), all important indications to potential candidates. Unfortunately for all concerned, candidates sometimes ignored these signs, preferring instead to do a kind of mass mailing for any job in French or even in Spanish (where the market for job seekers is much better). Surprisingly, many people who did not meet one or both of two major criteria—expertise in the field requested and PhD in hand by the specified date—applied for positions anyway.

On a more positive note, common practice has lately dictated that candidates include a description of their teaching philosophy with their letters of application, whether explicitly requested or not. This document gave the search committee insight into candidates' attitudes and priorities. Actual experience teaching the specific courses that constitute the load of a beginning assistant professor of foreign languages certainly trumped even the best-written teaching philosophy. Most foreign language PhDs have taught beginning and intermediate language courses as part of their training as graduate students. Indeed, these courses form the bulk of the teaching load for foreign language professors at comprehensive universities, and students from important introductory and intermediate courses become the majors and minors in the language.

But beginning assistant professors also will have to teach two different kinds of upper-level courses required for the major and minors: conversation and composition courses, in which the teaching skills they develop as TAs will need refinement and expansion to meet the special demands of these courses, and survey courses dealing either with literary history (e.g., The Golden Age of Spanish Literature) or with cultural history (e.g., Latin American Civilization). Many candidates, however, never gained experience teaching these kinds of courses in their graduate institutions. While some foreign language graduate departments have changed and while we have seen more candidates with experience teaching at least one section of each kind of course, most applicants have little, if any, concrete experience. Even those who do have some experience may only have led a discussion section or taught a small portion of the course. They have not been responsible for the nitty-gritty work of creating lesson plans, deciding how to evaluate mastery of the material and participation in the course, grading essay exams, and so on (see Papp; Shumway).

Valid reasons why graduate students do not, as a rule, teach upper-level classes probably exist, but, to provide their students with the training necessary to enter the profession and succeed, graduate departments must find a way to involve them in these classes. Perhaps mentoring, one of the most crucial roles professors play in guiding graduate students to successful academic citizenship, can provide opportunities for TAs to expand their teaching repertoire under the watch of experienced faculty members. I suggest a specific step that graduate departments could take with little or no structural change: using a mentoring system for upper-division teaching assignments only after the doctoral student reaches candidacy and has demonstrated success in teaching beginning and intermediate language courses. The student would either choose or be assigned to a professor who teaches a conversation and composition course and, in a different semester, to one who teaches a survey course in literature or cultural history. The professor would take the student through all the steps involved in creating the course: forming learning objectives, choosing textbooks, designing a teaching syllabus, writing daily lesson plans, designing and grading exams. This semester-long cooperative project would result in a course syllabus, along with sample lesson plans and exams.[2] A successful job candidate needs a detailed, well-rounded course portfolio in today's marketplace to demonstrate readiness to step into the role of assistant professor at a comprehensive college or university, a sector of higher education priding itself on excellence in teaching.

Clearly, teaching occupies center stage on regional comprehensive campuses, but I have seen more than a few candidates for assistant professorships on such a campus falter during the teaching aspect of the on-campus interview. We generally selected for the final interviews three or four of the perhaps twelve to fifteen candidates whom we interviewed at the MLA convention. They possessed evidence of excellence in teaching and gave fine answers to the interview questions pertaining to pedagogy. After arranging dates for the campus interview, we sent candidates information about a teaching demonstration for a beginning or intermediate language course. The candidates should show creativity and use a variety of teaching techniques, possibly even some technology, during their teaching demonstrations. Some job candidates would have benefited from the guidance of experienced faculty members when designing lesson plans for the teaching component of interviews, keeping in mind the peculiarities of the exercise, and they would have grown from the feedback of friends who might have acted as the students in a rehearsal. Some departments do indeed already mentor their job candidates in this manner, but this practice, surprisingly, is not yet the norm, at least in my experience.

The 2003 report of the MLA Ad Hoc Committee on the Professionalization of PhDs supports this impression, although, in terms of teaching as part of the interview process, it only describes research of English departments. When discussing the initial screening of applicants by English department search committees, the authors found that the most highly valued characteristics of candidates were " 'potential for making a positive contribution to the institution as a whole,' 'letter of application,' 'general teaching experience,' and letters of recommendation" (47). There is no mention of evaluating the candidate's teaching of an actual or staged class at the on-campus interview. The phrase "candidate's ability to relate well to students like ours" (47), a highly ranked characteristic of finalists, hardly describes an evaluation of on-campus teaching performances. My department weights this aspect of candidates' visits among the top three highly valued characteristics of potential colleagues. In the teaching demonstration, one gets a sense of the identity candidates have created for themselves. Of course, that identity will change with professional experience and maturity, but the newly hired assistant professor will begin his or her career at CMU with that identity.

Scholarship receives primary focus from many, if not most, job candidates and their faculty advisers. This focus should not surprise us, since those who complete PhD programs commonly aspire to follow in the career footsteps of their professional mentors (MLA Ad Hoc Committee; Debicki). Although attaining the holy grail of a tenure-track position at a preeminent research university is not a realistic result for most PhDs, many candidates have not altered their expectations significantly. The chances of finding employment as a full-time tenure-track assistant professor of foreign languages (other than Spanish) are approximately fifty percent, at best, with significant variations according to the specific language (MLA Ad Hoc Committee 51–52). Even those who apply to teaching-intensive institutions devote a great deal of space in their cover letters to expansive descriptions of their dissertations. The faculty members who write their letters of recommendation focus chiefly on the students' scholarly contributions to their field. Both the job seeker and the recommenders seem to write solely to an audience that inhabits the realm Robert Scholes describes in an article in the *MLA Newsletter*. At elite universities, he writes, the scholarship bar has been raised even higher: job candidates need not only an extensive record of publication to be hired but also not just one but two book publications, or at least substantial progress toward a second book, "including published articles on this second topic," to gain tenure.

The scholarship demands and opportunities at my university are typical of the profession at regional comprehensive universities. CMU requires refereed publications for tenure and promotion but not for hiring. In interviewing and hiring, we look for evidence of excellence in scholarship, but conference presentations or invited (possibly non-refereed) publications demonstrate excellence as much as refereed publications. The promise of scholarly achievement can be just as important as the publication of one or two articles.

Two issues come into play with respect to the role of scholarship once one joins the faculty of this kind of institution. First, there is the major issue of institutional support, which takes two forms: money and time. Money is, of course, always an issue, especially at institutions without large amounts of development funds to support research and professional development. Yet even in the periods of economic downturn that plague Michigan, faculty members find a surprising amount of financial support available to them for research endeavors. A lack of time, on the other hand, often hinders them from achieving their scholarship goals. Research-intensive universities have an advantage over teaching-intensive colleges and universities, where significantly lighter teaching loads (and often fewer students) allow more time for scholarly development.

Given the demands of teaching, professors in my department save research and writing for the summer since we do not teach in the summer terms. Many, especially the junior faculty members, spend a great deal of the summer abroad, working in libraries or archives while also catching up with family and friends in what are often their home countries or their "second home" countries. During the fall and spring semesters, one rarely is able to find the psychic space needed for developing an intellectual argument and writing an article. Teaching three courses four or five days a week, with language classes of up to thirty and upper-level courses of twenty or more students, becomes a time-consuming activity, especially when one is a new professor and each course requires a new preparation.

If institutional support emerges as the major issue relating to scholarship, institutional reputation seems to be a minor issue. But this second issue affects one's sense of identity as a citizen of the academy in a profound way. No college or university sees itself as an institution without prestige, but the nonelites are perceived as such, despite our decades of deconstructing hegemonic discourse and foregrounding the outsider (Debicki 16–17). I am reminded of this reality at every MLA convention I attend. As I walk through the corridors or circulate at receptions, I notice how one attendee after another, especially younger persons (job seekers perhaps), looks first at my name tag, not at me. Having observed this for years, I have learned to interpret their thoughts: "Hmm, I'm not sure if he is Somebody. That name's pretty generic. Let me see where he's from . . . Oh. He's nobody. Moving on." At first, I was offended by this behavior; now, I find it amusing. Maybe part of the aging process for academics involves accepting their places in the ivory-tower hierarchy. This nonverbal exchange strikes me as a sign of the overvaluation of status. We all have degrees from universities that produce PhDs, but we cannot all teach at those institutions, even if our mentors suddenly retired en masse. Yet we are trained for such institutions and often therefore view other colleges and universities as inferior. As successful graduate students, we had the stamp of approval from those highly ranked departments, so working anywhere but in equally hallowed halls seems like a demotion.

The system of ranking departments may not change, but we can change the training of future professors by consciously preparing them for the realities of the academic positions that will be available to them. They would benefit from working with the department's alumni at the end of their graduate student careers. These alumni, professors in a variety of academic settings, could provide information about what they learned in their first jobs after graduation, what they do in their present positions, and what they look for in new colleagues. Andrew Debicki writes that "mentoring in all aspects of students' lives and careers seems far more . . . successful in some areas of science than in the humanities" (17). Business schools have been mentoring their students and fostering alumni relationships for many years, but these practices barely exist at the PhD level in the humanities. We in foreign languages only manage to send our old departments a copy of the job ad when we are conducting a search.

I rank one last point about scholarship as a distinct advantage that I have enjoyed as a faculty member at my institution as opposed to a research university with very high research activity. Hired as an assistant professor of German, I was expected to publish in the field of German studies. I have done that, but I have also published articles on American and British AIDS fiction, on American gay and lesbian films, and on a variety of gay American authors. All these publications counted for various promotions (and tenure), and no one at any level of decision making questioned their relevance. I was not hired as a comparatist, nor do I teach courses in the English department. I did, however, define myself from the beginning as a scholar-teacher of gay and lesbian studies. I created my own identity, first as scholar and colleague and then as teacher. I doubt that the freedom to create this professional space and have it accepted by peers and administrators exists to such an extent at the top-tier institutions. There, the hiring practices are different—one is hired to teach and publish in a very specific area—and job definitions tend to dictate certain parameters to the inquiry faculty members conduct throughout their careers.

The more flexible identities possible in institutions that prize teaching have opened opportunities to teach outside my home department. I have cotaught, with a colleague in the history department, a large lecture course on the Holocaust. For me, this was a chance not only to teach in English about a topic central to my research but also to work in the large lecture format. I also organized an introductory course in gay and lesbian studies that I and several other faculty members (tenured, tenure-track, and non-tenure-track) taught. We divided the course into discrete topics relating to the expertise of the particular professor—for example, the history of gay and lesbian music from a musician's perspective or the nature-versus-nurture debate from a biologist's point of view. While I taught both courses on an overload basis, in addition to my three courses in German, these assignments provided me the chance to explore new modes of teaching and reinvigorated both my teaching and scholarship as a member of my home department. The likelihood of engaging in these kinds of experiments is somewhat greater at comprehensive institutions because the requirements of departmental structures—and rewards—for teaching are less rigid than they are at research-intensive universities.

Beyond teaching and scholarship, faculty members must demonstrate acceptable accomplishments in service to achieve tenure and promotions. Each member of my department participates in a wide variety of service activities, even if some colleagues outside my department devalue service and certain professors in graduate schools warn their students to stay away from committee work and concentrate on publishing and teaching until they have gained tenure. That advice does not address the reality of working at a regional comprehensive university like CMU. Valuable service is just as necessary as good teaching and recognized scholarship in demonstrating successful academic citizenship. To begin with, service encompasses far more than committee work, which is often the least of it, especially for junior faculty members. Because of the importance of this responsibility, we carefully review applicants' curriculum vitae for service, looking in particular for experience related to study abroad. What Pennylyn Dykstra-Prium wrote in 1998 still seems true today: "All too often, the service part of life as an academic is ignored in graduate training" (36).

New faculty members enter the realm of service by advising majors and minors, not a simple task for someone new to the campus. The academic requirements for undergraduates may not always be obvious or straightforward. Signing a major or minor form with students constitutes only one part of advising in a foreign language department. At the signing, faculty members explore study-abroad options with students. Although we do not require students to study abroad, the experience has become a necessary part of undergraduate foreign language education because students gain fluency and are better able to market themselves after graduation. The new assistant professor needs to know the programs available to our students, to recognize ways the courses taken abroad fit into the requirements of the major or minor, and to understand the monetary support available to finance study abroad. Each of these topics forms important parts of adviser-advisee discussions, and the new faculty member needs training to address these points with the requisite knowledge. Usually, we assign a faculty mentor to each new assistant professor, and the mentor works with the newly hired person for the first year or so, perhaps sitting in as a kind of coadviser during these student-faculty meetings.

From the beginning, we involve our colleagues in departmental committee work; otherwise, the department cannot function. Like every academic bureaucracy, we have our array of departmental, college, and university committees. After the first year, a kind of dipping one's toes in the service pool, we encourage new colleagues to become involved gradually in at least one committee outside the department. As the years pass, one is expected to wade farther into the pool, being careful to stay afloat. Although foreign language faculty members are heavily involved in service, committee work rarely threatens to drown anyone. Faculty members can always resign from committees, if need be, and no one thinks less of them.

There are, however, certain service activities in a foreign language department in which all faculty members need to become involved, such as study abroad and the coordination of weekly conversation hours, which enables undergraduate students from a variety of language levels (usually the third through sixth semesters) to come together in a dining hall or a local coffee bar to gain practice in speaking the foreign language. Professors may attend these sessions themselves and help direct the conversations or may arrange for native speakers, usually graduate students outside the department, to facilitate the conversations. Foreign language professors also typically arrange film showings outside class. They introduce the movie and sometimes discuss it with the students afterward. And finally, foreign language departments consider student clubs essential to the undergraduate experience. In my department, we have a club and an honor society for each language offered, and each student organization must have a faculty adviser.

I have attempted to outline here some avenues by which graduate students can become better prepared to assume the role of assistant professor, particularly at the level of a regional comprehensive university. Obviously, no single way to prepare for a successful career exists, and each kind of academic institution has its own culture. Despite published reports and raised voices concerning the crises of academic employment, graduate departments at PhD-granting institutions have not expansively addressed the areas in which our students need to become better prepared to enter our profession.[3] As the 2003 MLA report "Professionalization in Perspective" states:

> [T]hose seeking to enter our profession have increasingly felt obliged to learn to become professionals before they even begin their search for a job. Facing a tight hiring situation, they understandably want to be as prepared as possible, and many do not think that they get sufficient assistance from their departments.   (MLA Ad Hoc Committee 41)

Increased dialogue between and among different sectors of higher education can help graduate students ascertain the advantages and disadvantages of faculty life at various two- and four-year colleges and universities.

Certainly, there are disadvantages to the life of an academic at a regional comprehensive university. If I take my university as an example, I would have to admit that a multilayered kind of isolation distinguishes faculty life here. Mount Pleasant, Michigan, is about an hour away from the closest regional airport, and, although we have a local Wal-Mart and Target, the nearest shopping mall is also about an hour away. Unmarried and unpartnered faculty members, especially, experience a sense of social isolation in addition to the geographic isolation. I vividly remember my job interview here with the associate dean in February 1987. As he described the city ("Small, a nice place to raise a family, but we don't have a lot of things you're used to, having lived in big cities"), he was scanning my curriculum vitae. When he read my list of publications, all of which included the word "gay" or "homosexual," he looked up at me, eyes widening, and said, "Well, we don't have . . ." I knew he meant "a gay bar," so I just smiled and replied, "Yes, I know." There is also a certain intellectual isolation, simply because I am no longer in a community of people who share my interests and because I do not have immediate access to a research library. But one realizes all this when one begins seriously to consider living and working in this setting.

There are two important points that people may not realize until after they have begun their careers. The first is the opportunity faculty members have to introduce their research into teaching, which in turn can become a source of research. I am referring not to teaching seminars on one's dissertation topic but to including mini-units (one or two weeks long) in broader-based courses on specific topics germane to one's research. In my survey courses of German literature or cultural history, for example, students read several texts about Magnus Hirschfeld and the Institute of Sexual Science when learning about the Weimar Republic. Comic-strip stories by Ralf König become a way for us to discuss the role of gays and lesbians in present-day Germany. To help students learn what a professor does, besides teach, I also include encyclopedia articles I have written on these topics. That often leads to engaging class discussions and to rich conversations with individual students during office hours.

That personal relationship with students is the second important point I'd like to make about life as a professor at a comprehensive university. Even though a new faculty member may have had a strong mentoring relationship with a professor, the newly minted PhD is at a very different stage of development from the undergraduate student she or he once was. It is a challenge to remember that experience and at the same time to step into the other role. Faculty members in my department have much closer relationships with their students than I or my friends did with our professors. Back then, we never told our professors stories about our love lives or family tragedies. I never would have dreamed of asking one of my German professors what one of my students asked me: "So, Dr. Jones, just what is your story? When did you know you were gay?" It turned out the student wanted advice on what to say to a friend who was questioning her sexuality. Professors here have closer relationships and more personal conversations with students because they get to know each other better. After all, students take several classes from a single professor, and they likely attend movies and drink coffee with that professor. Our faculty members routinely invite their classes to their homes for pizza, and students may invite faculty members to their weddings or commitment ceremonies. Graduate school cannot prepare doctoral candidates for this kind of relationship, beyond encouraging them to meet with alumni who teach in a variety of academic settings. Like any satisfying career, though, life as a professor at a regional comprehensive university is endlessly challenging as well as abundantly rewarding. The challenges can at times seem overwhelming, but better preparation in graduate school for the realities of the job as a beginning assistant professor, along with improved mentoring, can make the transition more successful.

NOTES

1. The Carnegie Foundation for the Advancement of Teaching no longer uses the categories comprehensive university, research university, or research extensive. I have used the new nomenclature to describe my institution, which is a doctoral research university. There are two categories of universities at which research plays a greater role: research universities (high research activity) and research universities (very high research activity). I have, however, also found the previous distinctions useful in describing differences between my own institution, where teaching and service play very large roles, and that of the elite universities from which most of our faculty members receive their PhDs (e.g., the University of Wisconsin, Madison). For this reason, I use the term "comprehensive university."

2. This idea is by no means new or original. Pennylyn Dykstra-Prium described the need for graduate students to create portfolios of teaching, scholarship, and service in a 1998 article. More recently, the MLA Ad Hoc

Committee on the Professionalization of PhDs called for graduate departments to institute similar processes. Their 2003 report, "Professionalization in Perspective," focused attention on this area because "[t]he single
message the committee received most often from students concerned the
importance and value of mentors in professional preparation, in helping
them learn the ropes" (45). The report added that this is "the collective
responsibility of the department," not just the duty of the dissertation
adviser (45).

3. In discussing humanities PhD programs, the "Invisible Adjunct" (who received a PhD in history and described her experiences as a non-tenure-track
teacher in many articles published in the *Chronicle of Higher Education*
between 2003 and 2004) seems to speak to the crisis that has given rise to
some of her central objections to the present state of affairs: "Can't professors see that a system producing so many people who can't get jobs is not an
indictment of the aspiring faculty members, but of the system itself? Or if
you really think that these adjuncts aren't of high enough caliber to hire,
then the graduate schools are failures, not the students" (qtd. in Smallwood
A11). Her blog was extremely popular among both job seekers and those junior faculty members who had managed to land one of the increasingly rare
tenure-track jobs. Although she decided to stop adding to the Web site, the
archives are still available at www.invisibleadjunct.com.

WORKS CITED

Debicki, Andrew P. "Looking Back, Looking Forward: Preparing and Inducting
Our New Colleagues." *ADFL Bulletin* 32.2 (2001): 16–18.

Dykstra-Prium, Pennylyn. "Our Ethical Commitments to the Graduate Students We Train: A Modest and a Not-So-Modest Proposal." *ADFL Bulletin*
29.3 (1998): 34–38.

MLA Ad Hoc Committee on the Professionalization of PhDs. "Professionalization in Perspective." *ADFL Bulletin* 34.3 (2003): 41–53.

Papp, James. "The Stars and Ourselves: An Ordinary Person's Guide to the Foreign Language Market." *ADFL Bulletin* 30.1 (1998): 44–51.

Scholes, Robert. "The Evaluation of Faculty Members in the Culture of 'Excellence.'" *MLA Newsletter* 36.2 (2004): 3.

Shumway, Nicolas. "What Our Mothers Might Have Told Us about Upper-
Division Instruction." *ADFL Bulletin* 27.3 (1996): 15–16.

Smallwood, Scott. "Disappearing Act." *Chronicle of Higher Education* 30 Apr.
2004: A10–11.

AERON HAYNIE

ACROSS THE GREAT DIVIDE
Teaching in Rural Montana and Beyond

In 1994 I found myself, a doctoral candidate who had completed all but my dissertation, in the fortunate position of being offered a tenure-track job in English. There was a catch, though: the position was at a small, isolated, liberal arts campus in rural Montana. Feeling much like the protagonist of Bernard Malamud's *A New Life*, I ventured across the country alone, only to discover that this four-year branch of the University of Montana system was more a teachers' college than a liberal arts school. With little cultural life, few institutional resources, and a wide gap between the students and me, I feared I would never integrate myself into this small town. Even so, my graduate professors persuaded me to accept any tenure-track job, no matter where it was situated. I remember thinking, "But they haven't *seen* this place!" The on-campus interview left me with images of dusty, small-town streets out of *The Last Picture Show*, with men in cowboy hats driving pickup trucks through a downtown composed of a Laundromat, a hardware store, and a gas station. It was with a heavy heart and much foreboding that I drove my newly purchased sports-utility vehicle across the country, into the vast, underpopulated, postapocalyptic landscape of the Rocky Mountain West.

I'm sure there are people who would welcome the opportunity to live in the pristine wilderness, but I was not one of them. At the time, I would rather have been offered a job in Detroit or Cleveland, places that seemed more real to a person who grew up in the gritty, post-industrial landscape of Buffalo, New York. It took a couple of years before I appreciated the sublime beauty of the Rocky Mountain landscape and roughly the same amount of time before I developed a professional plan that eventually would get me out of Montana and into my current position at the University of Wisconsin, Green Bay, located in a setting different from Dillon, Montana.

No matter what the location, the day-to-day life of a professor at a four-year teaching-intensive college will feel remote from the concerns and training of graduate school. Since recent studies estimate that only five to ten percent of new PhDs will build careers at research-intensive universities (Gaff), most of us lucky enough to obtain tenure-track positions will spend our professional lives at community colleges or four-year colleges. How do we resist feeling demoralized when we accept positions that value teaching while our profession values research above all else? Expanding definitions of research and scholarship to include classroom-based inquiry and curriculum design can help faculty members at teaching-intensive institutions reclaim some of the scholar's identity. After all, such faculty members teach seven or eight (ten or twelve) courses each year, often requiring seven or eight different preparations. In Montana, I taught speech, composition, British literature, world literature, drama, gender studies, and literary theory. In Wisconsin, we routinely teach a survey of humanities course that covers the art, history, literature, philosophy, and music of the past five hundred years. I know instructors at community colleges who teach five or six courses a semester, some of them outside their disciplines altogether.

The disconnect between graduate school and most teaching jobs involves more than just desirability of location or workload: there seems to be a fundamental difference in educational philosophy between the universities at which future faculty members study and the colleges at which the majority of professors work. Research universities produce more researchers. Are we at four-year colleges as sure of our missions? The need to strengthen the connection between research universities and teaching colleges is important not only for the well-being of many new professors but also for the public that institutions of higher education serve. While many states cut funding to their public universities, academics need to rethink and publicize the ways we already serve (and always have served) our communities. Part of this effort involves clarifying our individual relationships to our local communities, our institutions' goals, and our concrete contributions to the intellectual, cultural, and economic lives of citizens in our proximity.

Although my particular case may appear extreme, it illustrates the traumas often attending the transition from graduate school to one's first teaching job. Generally speaking, new PhDs are unprepared for the emotional, social, and pedagogical demands of embracing foreign academic cultures as well as of becoming part of radically different communities. Graduate school encourages a state of limbo in all areas of the graduate students' lives; and although getting that first job, thus beginning something like a real life, at first feels liberating, it can also feel disorienting. Unlike the university towns where many graduate students live for six to ten years, the places where they secure first teaching jobs may be their homes for life. For those of us fortunate enough to get tenure-track jobs, there are no assurances that we will ever get another.

Despite my initial reservations and my confused mixture of emotions, in the five years I lived and taught in Montana, I became enmeshed in a rich and complex community made up of students, faculty members, and townspeople. As academics, we join de facto international communities of scholars connected by texts, conferences, and the Internet. Yet we also live in, teach, and join our local communities. In truth, the fact that the destinations to which the brutal job market delivers us appear random and out of our control complicates our participation in local communities. I admit that I arrived in Montana feeling somewhat victimized and not at all at home, as well as feeling at times like a missionary sent to spread the gospel to the unbelievers or like a mail-order bride. For many professors, the sense of alienation toward their communities never recedes; however, a faculty member's ability to create an authentic sense of community in the classroom is directly related to her willingness to engage the larger community.

My current job in Wisconsin is not as fraught with challenges—Green Bay is approximately forty times the size of Dillon, Montana, and this job is more suited to my teaching interests—yet the issues I face here resemble the struggles I faced in Montana: a heavy teaching load of general education courses, little institutional support for research, and the challenge of becoming part of a community that I would not have chosen apart from the job. Fortunately, the years I spent in Montana forced me to reconsider my relationship to the local community. A small town really illustrates the concrete ways each person's presence causes ripples in the community. One Dillon townswoman, a feminist health care worker, explained to me why she chose to stay there: "I know I could move to a place where more people shared my values, but I feel more needed here. And I need to be around people who disagree with me to hear what they have to say."

In a college town or classroom, faculty members should realize the many ways we influence those around us and the ways we ourselves change as a result of our surroundings. Surviving and thriving in a geographically and culturally alien place require one to clarify values and examine assumptions about people, particularly students. What values come into conflict when we middle-class, educated, "exceptional" students encounter first-generation college students who may have long histories of experiencing schools only as sites of degradation? How do these power imbalances play themselves out in the contact zone of the classroom, "the space in which peoples geographically and historically separated come into contact with each other and establish ongoing relations, usually involving conditions of coercion, radical inequality, and intractable conflict" (Pratt 6)? The coercive nature of the classroom goes beyond the power to determine grades: professors have the social power to designate some students smart and others below average. Whether we recognize this power or even accept it, students and society at large give it to us, and it should make us very cautious. Therefore, ethics command us to go beyond misconceptions and stereotypes when interacting with our students and when attempting to understand their cultures. The critical pedagogical theorist Ira Shor has argued that teachers should begin every semester by investigating students' culture:

> What do students talk about, read about, and write about? . . .
> What do they watch on TV, read about in newspapers, and listen to on radio? Do they think the media give them an accurate picture of events? What news are they *not* getting? . . .
> Were [their] parents . . . born in the United States? . . . How do they feel about schooling? Do they think they are getting a good education? What are the local schools . . . like? . . .
> What are [their] community conditions—density, housing, religion, health care, mass transit, crime, playgrounds, sanitation? . . .   (205)

Indeed, the students one teaches as a teaching assistant may be quite different from the students one finds at four-year or two-year colleges. Most of the students I taught while in graduate school at the University of Florida were the traditional age, single, part-time employees, full-time students from middle-class families. By contrast, the students I taught in Montana—and now teach in Wisconsin—were and are mostly first-generation college students, a sizable minority nontraditional (i.e., older), quite a few working full-time in addition to taking a full load of courses, many planning to remain in the region after they graduated, and a high number already with families. In Florida, I felt poor compared with many of the undergraduates whose sports cars and future earnings exceeded my own expectations, whereas as an assistant professor in Montana (with no family to support), I felt well-off. Most of the students in Montana expressed modest postgraduation goals: to make more than minimum wage, to buy an unassuming house, and to continue to live in Montana. The attainment of these goals in a poor community where family ranches barely survived and most mines had shut down often proved elusive for students. In Florida, I prided myself on maintaining strict policies concerning absences and late papers, but I had to rethink this attitude when faced with students at Montana who missed class because of a child custody hearing or who quit halfway through the semester when their money ran out.

As bell hooks has argued, universities and colleges rarely examine the struggles that working-class students face in college (145). She observes that while an increasing number of working-class students attend college, few professors come from working-class backgrounds themselves (see Rodriguez). Although I have not seen research to support or deny this claim, it seems safe to assume that many professors come from middle-class backgrounds and have families that support and encourage intellectual achievement. In addition, most of us excelled as undergraduates, making it difficult for us to understand fully students who carry the weight of labels such as "unmotivated," "stupid," or even "average."

I remember my undergraduate college classes fondly, but I recall that I was often one of the only students to participate in discussion, to read supplementary material willingly, and to express genuine excitement about literature. I came to college with a commitment to language; the excellent college English classes I took reinforced, broadened, and sharpened my love of literature. As a college professor, I now understand why my professors appreciated my presence in class: it's wonderful to have that rare student who enjoys studying the subject, who possesses acceptable writing skills, and who confidently speaks up in class. I'm sure I loved college, in part, because I was singled out as exceptional. Now that I teach, however, I see the classroom differently. I do not feel justified teaching to that small minority of outstanding students. I strive, perhaps unrealistically, for universal engagement. This commitment to most of the students one teaches might seem like an obvious goal for educators, but some faculty members and future faculty members endorse the misconception that teaching to the top five percent implies selectivity and rigor.

Professors who believe in their students and in their power as role models of the scholarly temperament must adjust pedagogically (and perhaps attitudinally) to ensure the success of working-class undergraduate students. Since most of my working-class students hold full-time jobs during the semester, few can participate in outside activities such as films or lectures, and many students miss classes because of work or family problems. Although the downside of working with students who fit school into busy and complex lives may be discouraging to instructors, it would be a mistake to categorize these students as unmotivated or uncommitted to intellectual life. Instead of lamenting the fact that our colleges produce "workers, not leaders . . . clerks, secretaries, [and] mid-level managers," as Terry Caesar does (4), we could see our colleges' teaching-intensive missions as radical opportunities for greater influence in community and personal transformation along economic and intellectual lines. Most of our English majors here in Wisconsin will become high school English teachers, some will work in business and marketing, and a small number will go on for advanced degrees in law or literature. Our students' career aspirations present faculty members with chances to affect the general population through our influence over future high school teachers, a sector of American educational labor not always held in high regard by college professors yet trained by, of course, college professors.

My colleagues and I work hard to keep the needs of future teachers in mind. When we discuss curriculum revision in Wisconsin, we invariably reveal our educational philosophies to one another. In a recent discussion of the requirements for majors and minors, my department members engaged in a typical argument about the relative value of our course offerings. One colleague exclaimed, "The way our requirements are structured, an English major could graduate without having taken

Spenser!" Others expressed concern for the uneven quality of our undergraduates' prose. We had a provocative discussion around one central question: Who are we educating and for what ends? We realized that we are not, primarily, educating future PhDs in English. Perhaps some professors find this position defeatist; after all, shouldn't we teach with the expectation that some of our students will join our ranks? Yet the dismal job market alone forces us to encourage only a small number of extremely motivated students to pursue graduate degrees. Faculty members from across higher education should ask what courses would most benefit a general public. Shall we devote more concern to ensuring that students read certain authors—Sidney, Shelley, and Spenser—or to developing their skills in critical thinking, reading, and writing? Just as my department did, our profession needs to clarify what we teach and how it might be useful to a larger public that exists in the varied cultural contexts in which colleges themselves reside.

Graduate school did not prepare me to confront these issues. When, as graduate students, we discussed teaching among ourselves, we mainly complained about the number of student essays we had to grade and groused about the poor quality of the students' writing. Looking back, I see that we enacted in those discussions an institutionalized contempt for teaching undergraduates, at times replaying the humiliations we experienced as students in our graduate courses. I sought advice on teaching elsewhere, from relatives who were dedicated teachers and from rare conferences, such as the annual Pedagogy and Theater of the Oppressed conference, which focused on teaching in a broader political sense (see Freire). Once just concerned with my performance in the classroom, I began to think about the broader ethical and political implications of teaching.

I now agree with the basic theses of "critical pedagogy": that "schools . . . work against the class interests of those students who are most politically and economically vulnerable within society" and that the "material conditions within the lives of students and teachers contribute to their understanding of who they are and how they are perceived within schools and society" (Darder, Baltodano, and Torres, "Critical Pedagogy: An Introduction" 11–12). Instead of defining students as "deficits" or empty containers to be filled with knowledge, I began to recognize that students possess preexisting cultures that influence ways they respond to material presented in class. Understanding what students bring to the classroom is not only politically sound but also pedagogically useful, since such understanding gives faculty members the ability to link course content to students' concerns. Just as the material conditions of students' lives affect their ability to learn course topics, so the economic, social, and political conditions of teachers' lives affect what we bring to the classroom. I have learned the necessity of dialogue between students and teachers, a simple realization, but one vital to an informed pedagogy.

The issue of student writing serves as a fascinating flash point regarding perceptions about students, since at most campuses, faculty complaints and dissatisfactions about student work coalesce around writing skills. As the director of composition in Montana, I heard numerous complaints about the quality of student writing. Most faculty members judged student writing as unacceptable, and they assumed the two required courses in composition, properly taught, would magically alter students' skills. In response to these complaints, and with a bit of a hidden agenda, I conducted a survey to ask faculty members about the nature of the problems they encountered in student writing, the kinds of writing they assigned in their courses, and the ways they encouraged the writing process. I found that most professors did not teach the writing process—there were no drafts, no revisions of papers, and no modeling of acceptable papers. I also asked professors, "Do you consider yourself to be a good writer? Describe your own writing process." This question revealed a great deal of the anxiety, disappointment, and even anger that faculty members felt toward their writing. While students can profit from recognizing that all writers struggle and that writing takes effort, as instructors we should realize that the attitudes and anxieties we bring into the classroom shape how we teach our subject.

Recognizing my investments in and concerns for public speaking (my ability to present myself orally in interviews and in the classroom enabled me to get jobs, after all) inspired me to become zealous about my speech class in Montana. This course was most obviously and immediately helpful to students. In Introduction to Oral Communications, I helped students achieve a sense of their voice in a direct way. Timid, plainspoken students got up, semester after semester, and shared compelling narratives about themselves and constructed well-reasoned arguments. One student described watching his best friend being mauled by a grizzly bear; another gave a eulogy for her grandmother; and a third got up in front of a group of conservative, macho young men and argued in favor of same-sex marriage. The ability to use language rhetorically—to select key details, to know what to omit, to discover a rhythm, to argue convincingly—was something these students valued. Yet this course became the most important I taught because it gave me an opportunity to listen to my students, understand their concerns, and learn more about their local culture and my new community.

A speech class can give students a direct way of presenting their stories, one unmediated by the formalities of writing. Although delivering a public speech causes an immense amount of anxiety—and I address this anxiety the first day of class—students have much more experience expressing themselves orally than in writing. The public speech also allows for a greater democracy of response, since each student's speech is heard and responded to by each member of the class as well as by me, something that only occurs with written texts in the most successful workshops. While the coercive power of the grade that supports the teacher as the authority still asserts itself, students cared at least as much about what their fellow classmates thought of their speeches as what grades they received from me.

In addition, the speech class has a clear advantage over other class discussion: every student has the exact same amount of time to speak. Although I encourage discussion in all my courses, I admit that class discussion is not always a democratic exchange of ideas. As Stephen Brookfield and Stephen Preskill note, unstructured discussion, instead of being a liberatory space, can become a place where inequities of race, class, and gender are reproduced (43). Classroom discussion often rewards glib and confident students, those who come to class already feeling entitled (because of class, race, gender, or other factors) to express themselves, whereas the same discussion silences students who are not as quick to formulate their ideas or whose confidence in speaking has been unduly eroded by cultural forces.

Speech classes also reinforce the value of listening, both for the students and the instructor. I find it immeasurably more difficult to listen actively in the classroom than to hold forth. Some of the hardest moments for me as an instructor are when students freeze up in the middle of giving a speech and become so overcome with nervousness or emotion that they cannot continue. If this type of paralysis occurs in a student paper, I can comment in the margins, give the paper a "rewrite" grade, and quickly move on. Yet experiencing student blocks in real time along with the student and the rest of the class forces me to be in the moment with that student, to witness silently his or her struggles into speech. I remember one student from out of state, Alan, who stopped two minutes into his speech, turned around, and exited the room. Since he had left his backpack in the classroom, I knew he would eventually return, and he did. I sat with him for an hour, listening to him explain his anxiety and reassuring him. I cannot remember what I said; I remember only that I felt a sense of limitless compassion and patience. The next day his speech was a success, and his subsequent speeches became more elaborate, even flowery in their diction; in fact, he became something of a star with the other students. I learned much about the power of listening in that class and an incredible amount of information about students' communities and concerns, as well as a great deal about the region. I began to see myself as a part of a community because I listened and learned, in a sense becoming a student again.

The communitarian ethos of a speech class took on weight in the institution, for I noticed that many of my colleagues in Montana seemed more passionate about improving the college and creating a more dynamic learning environment than they did about building their individual careers. Instead of focusing their efforts on trying to land jobs in schools with stronger liberal arts programs, many faculty members dedicated themselves to transforming the college's curricula. The kinds of changes effected in the last ten years would have been impossible at a large research university: University of Montana, Western, now has a strong liberal arts program; it has adopted the innovative immersion model of Colorado College, where students take one course at a time; it has established an honors program; it has changed its name, improved the campus grounds, and built a great coffee house. While this range of transformation is unusual in higher education, it has shown me the fallacy of first impressions and the intrinsically dynamic nature of a college.

Last year I invited a good friend who is working on her dissertation in medieval literature to visit me in Wisconsin for a few days so she could observe the realities of a tenure-track job. I thought it might be useful for her to see the differences between the rigors of graduate school and the more mundane and multivalenced pressures of being a professor. She sat in on my British literature courses and observed students probably less prepared and sophisticated than those she teaches at her research university in the New York City area. I worried about how I would appear to someone still in graduate school: Was I too manic in my attempts to get my class of forty-five general education students to discuss *Frankenstein*? Was my lecture on Dickens too biographical? Although I am a confident teacher, I do not feel as slick and edgy as I did in graduate school. I have had to adjust my syllabi, not dumbing them down but discovering which material will best connect to particular students' knowledge bases and concerns. I had to ask myself if it makes sense to teach Lacan to students who have not studied Freud. On the other hand, since many of our English majors are also studying education, they are capable of spirited debates about critical pedagogy.

Unfortunately for her, my friend happened to visit me during what was an unusually bad period of campus politics. In the car ride from the airport, I filled her in on the warring factions, the back stories, and my own minor involvement in weeding (or becoming a weed in) the groves of academe. I joked to my colleagues here, "Now she will never want to finish her dissertation!" I was also about to start my maternity leave, and I told her that she would probably learn more about what it was like to be eight months pregnant than about teaching. Yet these distractions from the real work of being a professor are in fact the real challenges of being a professor. One's personal life and relationships with colleagues influence, interfere with, and enrich one's job.

————

I don't know if my friend's visit to Wisconsin has sped up or slowed down her dissertation writing. She has begun to talk about moving away from the rarefied atmosphere of her graduate program to a place where she might start constructing her real life. My advice to her is not to put her life on hold any longer but to be open to the most unlikely job opportunities and not assume anything about a community until she lives there. On-campus interviews do not give candidates a true idea of a town because no community is completely static or fully knowable: they are all in the process of transforming, just as academics are in the process of becoming more open to other cultures. Although I did not choose to spend the rest of my life in Montana, the lessons I learned there I carried to my current position: the community one enters is a dynamic place that changes and is changed by one's presence in it.

WORKS CITED

Brookfield, Stephen, and Stephen Preskill. *Discussion as a Way of Teaching.* San Francisco: Jossey-Bass, 1999.

Caesar, Terry. *Traveling through the Boondocks: In and Out of Academic Hierarchy.* Albany: State U of New York P, 2000.

Darder, Antonia, Marta Baltodano, and Rodolfo D. Torres. "Critical Pedagogy: An Introduction." Darder, Baltodano, and Torres, *Critical Pedagogy Reader* 1–22.

———, eds. *The Critical Pedagogy Reader.* New York: Routledge, 2003.

Freire, Paulo. *Pedagogy of the Oppressed.* 1970. Trans. Myra Bergman Ramos. New York: Continuum, 2000.

Gaff, Jerry G. "The Disconnect between Graduate Education and the Realities of Faculty Work: A Review of Recent Research." *Liberal Education* 88.3 (2002): 6–13. 15 June 2007 <http://www.aacu.org/liberaleducation/le-su02/le-su02feature.cfm>.

hooks, bell. "Confronting Class in the Classroom." Darder, Baltodano, and Torres, *Critical Pedagogy Reader* 142–50.

Malamud, Bernard. *A New Life.* New York: Avon, 1961.

Pratt, Mary Louise. *Imperial Eyes: Travel Writing and Transculturation.* New York: Routledge, 1992.

Rodriguez, Sandria. *Giants among Us: First-Generation College Graduates Who Lead Activist Lives.* Nashville: Vanderbilt UP, 2001.

Shor, Ira. *Empowering Education: Critical Teaching for Social Change.* Chicago: U of Chicago P, 1992.

STEPHEN DA SILVA

ARRESTED INTELLECTUAL DEVELOPMENT?
An English PhD Teaches High School

An occupational hazard of writing a dissertation is that one tends to see one's topic everywhere. My dissertation explored how late-Victorian and modernist male homosexual writers challenged the association of same-sex desire with arrested development by appealing to idioms of Hellenism and primitivism. When I decided to accept a high school teaching job after a couple of unsuccessful attempts on the university job market, I must confess that I did so not willingly but because I faced immigration and personal constraints that compelled me to secure a job immediately. Framing the situation in terms of my dissertation, I felt like a victim of an arrested intellectual development. At some level, my initial preparations to teach high school precipitated a regression, as if I were reexperiencing high school, complete with its attendant adolescent awkwardness, social fear, and peer pressure. I could see why Emily Peters titled the article detailing her experiences as a PhD teaching high school "Back to High School."

A developmental narrative of sorts, this essay details my progression from a sense of alienation at the prospect of teaching high school to recognition of the particular rewards and challenges of this professional choice. The structure and scope of this volume warrant careful consideration of my professional training as preparation for high school teaching, as well as thoughtful deliberation about the differences between college and high school academic cultures. My experiences as a graduate teaching assistant and a community college adjunct instructor, combined with my doctoral course of study, prepared me for teaching high school and may very well serve the needs of

MA or PhD students who desire immersion in an alternative academic culture.

BACK TO HIGH SCHOOL

Let me start by considering the attitude many graduate English programs, and probably foreign language programs, hold apropos of high school teaching careers. When I began teaching high school, I considered the choice a professional failure. And I contend that my embarrassment and inadequacy, instead of rising from idiosyncratic symptoms of my personal snobbery, find institutional sanction and endorsement, consciously or unconsciously, in many graduate programs. My PhD program, for example, fostered among students an understanding that we undertook a doctoral course of study to prepare only for university-level teaching positions, the imagined professoriat. The most desired outcome of our labor, a job in a university with a graduate program, would enable us to create our own professional acolytes. To return to my dissertation analogy, being fully adult, according to heteronormative ideology, involves reproduction, so being a real academic involves having graduate students of one's own. The extended job crisis of the humanities professoriat has forced us to acknowledge that those lucky enough to be on the tenure track would probably end up in teaching-intensive colleges with undergraduate populations. And, horror of horrors, some graduate students might consider community colleges as a last resort. High school teaching wasn't even discussed in the pedagogy seminar required of all graduate students—the teaching job that dare not speak its name remained totally invisible to my graduate school mentors and to me.

My wrongheaded sense of high school teaching as intellectual and professional diminishment only grew when friends from graduate school or former teachers often could not hide looks of revulsion when my secret was outed. They would predictably follow up their looks of disgust with lines of consolation like, "Oh, they're lucky to have you as a teacher." The more politically correct would talk about high school as a profound time in students' intellectual growth. One of the few graduate students (who had graduated some years before me) who taught high school told me she began her job merely to get teaching experience, and then she stayed on because, unable to secure a position at a local university, she simply did not want to relocate.

Now university cultures in the United States are diverse, but when I was in graduate school my university had neither a concentration in English education nor a large education department, so the reaction to my job might have been stronger in my English department than elsewhere. Still, graduate English programs across the spectrum of university cultures would benefit from changing their generally negative disposition toward high school teaching. Program directors need to inform graduate students of the importance of the high school teaching option in a perennially tight job market—after all, the "number of public school teachers who hold doctorates in subjects other than education . . . increased from 0.5% in 1991 to 1.7% in 1996 (slightly more for high schools and private schools)," while "in 2000, 1070 new PhD's in English competed among themselves and with former graduates for 528 tenure-track assistant professorships" (Hanson-Harding 17). On a more anecdotal level, Peters points out that in the private high school where she teaches English, "70 percent of [the faculty members in her department are] PhD's" (C2).

Time can change the cultures of English and foreign language departments as well as their attitudes toward high school teaching. Since none of my university teachers had taught in high school or knew anything about high school teaching, my graduate program and my mentors therein operated on rumor and hearsay regarding high school teaching careers. Perhaps it would help faculty members and graduate students alike if university departments invited successful high school teachers, particularly successful high school teachers who hold graduate degrees, to discuss their careers. In this way, graduate students could get a better sense of the ways their training prepares them (or does not prepare them) for the challenges of high school teaching and could then consider rationally this professional option. Since I learned to be a scholar by modeling my mentors, to give successful presentations by imitating my most admirable teachers, and to teach as an adjunct by modeling my best teachers, it stands to reason that graduate students will import university values to college and high school settings. While not necessarily a negative, unreflective importation and hierarchical acceptance of such values can damage everyone involved in the academic enterprise. Simply put, graduate students need models from many academic cultures so that the values inherent in those cultures become transparent.

Another helpful opportunity for graduate students would be to assist high school teachers or to teach at local high schools—even if was just a sample unit—to expose future faculty members to an academic culture often foreclosed from university discussions, despite the historical K-12–normal school partnerships. I benefited enormously from teaching undergraduate classes at my university and as a part-time faculty member at a local community college, but I was sorely lacking high school teaching experience. While graduate students could seek teaching positions in dual-enrollment programs (community college classes that enroll high school students), teaching a college class to high school students is not the same as teaching a high school curriculum to high school students in a typical high school setting. I once taught a first-year college English class to a group of high school students for community college credit, but the dynamics and atmosphere of that class—with its Monday-Wednesday-Friday schedule and academically motivated students—resembled college teaching much more than it did high school teaching. For a graduate student to learn about high school teaching, he or she must shadow a faculty member in a regular class, following a regular high school schedule.

Just as important as, or perhaps even more important than, changing the cultures of graduate departments and the relations between universities and other academic institutions, graduate students should transform their attitudes toward high school teaching, a transformation that an expanded graduate apprenticeship might enable. Some graduate students might choose to be high school teachers, but those of us who initially join the profession with negative preconceptions and a degree of shame must then devote precious postgraduate time to unlearning our prejudices before we can recognize the excitement and challenges offered by high school teaching. Initially, I almost instinctively deprecated my own work when I responded to questions about my job with the line, "Oh, I'm chair of the English department in a little Catholic school." I *am* chair of the English department at a Catholic high school. But my response betrays both anxious aggressiveness—I mention that I am chair of the English department (there are only three of us in the department) to show that my training as a PhD has not been wasted—and the self-effacement of the throwaway "oh" and the unnecessary "little." Once I recognized this pattern, I made a conscious effort to avoid downgrading my job, and I soon began to get excited and engaged by the challenges it offered, different challenges from those I had expected from my academic career, but exciting and rewarding challenges all the same.

THE VALUE OF GRADUATE EDUCATION TO HIGH SCHOOL TEACHING

A PhD entering a high school community will likely encounter a range of different attitudes from colleagues and students, some of them taxing to the spirit. When I joined the faculty of my school, the English department consisted only of two teachers. My PhD qualified me to assume the chair of the English department, an appointment that inspired considerable resentment from a colleague who felt she had far more teaching experience than I did. She viewed me as an academician who knew nothing about life in the high school trenches. With tact, a willingness to listen, and a degree of self-assurance, one can turn most negative situations around. I have a fairly cordial relationship with that colleague today. Nevertheless, my first reaction to her suspicion concerning my qualifications for the chairship was to behave as though she possessed inerrant insight; she did, in fact, have more experience than I did in the high school setting. As a consequence, I learned a great deal from her about managing an unruly class, negotiating with parents and administrators, organizing a much heavier teaching load than I had ever experienced as a teaching assistant or part-timer. On the other hand, her degree in education, with a specialty in English, left her unacquainted with the discipline. For her, English consisted of grammar, mechanics, and a canon whose value she considered unassailable. Thus I had valuable insights to share with her, but for us to learn from each other, we first had to traverse the barriers my degree imposed, both for her and for me. Clearly, confronting a colleague is not identical to dealing with a class, but there are similar issues involved: in both cases, one's authority is challenged, and becoming defensive and authoritarian, or rebellious and resentful, deprives all parties of wisdom.

I also learned lessons from my colleague about working effectively and in partnership with my students' parents. In college teaching, faculty members have little to no contact with parents, but students' parents and guardians play an important role in high school teaching. Principals usually advise faculty members to keep meticulous records and to make good-faith efforts to stay in touch with parents. Pamela Grossman points out that "curriculum and instruction courses" stress "the importance of student ownership" in the learning process (110). I extend that useful concept to family, a collective that can take ownership of students' learning. As a high school teacher, it is not enough simply to send home numerical grades to the parents. Good faculty members reflect on the most effective and tactful way to communicate with parents, to help them recognize their child's strengths and weaknesses, and to encourage them to invest in reinforcing classroom goals. Beyond grades, I try to keep parents abreast of our classroom activities, pedagogical objectives, and the relevance of those objectives to their children's futures in college or in the work world. While this level of communication involves intensive work, the labor can lead to pleasurable outcomes. After all, as graduate students of English, we trained as professional communicators, so we can use our rhetorical skills to build strong partnerships with parents. I can testify that students whose parents care about their classroom performance tend to achieve academically at a far higher rate than do those students whose parents remain uninvolved. In that sense, high school teaching can be a far more communal affair than college teaching. It's not enough to strike an attitude as the highly qualified head of the village—you know the famous cliché of it taking a village to raise a child.[1]

A nuanced approach works with parents and students alike, especially in the light of the three academic tracks in my school: regular, college preparatory, and advanced placement (AP) or honors. Practitioners should neither fetishize these boundaries nor negate the dynamism and flexibility essential to student learning and cohesive community identities. Despite these qualifiers, I think teachers should recognize students' varied educational objectives so they can mold their courses accordingly. Let me begin with college-bound students— almost all the AP students and some of the students in the college preparatory section. PhDs have the most to offer these students. As Kathleen McCormick points out, "schools and universities seem [like] quite separate" worlds to students and faculty members alike (qtd. in Appleman 8). My own experience confirms Deborah Appleman's contention that teaching English in high schools is a mélange of Matthew Arnoldian notions of "cultural transmissiveness" (transmitting canonical texts and values to the students), reader-response criticism (with an emphasis on connecting subjective experiences to the assigned texts), and New Criticism (4). Most material published on teaching canonical texts urges teachers to make connections between the students' personal experiences and school texts. On the one hand, making literature relevant to students' lives disrupts their sense that they must crack some "artificial," "phony" code to interpret texts "correctly" (Scholes 23). On the other hand, I concur with Appleman's suspicion of the narcissism and intellectual circularity endemic to personal responses, when she asks, "Is the purpose of studying literature only to clarify our own existence and underscore our own unique personal attributes?" (28). Since many high school teachers remain generally unaware of the theoretical debates that energize university literature departments, they may not move students beyond subjectivism. Indeed, A. N. Applebee found that "72% of high school literature teachers . . . surveyed in schools that had a reputation for excellence reported little or no familiarity with contemporary literary theory" (7).

Having a graduate degree in English proves useful when introducing students to a range of reading techniques. I would never dream of terrifying my senior AP students by mentioning deconstruction or by making them read primary theoretical texts, but I have had success in asking my students to keep track of oppositions they encounter in a text (specifically, we were looking at the terms "black" and "white" in *Othello*). Then we closely read passages where these oppositions occur and worked through their contradictory, incoherent, mutually sustaining relations. Many of my students had never performed a close reading before, and some of them found it really neat. Suddenly literature appeared as something other than a collection of great boring ideas to which only the teacher had the key. A sort of accessible puzzle, students participated in the game of discerning literary patterns and of teasing out the contradictions in those patterns.

Graduate study of English, particularly of composition theories, can help high school faculty members move their students beyond simple expressive writing. Scores of high school students stop at the level of observation and subjective response in their essays. We spend a good amount of time in class talking about audience—to whom are you writing? Why is the argument you are advancing of significance to this audience? How does your argument relate to other arguments that have been made in relation to the same topic? Although my students have written research papers, their research has often been empty and mechanical. Teachers ask them to find five sources, so they obediently hunt down five sources and plug them into their papers. Less theoretically self-conscious teachers have not encouraged students to think about why they are looking at these sources or about the importance of situating their arguments in relation to a discursive history that inevitably precedes them. This lesson is particularly important in an American high school context because most of my students have an uncritical investment in myths of individualism.

At the same time that I work to use the benefits of my PhD on behalf of students and their nascent reading, writing, and critical abilities, I acknowledge one aspect of individualism that pertains to the high school teacher's profession: classes are composed of individual students who possess an enormously diverse range of skills. Faculty members must learn the virtues of pedagogical flexibility far more in high school than in college teaching. I depend a great deal on grouping in my sections—students are grouped on the basis of their abilities and are given different tasks to complete each class period. Preparation is therefore often far more time-consuming for my regular sections than it would be for a college class or than it is for my AP classes. I have to be sensitive about whether students are grasping concepts, and I have to remind myself constantly not to take students' knowledge for granted. Since adolescents are generally far too anxious about appearing foolish to ask questions, teachers must pick up cues or students will remain lost.

More often than not, retrieving lost students demands a teacher-as-entertainer model. A good part of all teaching involves being a skilled entertainer, but this is particularly important with high school students, who have shorter attention spans than college undergraduates. In planning my classes, I try to incorporate at least two or three different activities in my fifty-minute class periods because students often lose interest if one activity continues more than fifteen or twenty minutes. The lecture classes typically encountered on college campuses would just not work in a high school setting.

Whether lost or engaged, entertained or bored, high school students cannot be something other than adolescents. Discipline issues remain the most challenging feature of my high school teaching career, especially for me as an adult who has opted out of a reproductive-familial economy. Adult college students sometimes can be abrasive, but they are socialized; adolescents, by contrast, regularly test one's authority and sometimes unintentionally behave in inappropriate ways. I have no magic answers to coping with discipline issues, but here I offer a couple of suggestions. First, it took awhile, but I learned to pull back from confrontations and to develop a sense of humor and perspective. Anger places a faculty member at the level of the student who is acting out or is behaving in accordance with adolescent norms. Rather than rely on anger to discipline wayward students, I attempt to make the student see the subject's relevance to adolescent cultures or to read what is underlying the student's response: Is something going on at home, for instance, that inspires the student to act out? I strive to translate possible disciplinary confrontations into intellectual challenges. An analytic posture enforces some distance between a situation and my reaction, thus preventing me from being consumed by anger or petty irritation.

A second point I would make about discipline is that the graduate training we receive in rhetorical and literary theories pertains to high school teaching. When I first began teaching at this level, I often reacted reflexively to a student's lack of attention or disruptive behavior. Now I try to control myself and take a few moments to assess the situation. Humiliating or confronting an adolescent in front of his peers (and I use the male pronoun advisedly; the dynamics are often different with female students) often results in overtly recalcitrant insolence. It's far more effective to talk with the student after class, audience removed. Related to this issue of rhetorical communication is the issue of spelling out one's expectations. Someone just out of graduate school may make assumptions about schooling and learning behaviors that high school students need to have explicitly communicated. Students need to be told to bring their literature texts with them when class discussions focus on a piece of literature from it. Teachers have to instruct students to annotate key passages discussed in class and to participate in class discussions, an expectation common to college humanities classes but not fully understood by high school students. The same sort of rhetorical attention to audience can help faculty members write better assignments and class descriptions. Most high school students are learning basic study, academic, and social skills, in addition to the subject being taught, so faculty members must articulate all expectations in painstaking detail while concomitantly avoiding condescension. That's quite a rhetorical challenge.

Extracurricular activities, clubs, or athletic teams represent extra commitments common to high school faculty life, and sometimes they can enhance one's teaching. As the world's most unathletic person, I am pleased that I do not have to coach any sport, but this year I am one of the class sponsors for the seniors, which means I will need to acquaint myself with previous senior classes' fund-raising activities so I can help organize the prom and the senior trip. My first response to extracurricular work was annoyance. I saw these commitments as trivial, as taking me away from my classroom and my academic planning. After some experience, though, I came to view these obligations as opportunities to work with my senior students and know them better outside the classroom. I also communicate and work with the seniors' parents, and a strong relationship with parents only increases my effectiveness as a high school teacher. From the practical point of view of academic politics, teachers should make every effort to stay on the right side of their principals. Any high school administrator would be annoyed with teachers, advanced degrees or not, who zealously guard their time. Collegiality is vital in high school teaching, perhaps even more important than intellectual skills. That faculty members are stretched for time is undeniable, so they must learn how to prioritize and to be realistic. In organizing the prom, I will delegate a great deal to the seniors and their parents. Graduate school provides no training in prom organizing, planning, and execution, but effective high school teachers cannot afford to alienate their students, their students' parents, or their principals.

When I began teaching high school, I rather arrogantly imagined that I was regressing. Instead, I have entered a profession that demands that I grow. Coming out of graduate school, I possessed familiarity with a wide body of academic knowledge, but this job has taught me flexibility in my pedagogical and interpersonal skills that I did not know I had. The career offers equal measures of demands, rewards, and frustrations. My graduate training did not fully prepare me to teach at the high school level, but, in taking up this challenge, I have found that my professional development has been anything but arrested.

NOTE

1. Tchudi and Tchudi list ideas, some more practical than others, that have proved a useful launching point for me to think about communicating effectively with the villagers (213–15).

WORKS CITED

Applebee, A. N. *Literature in Secondary Schools: Studies of Curriculum and Instruction in Secondary Schools in the United States*. Urbana: Natl. Council of Teachers of English, 1993.

Appleman, Deborah. *Critical Encounters in High School English: Teaching Literary Theory to Adolescents*. New York: Columbia UP, 2000.

Grossman, Pamela L. *The Making of a Teacher: Teacher Knowledge and Teacher Education*. New York: Columbia UP, 1990.

Hanson-Harding, Brian. "Scholars in a Teenage Wasteland." *New York Times* 10 Nov. 2002, educ. supp.: 17–18.

Peters, Emily. "Back to High School." *Chronicle of Higher Education* 7 Nov. 2003: C2–3.

Scholes, Robert. *The Crafty Reader*. New Haven: Yale UP, 2001.

Tchudi, Stephen N., and Susan J. Tchudi. *The English / Language Arts Handbook: Classroom Strategies for Teachers*. Portsmouth: Boynton, 1991.

Douglas Scott Berman

OVERTURES FROM ABROAD
An Inside Look at University Teaching in Taiwan

"Globalization" has acquired a buzzword status on American university campuses these days as administrators, university presidents, and educators exhort students to avail themselves of different cultures by studying abroad and by developing greater sensitivity to the foreign students already in their midst. The nearly six hundred thousand foreign students who study in the United States foster a rich environment for cultural exchange and provide Americans with a timely reminder of their nation's interconnectedness with the rest of the world (Levin). The former Harvard president Lawrence Summers is correct to argue that "in an increasingly globalized world," students must have a sure "grasp of foreign cultures and global issues." In my case, I didn't begin to ponder what it means to live in a global world until after graduating with a doctorate in English and accepting an opening in Taiwan at Providence University, a private Catholic college, thus joining the growing pool of professionals abroad. A year later, I transferred to National Taiwan Normal University (NTNU). In what follows, I offer a brief overview of what it is like to teach in this country for aspirants to overseas professorships, and I also offer a consideration of ways my experience encouraged me to rethink the value of the humanities doctorate in a global world.

Taiwan, or the Republic of China, a small island located approximately ninety miles off the coast of China in the Pacific Rim, was my home from 1999 to 2004. In the West, Taiwan is mainly known as a major manufacturer of computer chips and as the base of the Kuomintang, the once dominant political party that fled China in 1949 to take up residence in opposition to the Communists on the mainland. After the introduction of direct presidential elections in 1996, the Democratic Progressive Party, run by President Chen Shui-Bian, has governed the country since 2000. Once a Dutch outpost, then a Japanese colony (1895–1945), Taiwan has recently emerged as one of the dominant economies in the world, ranking fourteenth on the World Economic Forum's index of most competitive countries for 2007–08.

Most of the nation's elite, including nearly all the top politicians, were educated abroad, primarily in the United States. In Taipei, the capital and a bustling, hectic metropolis of over three million people, one finds many of the conveniences of a Western city: fine dining, hotels, nightlife, and cultural events. Young people in Taiwan (as in Singapore, Hong Kong, Japan, and elsewhere in Asia) are keen on Western culture, as seen by their ready acceptance of American movies of all stripes, Western cuisine, books, magazines, and newspapers and by the amount of Internet activity (one of the highest in the world).

Yet Taiwan's enormous success has come at a price, both politically and environmentally. In the capital, space is at a premium, and a weak infrastructure, a scarce water supply, an abundance of air pollution, and a lack of resources in a country that has one of the greatest population densities in the world conspire to make life difficult for many residents (though in recent years the government has begun to enact eco-friendly policies and improve the island's infrastructure).

With regard to language, the majority of people speak Taiwanese (a variant of the language spoken by the people in the southern part of Fukien province), and a minority speak Hakka. Aborigines, who mainly reside in rural and mountainous regions, speak Austronesian. Mandarin is the language of the media, instruction, and formal use. Though not an official language as it is in Hong Kong or Singapore, English has become incredibly popular in Taiwan, as evidenced by the tremendous sums of money parents spend yearly on "cram" school tuition, English language instructional materials, and Test of English as a Foreign Language prep courses. For foreigners, any ability in a native language goes far in easing distrust (not to mention facilitating conversation). However, many foreign English professors have no experience with Mandarin and still manage to cope. Since I had studied the language as an undergraduate in the United States, I had an additional incentive to return to the country I had already visited once before, in 1990.

Since 1990, the Taiwanese government has undergone a shift in its approach to education, another incentive for me to return to Taiwan. The number of universities and colleges has grown from 50 to 144, and over half of these now boast PhD programs—an enormous expansion in a few short years (Lin-Liu A43). At National Taiwan Normal University, where I taught for four years, the level of English proficiency is arguably the best on the island, and the students are likable, open to new intellectual experiences, and exceptionally well prepared for a rigorous course of study. NTNU's traditional mission of training future teachers, once the only channel to careers in education, has changed now that other universities are also allowed to produce teachers. Nevertheless, most students, many of whom come from southern Taiwan, which is considered more traditional than the north, begin their studies here with the intention of becoming teachers. In a land where Confucius is praised as a great teacher, teaching has long been considered a stable, noble, highly moral occupation.

The cultural value assigned to teaching and teachers dramatically affects classroom dynamics. It is relatively easy for foreigners to recognize differences and similarities between Taiwanese and American students. Students here are more homogeneous than students in the United States, and they are generally shyer in the classroom, unaccustomed to expressing their opinions. At a conference on English education in the United States, a Taiwan-born academic explained to me that as a student, she judged any questions she might pose as unimportant, as impediments to the entire class's progress. As a result, she would wait until after the bell rang before approaching the professor and asking her question. Of course, the uncomprehending Western professor beseeched her to ask her question during class time so other students could benefit from the discussion, but to no avail. In Taiwan, the foreign teacher quickly learns to avoid ending a lecture or long explanation with the query commonly heard in the States: "Any questions?" A better strategy, quizzing selected students on their understanding of the material, provides teachers with a more accurate assessment of their learning than do verbal cues. At times, when many students do not comprehend class assignments, they may elect a single representative to bring these concerns to the professor; however, my experience suggests that certain students often remain lost until after the class, at which time they attempt to gain the missing information from other classmates.

While ideologies of individualism inform American students' class-room behavior, Taiwanese students demonstrate keener understandings of interconnectedness, steadfastly refusing to shame another classmate or demonstrate their own abilities at the expense of another. Given the importance of face to Taiwanese students, foreign teachers should exercise restraint in judging them. The tremendous stress associated with getting into high school and college can drum out any incentive to learn for the sake of learning. Close family ties also ensure a prolonged adolescence, and foreign teachers may be struck by students' relative immaturity—understandable, though, once we realize that most Taiwanese have sacrificed much of their childhood to getting into the best high schools and colleges. In general, foreign teachers value their encounters with students, often considering these experiences the most pleasurable part of their stay.

The kind of teaching assigned to foreign faculty members depends, of course, on the institution, though one should expect a certain amount of ESL-type courses, particularly at national universities. I have taught skills courses in listening, writing, public speaking, and conversation in addition to graduate and undergraduate courses in literature. Except for a few universities, rhetoric and composition has yet to catch on as a distinct subfield, yet foreigners should have competence in teaching composition, regardless of their research concentration.

Before negotiating for classes, however, one must first obtain the position. At Providence University, the interview procedure was fairly straightforward, emphasizing teaching effectiveness over scholarly potential. I forwarded a teaching video and curriculum vitae before completing the dissertation and was duly hired, pending completion of the doctorate. At NTNU the process is geared primarily toward research. Interviews involve a short, twenty-minute presentation on research background and interests followed by questions from the floor. In general, only large, public, research-oriented schools stress research as a condition of employment (evidence of the high caliber of the mostly foreign-trained faculty members coupled with recent pressure from the Ministry of Education to increase publication in international journals). In practice, however, course loads at the elite public institutions are just as heavy as at the private ones, though class sizes may be smaller. Regardless of research demands placed on faculty members, job seekers should know that Taiwan has no tenure-track system per se. Contracts are yearly; the first year is probationary, but after the first year, provided one conducts oneself in a professional manner, employment is almost automatic. The lack of tenure may create apprehension among foreign staff members; yet it is uncommon for a foreigner to lose employment, except in cases where teachers have clearly violated professional norms.

Provided a candidate successfully navigates the waters of applying and interviewing for a faculty position in Taiwan, the newly hired professor should set realistic goals during the first year or two on the job. As one of a fairly elite group of professionals with a native command of English, a new faculty member may feel compelled to take on more extracurricular tasks than is reasonable. Although a university contract guarantees a fixed number of classroom hours, many professors (foreign and native) supplement their income by teaching outside courses (something generally not allowed at Western universities), translating documents, editing and publishing English-language textbooks, and running "cram" schools (tutorial centers that offer training in different academic subjects to prepare students for tests). University professors have long taken advantage of the premium placed on their English skills to moonlight, but new faculty members should focus on their university obligations. In a collection of essays on Taiwanese education (the most comprehensive work in English to date on the subject), Erwin Epstein and Wei-Fan Kuo comment on the detrimental effects of moonlighting on college teaching:

> [T]he incentive to enter the faculty ranks is clearly the high prestige conferred in Chinese society to acknowledged scholars. Yet relatively low salaries impel many faculty members to supplement their salaries by teaching additional courses, which tends to reduce their overall effectiveness.   (195)

One should note, however, that the years since the book's publication have seen numerous reforms in higher education, such as the introduction of the rank of assistant professor (the absence of which is duly noted by Epstein and Kuo). The Ministry of Education, in an effort to stimulate research, has also reduced the maximum number of hours university instructors can teach. Course loads still remain heavier than in the West, and the restrictions on outside teaching are not consistently enforced. Given the leniency of the earlier system and the seemingly insatiable demand for competent English teachers, it is uncertain whether the current proposal to restrict all teaching hours to nine will succeed.

What do these reforms mean for future faculty members? Professors in Taiwan may assume extra assignments—anything from editing journal articles and directing dissertations to recording English-language dialogues—in addition to attending committee meetings, interviewing job applicants, and sometimes serving as student counselor. All these tasks provide additional financial remuneration, but they need to be balanced with one's regular duties. At top universities, a faculty member normally has the opportunity to teach at least one graduate course a semester, which has allowed me to teach my research specialty to strong students. Yet even the nuts-and-bolts English-skills courses allow teachers to incorporate previously learned pedagogical methods. Teaching public speaking, for example, required that I draw on my interests in rhetorical and performance theory and my background in the theater. Though few schools offer course work in creative writing, one may be able to tailor a literature or writing course to incorporate such an element. As an ambitious new hire, I offered a volunteer workshop in poetry composition. Only a few students signed up, and even then they expected the course to prepare them for literature tests rather than provide a forum for experimenting with their own work. As time went on, this mind-set changed, and by the end of the semester, students enthusiastically wrote poetry of their own.

The teacher should not expect poetry or prose from English language classes to entertain big ideas, since students are somewhat less receptive to political philosophy or to philosophy in general. In some of my writing classes, I have attempted to discuss the meaning of freedom and rights through such diverse writers as George Orwell, Karl Popper, and Martin Luther King, Jr. Some students responded well to certain texts, but most were not accustomed to reflecting on the role democracy might play in their lives. This intellectual roadblock traces back to Taiwan's recent history, the manner in which democracy was implemented (from the top down), and the educational system itself. As time goes on, however, and Taiwan's democracy deepens, I will be interested to find out whether the relative passivity among students continues.[1]

Student passivity may decrease as university curricula include study of newer fields of inquiry such as postcolonialism and cultural studies. Under the influence of these bodies of work, faculty members appear to pay less attention to teaching canonical literature, even though the undergraduate curriculum includes traditional survey courses known in the West. In my survey course on English literature, which is taught with the standard Norton anthology, I accompany my teaching of famous British authors with a thorough historical and philosophical background to the works we read, a pedagogical move made more compelling by the students' general lack of knowledge regarding Western historical periods. I teach the period course as a reflection on the meaning and importance of periods themselves, made more meaningful by the fact that Taiwan is a country with its own ongoing and historical dispute with the Chinese on the mainland over boundaries and sovereignty.

This brief glimpse of life in a Taiwanese university may intrigue readers and encourage graduate students to consider foreign markets in their job searches. For those planning to teach abroad, or even those who wish to broaden their education, I have some suggestions—but first, a warning: teaching abroad, particularly after earning the doctorate, is a decision that should not be taken lightly, as it carries implications that can affect an entire academic career. Even in the age of globalization, it is possible to lose one's lifeline back home. For one thing, moving abroad makes returning to a formal academic track in one's home country appreciably harder, a factor that may account for the relatively small number of new doctorates pursuing employment here. University schedules in Taiwan conflict with conference and hiring sessions in the States. The MLA Annual Convention is held at the end of December, which coincides with semester exams here. Research materials may be limited in overseas institutions, and the distance between Asia and the United States makes travel to conferences arduous. Finally, a psychological barrier comes into play once one has left the country. Now, my suggestions: I encourage aspiring teachers to learn at least the rudiments of ESL or EFL before they arrive in a foreign country. I would have benefited from a thorough course in how to teach foreign students. Future overseas faculty members should have some goal that can best be accomplished in the foreign country beyond the immediate one of securing employment. Ideally, a professorship in another country should parallel candidates' academic areas of expertise.

For the small number of faculty hires who forge lifelong careers abroad, my remarks may be less useful. These hardy souls will have plenty of time to acclimate themselves. For those less intrepid, I offer a few reasons why they, too, might consider a stint teaching in Asia. The availability of positions to foreign-trained PhDs is important. Mary Heiberger and Julie Miller Vick note that "in recent years, some Asian universities have recruited Americans very vigorously for positions." Just as important, a short-term appointment abroad allows new PhDs to fulfill the goal of graduate training by researching and teaching for pay. Along with other Asian countries, Taiwan has opened its doors to overseas faculty members, and its recent accession to the World Trade Organization has made possible academic partnerships and joint consortia between Taiwan and Western universities, some of which have now begun to establish branch campuses in the host country staffed with foreign faculty members. Even as the demand for practical English skills continues to dominate higher education curricula and hiring in Taiwan, the importation of current intellectual subjects such as postcolonialism and cultural studies benefits Western scholars adept in these areas as well. Some other benefits of working overseas are obvious: learning about another culture, reaching out to students who are inquisitive and eager to learn, and seeking out enriching experiences—spiritual, intellectual, and otherwise.

I could mention many other aspects of faculty life in Taiwan, but those who arrive on these shores will have ample time to discover their purpose and its connection with their previous training. Instead of elaborating all the details of academic appointments in my host country, I conclude by considering how my time abroad has helped me consider some of the ways university departments can encourage students to think beyond immediate disciplinary and geographic borders toward a more expansive, productive view of the humanities in a global world, even as they remain mindful of the tremendous challenges ahead in funding and staffing such programs. While my experience may or may not represent a new kind of global education taking place today, it gave me a different vantage point to contemplate my educational choices and how these choices did, and did not, prepare me for life after the doctorate.

If we trust the growing number of social critics and educators, change is certainly afoot in the professoriat. A recent survey by the Pew Charitable Trust reported in *Academe* suggests that graduate education is increasingly out of touch with the reality of postgraduate employment. Accordingly, the editors cite what has by now become obvious to many: "PhD programs persist in preparing graduate students mainly for academic careers at research universities, despite an ongoing shortage of such jobs" ("Graduate Education"). Teaching over-seas can be a justifiable alternative to the brutal job market at home; however, establishing a global curriculum in the United States will not ultimately ensure an adequate supply of academic positions for those PhDs who wish to stay in the country.

My recommendations for preparing future faculty members and for broadening graduate education are scarcely radical. I do not recom-mend that we dismantle literary curricula or abolish the dissertation. I believe specialized research should continue to constitute a significant part of the doctoral degree for obvious reasons: a graduate degree trains candidates to think clearly and exactly on a complex subject while mastering higher-level research, experimentation, and organization skills. Doctoral programs can improve their discussions of overseas teaching opportunities, according positions abroad the same respect as stateside professorships. Postdoctoral teaching internships could en-courage recent PhDs to teach for a year abroad, and doctoral course work could include "global English" to prepare candidates for their in-ternational experience. English and foreign language departments can work more explicitly to link theory to practice, teaching to cultures, and inquiry to practical politics.

Faculty members and graduate students of the humanities do much to champion the causes of globalism and civic responsibility. I am attracted to Mary Louise Pratt's proposal to change the model of the humanities department from one where the "farmer [is] always walking the fences and patching them up to make sure nothing wild gets in, nothing valuable gets out," to one where "animals . . . move from pasture to pasture and pen to pen" and where "strange matings will occur and new creatures [will be] born" (58). I have seen the re-markable adaptability, open-mindedness, and capabilities of students in the humanities. I hope it is possible for them to stand on the ground between cultures, between languages, and between teaching and schol-arship, so that cross-cultural mediation and reciprocity can replace provocation and chauvinism.

NOTE

1. According to the article "An 'Accidental Dissident' Tries to Reform Tai-wanese Education" (Xueqin), a former Taiwanese dissident has already re-turned from the United States in an attempt to develop community colleges that teach civic values for nontraditional students and to provide students

at elite universities with an introduction to founding democratic Western thinkers such as Locke, Hobbes, and Jefferson. So far, his efforts have had mixed success.

WORKS CITED

Epstein, Erwin, and Wei-Fan Kuo. "Higher Education." *The Confucian Continuum: Education Modernization in Taiwan.* Ed. Douglas Smith. New York: Praeger, 1991. 167–219.

"Global Competitiveness Index Rankings and 2006–2007 Comparisons." *Global Competitveness Report, 2007–2008.* Geneva: World Economic Forum, 2007. 10. <http://www.weforum.org/pdf/Global_Competitiveness_ Reports/Reports/gcr_2007/gcr2007_rankings.pdf>.

"Graduate Education Flawed, Study Finds." *Academe* 87.4 (2001): 14.

Heiberger, Mary, and Julie Miller Vick. "Finding a Job Overseas." *Chronicle of Higher Education* 6 Aug. 1999. 26 June 2007 <http://chronicle.com/jobs/v45/i49/4549career.htm>.

Levin, Tamar. "Foreign Students Contribute a Lot to U.S. Economy." *International Herald Tribune* 12 Nov. 2007. 26 Nov. 2007 <http://www.iht.com/articles/2007/11/11/america/students.php?WT.mc_id=rssamerica>.

Lin-Liu, Jen. "Coming Home to Taiwan." *Chronicle of Higher Education* 18 Oct. 2002: A42–44.

Pratt, Mary Louise. "Comparative Literature and Global Citizenship." *Comparative Literature in the Age of Multiculturalism.* Ed. Charles Bernheimer. Baltimore: Johns Hopkins UP, 1995. 58–65.

Summers, Lawrence. "Our Next Assignment." *Newsweek.* Intl. ed. Spec. issue. Dec. 2002–Feb. 2003: 77.

Xueqin, Jiang. "An 'Accidental Dissident' Tries to Reform Taiwanese Education." *Chronicle of Higher Education* 22 Mar. 2002: A41–43.

Lynnell Edwards

GROW WHERE YOU'RE PLANTED
The Invitation to Work at a Conservative Lutheran University

The war in Iraq has begun, and I am in chapel listening as the choir's haunting sounds of *Ubi Caritas* float through the stone sanctuary of Saint Michael's Lutheran Church. I was here on the morning of September 11, 2001, and I am here occasionally throughout the semester on days absent of national tragedies, personal crises, or existential voids that too much time spent thinking can create. The chapel service is a little fuller than usual, the message delivered by a member of the theology department more sobering, and the prayer time a little longer, though individual requests are perhaps fewer. The words of the Latin hymn are projected above the choir: "Where there is sincere love, God is there." The sound of harmonies, the sight of my students gathered for these twenty minutes of peace, and the opportunity to take a deep breath and admit I am afraid and sad and small in the face of war moves me nearly to tears. I realize I can write this essay now. Here is the distinctive feature of teaching at this Christian university: In this community, we open ourselves to the presence of God; we breathe in the divine presence and radiate its power. Concordia University, Portland, honors this commission and seeks, above all, to invite others with similar mind-sets and fundamentalist—or, as with many faculty members and some students, mainstream—Christian religious affiliations into our distinctive academic culture.

I have taught at Concordia University, which is governed by the conservative Lutheran Church Missouri Synod (LCMS), for nine years and have never stopped asking why I am here, even as I recognize the inherent worth of my work here. Many attributes of far-right institutions such as mine make it difficult to call this a good job. Faculty members here brave challenges to academic freedom wholly unlike those my colleagues from other institutions endure, and an empowered core of students drives the public, conservative face of the university in ways that invariably move me to apology and explanation when I am in other academic settings. Furthermore, faculty members face all the frustrations that characterize working at many small, not particularly competitive liberal arts colleges. We worry about competition from the University of Phoenix and other proprietary colleges marketing themselves to our demographic. We work long hours (a four-four teaching load) for low pay, very low pay. Our library is too small, our student center is nonexistent, and our students are stretched too thin trying to work too many hours to pay for their own educations and taking more credits than they are academically prepared to complete successfully. I have only two faculty colleagues in English studies and another two in history, and together we constitute the humanities department.

But the five of us delight in being true generalists and in the intellectual rewards of exploring unfamiliar questions and unsuspected connections in our community. Initially, my position was construed broadly as composition and rhetoric, and the job description included responsibilities as diverse as teaching English as a second language (with the opportunity to grow and lead the international program), teaching the Secondary Language Arts Methods course (with the opportunity to lead and grow that curriculum), developing and administering a writing center (with the opportunity to lead and grow a complete tutoring program), as well as teaching a variety of literature and writing courses, including first-year composition (with the opportunity to lead and grow that curriculum, taught mostly by adjuncts and in a variety of modes). At any university and at many larger liberal arts colleges, not only are each of these responsibilities assigned to a different position, but one or more of them may stand at intellectual or professional odds with another. Writing center faculty and staff members sometimes demand to see their roles (and their funding) as distinct from tutoring or learning centers in other subjects. Literature scholars often try to distance themselves from colleagues in composition, who likewise may be quick to diverge philosophically from the work of their counterparts in secondary education language arts. Concordia, however, like many small liberal arts colleges, has a terrific need for experts in a variety of fields who must perform as needed across the curriculum and assume leadership roles—both curricular and cocurricular—in the community as well.

Once the interview for my position began, I discovered there was not necessarily an expectation that a single individual would, in fact, take on all these responsibilities in equal measure, so I made it clear that the work in ESL and in secondary language arts would be an unfortunate stretch for me. Thus the position and my role at Concordia have become tied to the teaching of writing—of all kinds—and to the development of a comprehensive writing program, which includes the work of the writing center, the general education writing curriculum, and the literary magazine. Taking to heart the adage "Grow where you're planted," I am continually surprised by the number of blooms in various stages of bud and blossom. In my time here, I have taught journalism, introductory composition, introduction to women's literature and history, creative writing, introduction to poetry, creative nonfiction, and playwriting. I direct the writing center, and I advise the student literary journal. I have served on all but one of our faculty committees and have been part of advisory councils for faculty development and general education. My scholarship has included a qualitative study of student discourse in a biology course on evolution; essay reviews of recent scholarship on plagiarism, writing program administration, and writing center research; a narrative history of feminism and composition studies; and a book of poetry. I have written (and had staged at Concordia) an adaptation of *The Yellow Wall-Paper*.

Certainly there is a danger here of becoming so professionally diffuse that no scholarly agenda of any substance materializes, and one might look back, after a very fast twenty years of service at such an institution, and rightly proclaim, "What on earth have I really accomplished?" Because the limited pressure from the institution to publish or produce traditional scholarship (publication is generally met with a mixture of surprise and delight by colleagues and administrators, whereas the decision not to publish implies a deep commitment to teaching), the young academic should develop a real vision for scholarly growth and contribution. In addition, the macroperspective afforded by the small college suggests scholars will come to see the connectedness of differing responsibilities, thus redefining their own professional identities and their notions of scholarship. Though the juxtaposition of assorted responsibilities arises out of economic necessity, the symbiotic relations among, for instance, the writing center, a writing-across-the-curriculum program, and some features of a modest creative writing program can invigorate professors' intellectual lives in ways the architecture of universities and graduate programs generally disavows. I experienced no greater reward for the various work I have done than when, after having brought a particularly well-received poet on campus to read at an open forum, a longtime staff member remarked to a colleague, "It just seems like there are so many good things going on with writing here these days."

That this staff member was not part of the teaching faculty also points to a key feature of Concordia's Christian community: its oddly democratic and nonhierarchal structure. In some measure, the Christian promise to "make all things new" and to reorder, if not dissolve, some hierarchies, undergirds the implicit community structure at the university. In daily, observable ways, faculty and staff are not divided in their allegiances, whether in the dining hall, at the noontime pickup basketball games, at sports events where we serve as ushers, or at the orientation picnic where we good-naturedly position ourselves on the receiving end of water balloon tosses. The entire faith community celebrates arrivals and departures or personal and professional achievements, and policies that affect job welfare simultaneously consider faculty and staff needs. It is not just that we're nicer in some way or that our particular Christian community is less politicized than typical academic communities. In fact, to our detriment, we do not have a history or practice of productive dissent that would likely allow us to move forward in wiser and more economically efficient ways on matters of curriculum change, facilities development, or public outreach and awareness. But these shared community values of humility and service do drive our deep sense of mission and help dissolve emergent, and false, hierarchies.

The view of Concordia's conservative Lutheran community as both intellectually engaging and personally satisfying was some time coming for me, but I can now adopt an accommodating perspective. For the first two years in my faculty position, I considered Concordia's professional community inferior to my graduate school's community. I wanted special treatment as a member of the faculty, and I also expected a continued immersion in the specific, disciplinary activity for which I had been trained. Mark Schwehn, in *Exiles from Eden*, describes the shock young scholars experience when they leave the intellectual enclaves of graduate programs and find themselves, particularly in appointments such as mine, immersed in the messy realities of department membership and student mentoring. He points out that "faculty at all colleges and universities are trained and socialized at modern research universities where the supreme value of making and advancing knowledge is deeply instilled within them" (5). Schwehn explains that this core value comes from Max Weber's notion of *Wissenschaft*. Developed in his address to Munich University in 1918 titled "Wissenschaft als Beruf," it "remains even today the *locus classicus* for the elucidations of what has become the predominant understanding of the academic calling" (6). Weber's address to the students in Munich responds to their demands "that their teachers should become seers and prophets, asking professors to assume roles they could not responsibly perform" (7). Accordingly, "[i]n refusing the role of prophet, and in defending methodical intellectual procedures, Weber was reaffirming what he took to be the great legacy of the Enlightenment against the perilous irrationality of his contemporaries" (7).

So began the abandonment in the modern university of the nineteenth-century German learning tradition that had "emphasized the cultivation of the mind and the spirit *(Bildung)*" (7). Previously, a spiritual dimension had not been foreign to a focus on character development in the traditional model, and for its greatest proponent, Karl Jaspers, education was most certainly "involved [with] 'forming of the personality in accordance with an ideal of *Bildung* with ethical norms. . . . Education is the inclusive, the whole' " (qtd. in Schwehn 7). Schwehn points out that, unlike Jaspers, Weber argued against this kind of synthetic model of learning and character, insisting that "separate departments of learning were finally so many warring gods, self-sufficient spheres in permanent and irreconcilable collision" (7). In consequence, "[a]cademics were . . . true to their own calling when they steadfastly refused to address questions about the meaning of the whole or the purpose of human life" (7).

The rise of this Weberian model in American higher education stems from similar debates about the relative priority of character formation versus creation and transmission of knowledge and can largely be traced to debates at Harvard in the 1870s and 1880s and, even more recently, to Derek Bok's assumption that "teaching and research have little or nothing to do with character formation" (Schwehn 8). Schwehn asserts that this Weberian model *(Wissenschaft)* for faculty work enjoys a privileged position in the modern research university, and, as a result, the goals of caring for and mentoring students have become alien to junior faculty members' visions of success. From my perspective, then, fresh from the *Wissenschaft*, it seemed that no one was doing important work at Concordia. What's more, a Christian paradigm, particularly the fundamentalist and conservative position of the LCMS, appeared to make real, skeptical, academic inquiry impossible.

In a longer discussion, Schwehn finally believes that the articulation of Weber's model as void of any dimension of character formation is ultimately misplaced; Weber appropriates the Protestant work ethic to the model and in his rhetorical method does not divorce character formation from the business of the *Wissenschaft*. Schwehn goes on to note that the Harvard legacy has begun to dissolve somewhat, as educators and philosophers such as Alasdair MacIntyre, Parker Palmer, Richard Rorty, and Wayne Booth have explored the symbiotic nature of knowledge production and character formation. Ultimately Schwehn's project leads him to believe that "[t]his present-day discourse about higher learning among both the religious and the secular intellectuals in our midst should lead us not so much to solve the problems of the Weberian legacy as to reconceive them in fresh and productive ways" (19).

When a Christian university such as Concordia can stretch beyond its proselytizing and evangelistic impulses, it offers a reconceived vision of education for academicians from a range of institutions. Religious scholars point out that Christians who claim allegiance to diverse denominations share a common life within the paradoxes of the gospel: the least shall be first; salvation comes in the form of a helpless infant; there is death so that we may have life everlasting; the wise shall be rendered foolish, and the foolish, wise. And professors who work at Christian institutions—whether evangelical, fundamentalist, conservative, or liberal—wrestle continually with the paradox of faith and learning: Are the two mutually exclusive? This struggle, as anyone who works in a Christian university will quickly discover, has a long, complex, and intellectually rigorous history.

Richard T. Hughes responds to this history of struggle in his work *How Christian Faith Can Sustain the Life of the Mind*, in which he outlines the paradigms for scholarship, teaching, and service in the Roman Catholic tradition as well as in the three post-Reformation traditions: Reformed, Anabaptist (his example, the Mennonites), and Lutheran. Each of these traditions confronts the problem of faith and learning to arrive at different models for the modern university and its scholars' search for truth. His conclusions, no matter how the particularities of a denomination affect a campus and classroom experience, suggest that this fundamental paradox of faith and learning in a religious academic context allows scholarship and teaching (both implicitly service) to flourish in unique ways. He writes:

> If we wish, therefore, to teach from a Christian perspective— indeed, if we wish to honor the integrity of the academy and the integrity of the Christian tradition, and to honor them both simultaneously—then we must take upon ourselves the paradoxical vision that stands at the heart of the Christian gospel. . . . If we are comfortable with paradox, we no longer feel compelled to resolve a dilemma, to foreclose on a student's question, to eliminate ambiguity, to transform all shades of gray into black or white, or to tie up every loose end before the class concludes. Again, if we are comfortable with paradox, we can be comfortable with creativity and imagination on the part of our students, even when their creativity forces us to occupy unfamiliar ground.   (99–100)

Schwehn also finds values for the work of the academy in his notion of a Christian paradigm and thoughtfully considers "the extent to which the conduct of academic life still depends upon such spiritual values as humility, faith, self-sacrifice, and charity" (45). He makes the provocative suggestion that "[s]ome degree of humility is a precondition for learning" and asks the important question, "If I have grown to treat my colleagues and my students with justice and charity, am I more or less likely to treat historical subjects . . . in the same manner?" (49).

On this point, the small, conservative Lutheran university offers an intellectual life distinct from the small, nonreligious liberal arts college. At Concordia, the question of intellectual curiosity and paradox has been most strikingly explored in a series of seminars devoted to locating and articulating the intersections of faith and science. Without doubt, questions of faith trouble the study of many students at any institution investigating complex, cross-disciplinary issues such as homosexuality, evolution, or war. And on precisely those three topics, we have offered packed-to-the-limit seminars, cross-listed, as appropriate, in religion, humanities, psychology, and biology. Team-taught by two or three faculty members, the seminars invite vigorous debate across disciplinary, philosophical, religious, and personal lines. All students are necessarily moved to unfamiliar ground and expected to respond to scholarship that stretches their individual paradigms. Such classes aim to foster in students humility and respect for a variety of positions. Consequently, fundamentalist students (though some undoubtedly become more entrenched in their worldviews) confront the face of diversity, often through invited guests, and no longer direct their paradoxically "Christian" anger and indignation at abstractions. Liberal and even nonreligious students (of which there is a significant population) must likewise recognize the depth and complexity of conservative Lutheran religious claims and seek rational rather than angry responses to them that bring integrity and respect to these conversations, which ultimately remain in a paradoxical state. Final answers to the questions of why we go to war or determinative answers concerning human sexuality never issue forth from these seminars. Nor do the seminars allow participants to say with certainty whether a plan or design for our origins or future exists or does not exist. Hughes's explication of paradox suggests that a Christian scholar aligned with his version of Christianity might more fully contain this kind of intellectual discontinuity, particularly when coupled with humility and respect for both the subjects of study (all, implicitly, part of creation) and the members of the community (all, implicitly, our brothers and sisters). I cannot, of course, make claims that this model of inquiry or collegiality persists in every classroom and in every conversation, but I do know that while these interdisciplinary seminars have been a source of some controversy for Concordia among church leaders, they are also held up locally as models of curricular excellence and are overwhelmingly popular with students.

Justice and charity also characterize the work of the faculty community on matters of policy and student life. These values have been most apparent in Concordia's continuing conversation across the curriculum about plagiarism and academic integrity. The issue has come to the fore at many institutions, as plagiarism scandals garner headline news and the public's lament of the moral decline of today's students takes center stage in the drama of higher education. Pundits and scholars have considered every possible source for the problem: lack of moral integrity among corporate leaders impresses itself upon young adults; grade inflation and pressure to succeed at any cost inspire dishonesty; poor critical thinking skills breed ignorance of honesty; overworked (and undersupervised) faculty members pass students along; and, naturally, the general decline of Western civilization manifests itself in student cheating. Not a few times, the question of character surfaces, and colleges are challenged on the editorial pages to restore this feature of education to the public university. Evangelical and conservative Christian universities have always provided a faith-based version of character-infused curricula, though little research has documented its effectiveness and there are few models for implementing character education—faith-based or otherwise—into the college curriculum. Though we might be smug about our edge in this area, we found ourselves, when we began looking closely, just as troubled by plagiarism as our secular counterparts. For whatever reason, Christian students taught by Christian faculty members had no trouble reconciling plagiarism with their love for Jesus.

To consider the issue, Concordia created a task force consisting of faculty members from across the curriculum and from student services. Its members researched the problem, examined effective plagiarism and academic (dis)honesty models and policies, recommended changes to our official policy, as well as commenced a cultural change at the university. I headed the group as the expert on plagiarism, and we began our conversation in the way most task forces might. There was some venting about what we saw happening in our classrooms, some research into what other colleges had done to encourage academic honesty, and some airing of opinions about the need for honor codes and single-strike punitive responses to plagiarists. Ultimately, though, we concerned ourselves with effecting changes to the culture of academic integrity through three vehicles: a clear definition of "breach in academic integrity"; a just and specific process for sanctions; and a variety of curricular and cocurricular protocols and forums that would shape values and behaviors among community members. Our process was no different from the deliberative process at many institutions, I suspect. But our community's commitment to those chief values of justice, charity, and humility influenced our discussion and subsequent actions in significantly different ways than did the models for civic freedoms and responsibilities that inform other institutions.

Perhaps most concrete, the first part of our policy, the definition and explanation of "breach in academic integrity," offers a passage from the scriptures as the justification for and underlying value of maintaining academic integrity. Rather than cite an admonition ("Thou shalt not steal"), we hold up Philippians 4.8, which states, "whatever is true, whatever is honorable, whatever is just, whatever is pure, whatever is pleasing, whatever is commendable, if there is any excellence and if there is anything worthy of praise, think about these things." Though initially we disagreed about the sanctions process, there was immediate and full agreement that these words identified the value of our work. Without detailing the discussions that followed about punitive response, I can say that we sought to balance a measure of grace against the need to maintain order and justice. As we go forward with the articulation of a sanctions and grievance process and the development of community and cocurricular education, love, service, and commendation will be at the forefront of our movement.

Entering the community of a Lutheran university with Concordia's fundamentalist values also means learning to reckon with a kind of religious diversity that confronts one's sensibilities. The religious convictions I share with the tenets of Concordia's sponsoring church probably stop with "Jesus loves me, this I know." And even on that point, we would likely disagree about just who and what Jesus was. As a fundamentalist institution, the church does not ordain women, it flatly condemns homosexuality, and, perhaps most problematic, its official doctrine states that scripture is inerrant—we should understand events described in the Bible as literally, factually true: a six-day creation period, a world-destroying flood, an apocalyptic end to time. I can reconcile none of this with my understanding of the Judeo-Christian tradition and my practice of the Christian faith. I have learned the astonishing otherness of a faith community that divides all the peoples of the world into two types, Christians and pre-Christians; that considers the fossil record, scientifically dated as millions of years old, as a God-given test of our faith in the inerrancy of the Genesis account of creation; and that loves the sinner but not the sin.

Most of my immediate colleagues wonder about these positions as well, and the collegial spirit on campus, when explicitly religious, tends toward the ecumenical. Traditionally, and in my department, the university constituency locates itself considerably to the left of what the church officially proclaims as doctrine, and so relatively free inquiry characterizes the intellectual climate at Concordia University. However, the presentation and discussion of material that clashes with students' religious values lead to trouble. Compared with their religious peers at other colleges, our students are uniquely empowered to voice and act on their concerns. A film in a humanities class that contains some nudity, a discussion of social policy that considers homosexual rights, or an understanding of origins that suggests an age for the earth greater than the generations of Adam can cause, and has caused, an official grievance against a faculty member and a demand for the fundamentalist Lutheran perspective to prevail.

As a result, my colleagues in biology and theology have suffered the worst sort of academic inquisition. Because the church-university relation allows an unnamed clergy member to level charges of heresy at the highest level, the burden of proof of innocence rests with the faculty member. Even when charges come secondhand through disgruntled students or by hearsay, they must be taken seriously and given due process. Not surprisingly, the term "academic freedom" is as alive and raw to us as the word "democracy" is to a battered nation struggling under a dictatorship. And though on our side none has taken up arms, working at Concordia can mean witnessing the ugliness of church politics and the pettiness of power as it shifts from one faction of a governing body to another. At some distant time, I will no doubt look back and consider the depth of information I have about the inner workings of a church that is not my own, and I will marvel. For now, it is both frustrating and fascinating to see ways in which the politics of a church consume its members and shape their every communication.

Less consequentially, teaching at Concordia means engaging with the day-to-day religious rhetoric that characterizes official communication: faculty meetings begin with a devotion; committee meetings often open with a word of prayer; communications from the synod and the Board for Higher Education are always signed "For His Students" or "In His Service" or, when the news is particularly somber, "In the Service of the Risen Lord." Informal communication is similarly infused with the spiritual: the dean of students signs communications "Vaya con Dios"; at least two members of the theology department, perhaps in a deliberate attempt to be ecumenical, close e-mails with "Shalom." Students share favorite passages from scripture as their signature file, wish me "blessings," acknowledge their requests "for Him," and intend no irony when they wish me "God's Peace" and ask for an extension on a paper in the same e-mail. Prayer requests and thanks to God join notices of changes in dining services and spring registration as part of the daily flow of institutional communication. This is certainly no place for the person who cannot tolerate religious rhetoric;

for me, it alternates between being a kind of spiritual white noise and being an expression of the genuine affection of a community for its members.

The struggle, then, has always been whether the balance of what I share with the central mission and these ideals of what a faith-based institution might be can offset the fundamental differences between my convictions and the official doctrine of this church body. Some believe that employment by an institution that takes such a strident stand against homosexual rights or that holds up scientific incoherencies as truth is flawed enough in principle to merit dismissal, if not active disdain. To be sure, this faculty position has caused me to consider deeply my religious and civic convictions and even the matter of whether one can bracket these convictions in the pursuit of a vocation. It being no small dilemma, I have wondered more than once whether I keep this position simply because it is a full-time job, something more and more scarce in the humanities, or because the work I am doing here matters at some level beyond my own intellectual and professional satisfaction. Perhaps, though, this too is an example of how paradox shapes the life of the scholar in a Christian university, and so no final resolution is needed. Ultimately, having had to reckon with the dilemma is what gives meaning to the life.

In chapel once again, I join the community in its yearly anniversary celebration to praise the service of faculty and staff members who mark their ten-, fifteen-, twenty-, and forty-year anniversaries. There is no other way to characterize the special service than as joyful. We sing uplifting hymns (no small accomplishment for Lutherans, who, as Garrison Keillor has noted on more than one occasion, are a particularly somber bunch), and we recognize these members of our community and the families who have supported them. Our president makes a brief, personal statement about each honoree that is sincere in its gentle humor and deep appreciation. A representative from the board of regents brings greetings and praise thick with "the Lord's blessings," and the "joy of service in Christ," and "praises for our Lord and Savior," and we proceed out to the sturdy strains of the school song, the first and only school song I have ever known.

In the reception that follows, I visit with the honorees and my colleagues who have attended the celebration and then press on to the cafeteria where I am scheduled to meet with two students whose creative writing theses I am directing. As I have no classes scheduled this day, the rest of the morning and the early afternoon are spent taking care of minor administrative tasks associated with directing the writing center. I read and consider a response to the scholarly electronic discussion list to which I subscribe. I decide to procrastinate another day before cracking a stack of papers from my creative nonfiction class. Has the day been really different from a day teaching at any small, not particularly competitive liberal arts college? Perhaps not, unless I have made it so. The invitation from the community to make the day different, by filling it with the divine, is always there at the heart of a fundamentalist Christian university honoring its mission. For some, it is an invitation that is worth considering, a vocation worth pursuing.

WORKS CITED

Hughes, Richard T. *How Christian Faith Can Sustain the Life of the Mind.* Grand Rapids: Eerdmans, 2001.

The New Oxford Annotated Bible. Oxford: Oxford UP, 2001.

Schwehn, Mark R. *Exiles from Eden: Religion and the Academic Vocation in America.* New York: Oxford UP, 1993.

Part II

REFLECTIONS ON CAREERS AT TEACHING-INTENSIVE COLLEGES

ROBERT CHIERICO, FABIOLA FERNÁNDEZ SALEK,
EVELYNE NORRIS, AND VIRGINIA SHEN

UNDERGRADUATE FOREIGN LANGUAGE INSTRUCTION
A View from an Urban Campus

Originally founded in 1867 as an experimental teacher-training school, Chicago State University (CSU) has evolved into a multipurpose university committed to meeting the needs of its urban community by adhering to a clear mission that emphasizes high-quality teaching. CSU is sensitive to its multiracial student population, one reflective of the demographics of the Chicago metropolitan area, particularly the southern and western areas of the city and its adjacent suburbs. The student body currently consists of more women than men, many part-time students who work full-time, many students from low-income backgrounds, and a good number of returning students (*Chicago State University* 15). Cognizant of the need to consider the dialogic relationship between CSU's academic culture and students' cultures, the members of the Department of Foreign Languages and Literatures have developed strategies to enable student success. These strategies include designing and delivering a high school–to–college transition program for minority students, providing special Spanish courses for native speakers, ensuring a strong study-abroad program, and offering a complete range of foreign language course offerings, including less commonly taught languages such as Chinese and Arabic.

The purpose of the department reflects the mission of Chicago State University in that it stresses preparation in the humanities; provides access to traditionally underrepresented populations, especially Hispanic students; and contributes to the economic and social welfare of CSU's community. A collaborative effort, this essay represents voices from a specialized academic culture—the urban university, whose faculty is devoted to serving underrepresented groups of students—and indicates some of the innovations possible in that culture. Small foreign language departments across the country can implement programs aimed at increasing student success and at transforming the communities to which such departments pledge their service.

HISPANIC FUTURE PROFESSIONALS ACADEMY

After members of the department surveyed some of the most pressing needs of our community, we collectively agreed to address the challenge of ensuring student access to the university. CSU has a liberal admissions policy—18 ACT score and a 2.5 GPA—but a number of minority students fell slightly below this standard. Anecdotal information suggests that borderline students contribute positively to the university environment when provided the additional support necessary to transition successfully from high school or employment to college-level study. With this information in mind, the Hispanic Future Professionals Academy was born.

The program represents a joint effort among the Department of Foreign Languages and Literatures; the Department of English, Communications, and Theatre; the Department of Math and Computer Science; and the Office of Academic Support. The original concept was simple: while students were still in high school, they would be offered English and math courses to improve their basic skills, as well as advanced Spanish classes to maintain and strengthen their native language. Students would then participate in a summer bridge at CSU to prepare for the ACT. Once they matriculate at the university, Hispanic Future Professionals Academy faculty and staff members would track and counsel them to ensure their success throughout the first year of study. To make our simple concept a reality, we submitted a grant proposal to the Illinois Board of Higher Education (IBHE) in 2003 as a New and Expanded Program Request, which met curricular approval without funding. Consequently, in 2004 the departments proposed to fund the project through an IBHE-sponsored Higher Education Cooperative Act grant. Funded at about one-third of the original request, faculty members who ran the program chose its most important components, given the budgetary restrictions. They focused on strong ACT preparation to help students enter the university in the first place, followed by a substantial summer bridge to enable mastery of basic English and mathematics skills.

After several months of extensive recruiting at area high schools, our pilot project of Saturday classes began in spring 2004; the students attended intensive English from 9:00 to 11:00 a.m. and intensive math from 11:30 a.m. to 1:00 p.m. Results from this initial effort were mixed. Three of the ten students in the class completed the twelve weeks and retook the ACT in June. Of those three, one attained a score high enough for admission to CSU, while the other two were counseled to attend a community college. Evaluations indicated a one hundred percent satisfaction with the program: after participation in the Saturday classes, students reported higher levels of internal motivation and interest, along with better understanding of the disciplines.

The summer experience yielded more positive results than did the spring pilot. Faculty members focused on serving one population of students, University College students, or those who have slightly lower ACT scores or lower GPAs than are required for entrance. Students sat for placement exams in reading, math, and English to identify target areas for improvement during their course of study in the summer bridge. The remedial courses yielded success: 72% of students passed Basic Mathematics, 100% passed Basic Algebra and Intermediate Algebra, and 82% passed Writers' Workshop II. The formula for this success was to create small classes and offer students intensive academic and personal support. The summer classes averaged ten to twelve students; the maximum was fifteen. Tutors were available for students all day in a drop-in facility, and some tutors attended class sessions to follow lectures and then met with students directly afterward. The director of the Summer Bridge Program monitored students' work carefully, consulted with students often about their progress, and provided counseling and academic advisement.

The following year saw a grant renewal at the 2004 level of funding, an amount that greatly limited the project. To increase the program's effectiveness and to build on its previous successes, CSU's faculty enlisted the help of the university's Office of Academic Support. In addition to working closely with the summer bridge students, staff members from this office agreed to conduct a carefully designed follow-up review throughout students' first year, monitoring progress, tracking grades, and counseling students regularly. If students showed any weaknesses in certain classes, their instructors would receive a request for specific information about the cause of students' poor performance, and counselors from Academic Support would then conduct a follow-up analysis.

Since the guidelines for renewal of the Higher Education Cooperative Act grant required the program to demonstrate development, additional CSU funds allowed us to reorganize the Summer Bridge Program experience into a learning community, one that would place Chicago State University's principal student groups, African Americans and Hispanics, into contact with each other, especially since evidence suggested self-segregation had limited cross-racial interaction. Keeping this in mind, we introduced diversity as the theme for the program. Students in English and Spanish classes studied this core theme while fulfilling requirements for their classes. To understand diversity more fully, students read short stories and the instructors lectured on the American experience from a variety of perspectives: Mexican, Puerto Rican, Cuban, and African American. Students recorded their reactions to what they learned in a cultural journal, insights that formed the basis of public presentations they delivered at an end-of-the-course celebration.

Although our Summer Bridge Program gave us cause to celebrate, minority students, especially heritage speakers, continued to face challenges after they matriculated at the university. The Department of Foreign Languages and Literatures responded to these challenges by creating an array of course offerings, some of which are described below.

SPANISH FOR NATIVE SPEAKERS

In response to Chicago's large—28.2% in 2006 ("Chicago City")—Hispanic and Latino population, Chicago State University's Department of Foreign Languages and Literatures offers two Spanish majors, Spanish, liberal arts, and Spanish, K–12 teaching. The department also serves bilingual education students as well as students who opt for the Spanish certification through the College of Education. In 2005 the distribution of students in the Spanish program was 66.7% heritage speakers and 33.3% native English speakers ("Fall Enrollment"). Since the level of fluency among native speakers varies widely, the classroom becomes a site of communication and miscommunication.

Before we continue, it is important that we define the key terms of our discussion. A *native* or *heritage* speaker, according to Guadalupe Valdés, is defined as "a language student who is raised in a home where a non-English language is spoken, who speaks or at least understands the language, and who is to some degree bilingual in that language and English" (38). To address the needs of our heritage students, our department created two courses: Spanish for Native Speakers I, "an accelerated review of language skills for native and near-native speakers of Spanish," and its continuation, Spanish for Native Speakers II (*Chicago State University* 589). These courses are designed for the native speakers, most of whom acquire language skills in informal settings, which usually leads one to "speak what may be interpreted as rural or stigmatized varieties of Spanish." Although teaching "the prestige or standard variety [of Spanish] involves developing metalinguistic awareness about the differences between the standard and other varieties" (Peyton, Lewelling, and Winke 3), these courses by no means attempt to undermine the rich backgrounds students bring with them into the Spanish classroom. Instead, they facilitate the transition from informal settings to formal educational settings by addressing issues such as bilingualism, grammar, syntax, and writing on par with oral skills. Our heritage courses move well beyond concerns of grammar, though, when they implicitly and explicitly capitalize on students' knowledge bases, ultimately increasing cultural diversity awareness and building bicultural individuals capable of bridging cultures in the classroom and in society.

MEETING THE NATIONAL DEMAND FOR CHINESE-LANGUAGE INSTRUCTION

Always aware of our role in cross-cultural exchange, CSU's faculty members strive to keep abreast of new trends in foreign language instruction and scholarship, something hardly unique to us, even though teaching-intensive colleges sometimes suffer from being mislabeled "intellectual outposts." The small size of CSU's Department of Foreign Languages and Literatures does not preclude its faculty members from teaching a variety of languages. Since the implementation of a six-credit-hour foreign language requirement for undergraduates in 2003, the department has offered a variety of language courses, primarily at the elementary level, including German, Arabic, Wolof, Japanese, and Chinese. The latest addition to our course offerings is Chinese.

As China has moved toward superpower status in recent decades and as Taiwan and Singapore, where Chinese is also the official language, have assumed leadership roles on international political and economic stages, the United States State Department has designated Chinese a critical language. The rise of China is driving new demand for Chinese-language speakers across the business and social sectors, creating an urgent need for American students who can demonstrate a functional proficiency in Chinese. Citing a survey conducted by the Modern Language Association that fixes the number of college students studying Chinese in higher education in 1998 at 28,456, the Asia Society,[1] in its annual report for June 2005, lists Chinese as the sixth most commonly studied foreign language in the United States (*Expanding*). The same MLA survey shows 34,153 students studying Chinese at American institutions of higher education in 2002, representing 3% of college students taking foreign languages and a 20% increase from 1998 (Welles).

Schools throughout the United States remain largely unprepared to meet the need for Chinese-language study, lacking qualified teachers, sound programs, and creative uses of modern educational technologies. A report in the *Chicago Tribune* indicates that Mandarin Chinese, the most widely spoken form of the language, has become the new "it" language among students, business executives, and others trying to gain useful career and life skills (Aduroja). The Asia Society's report calls for a national commitment to teaching Chinese language and culture and suggests short- and long-range strategies to address the question, What would it take to have 5% of American high school students learning Chinese by 2015? To meet this goal, the Asia Society indicates critical issues that require systematic attention from American colleges and universities, such as the creation of qualified Chinese-language teachers, an increase of the number and quality of Chinese programs, and the development of appropriate curricula, materials, and assessments (including technology-based delivery systems) for Chinese-language instruction (*Expanding*). Interest in learning Chinese is steadily growing among American youth, but the small number of school programs and a weak educational infrastructure conspire to limit the demand for Chinese-language instruction.

To address the disparity between the increasing need and limited capacity for Chinese-language instruction, CSU is building the foundation to support a pipeline of Chinese-language learners who will meet regional and national demands for fluency in Chinese. The Department of Foreign Languages and Literatures has developed various programs to concentrate on the service area of the Chicago Public Schools (CPS), since the CPS system is implementing world-language programs in fifteen languages, including Chinese, at elementary and secondary levels. To partner effectively with CPS, our department now offers a certification in Chinese, which requires thirty credit hours in the areas of language, culture, literature, and the professional fields of students. This certification will prepare students and other citizens to conduct business and to establish professional ties with the emerging Chinese markets. Another of our projects, an endorsement program in Chinese to fulfill the immediate need for certified teachers of Chinese, is available to persons already certified to teach at the secondary level. The department's endorsement offers teachers twenty-four hours of course work in Chinese, which we hope will lead them to successful completion of a state content-area exam and a score of Intermediate High on the oral proficiency exam.

The CSU Department of Foreign Languages and Literatures currently offers elementary- and intermediate-level language courses in Arabic, another language the United States State Department identifies as critical. We intend to expand Arabic offerings to support an Arabic certification, which will require thirty credit hours in the areas of language, culture, literature, and the professional fields of students. This certificate will prepare students and other citizens to conduct business in, and establish professional ties with, Arabic-speaking nations.

Given the urban student body of Chicago State University, pipeline programs in Chinese and Arabic languages reflect the mission of the university by preparing students to shape discussions about global diversity. These programs also contribute to the economic and social welfare of the community, offering learners unique opportunities to keep abreast of critical languages and to understand more deeply the cultural knowledge necessary to succeed in business and social sectors.

We hope to establish in the department the model higher education Chinese program in the Midwest. As American schools and government officials grow increasingly concerned about the lack of expertise in languages considered critical to national prosperity and security, the programs at CSU address the need for an expanded national commitment to world languages and international studies.

CROSSING CULTURAL BRIDGES: STUDY ABROAD

Our department's faculty prides itself on establishing dynamic study-abroad programs that enable CSU students to enhance their learning of languages and cultures. The department offers summer study-abroad programs at La Universidad Castilla–La Mancha in Toledo, at the Université Internationale d'Eté in Nice, and at the National Kaohsiung University of Applied Sciences in Taiwan.

The complex nature of language learning and cultural study demands multifaceted programs to meet students' needs. The required predeparture language and cultural sessions help students prepare for their experience. For the Spanish and French programs, session leaders stress functional uses of language, role-playing scenarios from everyday life (e.g., ordering food in restaurants, banking in town, asking for directions). Students review grammar and vocabulary independently with multimedia programs such as the *Rosetta Stone Language Library*. The Chinese program stresses basic Chinese vocabulary and expressions as well as simple Chinese writing and numbers, primarily because most students in this program have no experience whatsoever with Chinese. All predeparture sessions include in-depth discussions of culture and society. Information about customs, social issues, politics, geography, and history is gathered through authentic reading materials, the Internet, films, and documentaries. When students familiarize themselves with nuances of their new environment before their arrival, they often experience less stress and more confidence in the host country.

Predeparture orientation sessions also prepare students to deal with the inevitable culture shock associated with studying abroad. As noted in *Maximizing Study Abroad*:

> While we often talk about learning a language as if it were just one skill, it's really a number of skills. Thinking in terms of

strategies for dealing with different elements of language helps
to make language learning a more manageable process.
(Paige, Cohen, Kappler, Chi, and Lassegard 164)

Faculty members suggest strategies for students to improve their listening comprehension, vocabulary growth, communicative clarity
(oral), reading comprehension, and writing fluency while living in the
host country. We also articulate strategies for resolving intercultural
conflict so students can manage the interplay of social and linguistic
skills foundational to a successful study-abroad experience.

In language and intercultural preparation CSU's predeparture program is similar to many programs nationally. But it also includes content on the representations of Americans and of our minority cultures
abroad. In particular, African American and Latino students abroad
most often do not correspond to the stereotypical American that
French, Chinese, or Spanish hosts imagine. These students may be confronted with certain stereotypes their hosts have internalized about mi-
norities in America. Just as our students want to learn more about the
peoples and cultures of the host country, French, Chinese, or Spanish
hosts want to know more about Americans. Critical reflection on our
identities, backgrounds, and values helps minority students become
true ambassadors of culture, dispelling along the way some of the many
destructive stereotypes of African Americans and Latinos and introducing hosts to the rich cultural diversity of the United States.

When students return home, they assess the strengths and weaknesses of the study-abroad experience and review their learning. We
ask, Has the experience increased their ability to communicate and
understand the target language? What have they learned about the
peoples and cultures experienced? How has the experience helped
students view the world and the United States differently? How have
they changed as a result of their contact with other cultures? What
additional skills and dispositions have students developed? Renewed
outlooks of the world and their own cultures and identities are often
made evident in students' presentations and journal entries. They
particularly mention the challenges of uncertainty, the awareness
of differences and similarities between the host culture and their
own, and above all the decentering of the United States and Americans. CSU and other colleges in the United States must redouble efforts to close the gap between opportunities offered to mainstream

American students for study abroad and those offered to minority students.

———

CSU continues to offer more opportunities to help its minority student body develop strong foreign language and cross-cultural skills. These important initiatives (Hispanic Future Professionals Academy, Spanish for Native Speakers, new Chinese and Arabic programs, and study abroad) from one of the smallest departments at Chicago State University reflect its faculty members' strong commitment to offering unique and academically sound programs to African American and Latino students. Universities nationwide develop the new global citizen, one rooted in and knowledgeable about local realities while open to the world and its interconnectedness. In these exciting times, Latinos and African Americans will not be left behind, should the efforts of our faculty and faculties from similar colleges and academic cultures continue.

Recent PhDs have strong preparation in the knowledge base of the discipline as well as in their areas of specialization, but new assistant professors may not realize the challenges early years of a professorship pose, especially in the realm of pedagogy, the intersection of theory and practice. The graduate school experience of new PhDs leads them to expect that their students will discover the laws and principles governing a discipline without fairly constant professorial intervention. When the new professor leaves graduate school and transitions from student to professor, the opposite situation soon becomes painfully clear. One realizes that many undergraduate students cannot always grasp from the beginning a particular lesson. New instructors necessarily rework the course's material, revisit many concepts in diverse ways, and immerse their students in the subject matter. All this requires labor-intensive experimentation with new pedagogical methodologies and approaches.

In a teaching-oriented institution such as CSU, faculty members encounter a heavy teaching load, typically consisting of four classes a semester, for a total of twelve contact hours a week. As well as holding office hours and counseling and advising students, instructors often take on additional classes to cover a broad curriculum and to enable majors to graduate in a timely manner. Faculty members experience a conflict between teaching responsibilities and pressures to engage in research and publication for retention, tenure, and promotion. The ever-dwindling resources at state-funded universities compound this problem.

Fortunately for CSU's new faculty members, the university's Faculty Development Program eases the transition into the CSU culture. New faculty members from across the university participate in a program of orientation focused on learning about the characteristics of the CSU student body. In addition, a monthly discussion group concentrating on classroom instruction allows new faculty members to share the teaching experience. As the year progresses, faculty members take part in workshops on learning styles, cooperative groups, multiculturalism, and classroom assessment.

Despite the challenges of building an academic career at an urban university with a teaching mission, rewards that cannot be measured in concrete terms abound. These rewards may take the form of helping a student-teaching candidate become a competent, gifted teacher or seeing the joy of the student traveler who steps on foreign soil for the first time and realizes the power of communicating in a foreign language. The most important reward for faculty members who dedicate their professional lives to urban universities, perhaps, is enabling first-generation college students to achieve new heights, both intellectually and materially. Chicago State University is the appropriate place for this dream to become a reality.[2]

NOTES

1. Asia Society is the leading not-for-profit educational institution in America that promotes understanding of Asia and facilitates communication between Americans and the peoples of Asia and the Pacific.
2. We would like to acknowledge the helpful comments and suggestions from Eddy Gaytán regarding the faculty experience at Chicago State University.

WORKS CITED

Aduroja, Grace. "The 'It' Language." *Chicago Tribune* 27 Sept. 2005, sec. 1: 1+.

"Chicago City, Illinois." *2006 American Community Survey*. United States Census Bureau. 27 Nov. 2007 <http://www.census.gov/acs/www/>. Path: American FactFinder; Chicago, Illinois.

Chicago State University Undergraduate Catalog, 2004–2006. Chicago: Chicago State U, 2004.

Expanding Chinese-Language Capacity in the United States. Asia Society. June 2005. 6 July 2007 <http://www.internationaled.org/publications/ChineseLanguage5.pdf>.

"Fall Enrollment Report for Majors, 2005." Office of Enrollment Services, Chicago State U. 2005.

Paige, Michael, Andrew Cohen, Barbara Kappler, Julie Chi, and James Lassegard. *Maximizing Study Abroad: A Student's Guide to Strategies for Language and Culture Learning and Use*. Minneapolis: Center for Advanced Research on Lang. Acquisition, 2002.

Peyton, Joy Kreeft, Vicki W. Lewelling, and Paula Winke. "Spanish for Spanish Speakers: Developing Dual Language Proficiency." *CAL Digest* 1.9 (2001): 1–7.

Valdés, Guadalupe. "Heritage Language Students: Profiles and Possibilities." *Heritage Languages in America*. Ed. J. K. Peyton, D. Ranard, and S. McGinnis. McHenry: Center for Applied Linguistics, 2001. 37–77.

Welles, Elizabeth B. "Foreign Language Enrollments in United States Institutions of Higher Education, Fall 2002." *ADFL Bulletin* 35. 2-3 (2004): 7–26. <http://www.adfl.org/resources/enrollments.pdf>.

ELLEN COHEN

"WHERE IS THE CENTER OF THE WORLD?"
Teaching ESL at a Border College

To break the ice, people just meeting me often ask, "What do you do?" Rather than provide a one-word answer, I reply, "I help students map out plans to accomplish their long- and short-term educational and life goals." This is how I spend most of my time in the classroom and in my office, which overlooks expansive green-and-brown-checkered fields of cauliflower, lettuce, broccoli, and cotton that are, or have been, cultivated by 50% of my adult English-as-a-second-language (ESL) students and their families. The backbreaking fields, bordered by the thirty-miles distant Kofa Mountains and with a horizon of endless blue skies, ironically inspire Arizona Western College (AWC) students' dreams of employment beyond the hundreds of irrigated acres. This view and those dreams remind me every day to keep myself focused on the long-term perspectives and goals of our ESL program and its students and on the mission of our community college—"to offer educational, career, and lifelong learning opportunities through innovative partnerships which enhance the lives of people in Yuma and La Paz counties." That mission statement took an advisory committee of community educators, business people, college students, and staff and faculty members a full year to agree on. After much debate, "people" replaced the word "citizen," and the statement was approved by the Arizona Western College Governing Board. It appears on every college publication and business card so that our 12,000 students cannot miss it. The composite student profile at our college is a thirty-three-year-old, married, working Hispanic mother who studies part-time. This profile mirrors our ESL population. ESL faculty members guide students toward mastery of linguistic competencies and help them use the vast network of resources available to them in the classroom and throughout our campus and service area.

From twenty-five years of teaching ESL to adults from eighteen to eighty, a simple set of guiding principles has emerged that governs the ESL exercises, class plans, program designs, committee meetings, and workshops in which I participate. I call it the Ladder of Questions: Who, What, When, Where, Why, How. Applying the Ladder of Questions to my work helps me manage the class load, committee work, professional development, and community service that make up the life of a community college professor.

Where Is the Center of the World?

At the beginning of a semester, I want to learn about my students' lives and assess their knowledge of the college's ESL community. To these ends, a quick, humorous geography quiz reduces students' classroom anxiety and enables them to establish a rapport with one another. Students ask one another, the questions, "From which direction does the Colorado River flow?" "Where is the center of the world?" "Where can you climb the stairway to heaven?" The answers are fun, and they provide a convenient springboard for explaining three question formations included in the core competencies for this particular ESL level: *be, do* or *does, can.* When I bring out the map, students are surprised to learn that in this part of the world the Colorado River trickles from the east to the west (not north to south, as it does just about everywhere else), linking southwestern Arizona to California, Sonora, and Baja California del Norte, Mexico. It brings us to miles of sand dunes and the self-proclaimed center of the world: Felicity, California, population five, home of a three-person substation of the California Highway Patrol, a pyramid, and a thirty-foot-high wrought-iron spiral staircase from the Eiffel Tower that sits alone in the middle of a sandlot and stops in midair. If you climb to the top, you will be halfway to heaven and thirty miles west of Arizona Western College, where the students are the center of my world.

WHO ARE THE STUDENTS?

In a typical ESL class of 25 or 30 students, 90% are Latin American women between eighteen and sixty-five who possess varying degrees of formal education. Five percent are Latin American men, and 5% are men and women from Korea, Japan, Malaysia, and Indonesia; an occasional student comes from Croatia or Israel. This last 5% often consists of military spouses or people connected to the management teams of the *maquiladoras* in Sonora or Baja California del Norte. ESL classes commonly have students with sixth-grade educations sitting alongside students who studied accounting, computer science, nursing, education, medicine, or law in their home countries. In every ESL class, there are graduates of local high schools. These students usually have a broad range of vocabulary and high oral and aural abilities but low written skills. Most students have come to the Yuma area because they or someone they know is connected to work in the fields. English is their common goal and their ticket out. Before 9/11, students were quickly waved through the border checkpoint on their way to class at one of our satellite centers a few blocks from the Arizona-Sonora border, but now they must obtain a student visa and have proof of insurance, thus making the ticket out all the more difficult to obtain.

One student, Francisco, moved to Yuma from Mexicali, Baja California del Norte, where he had been in charge of a large computer system in a factory. He had two children, and his wife was trained as a teacher. He thought that since 56% of the Yuma area population was Hispanic, he and his wife would not have any trouble finding jobs. It had not occurred to him that he would need to learn to read and speak English to secure one of those jobs. After working in the fields for a few seasons, Francisco noticed a big swash of trees on a hill in the distance and discovered AWC. After the family scrimped and saved, he enrolled in and completed four semesters of ESL classes, had his Mexican university transcripts translated and evaluated, took a few computer courses, and graduated from our community college with an associate's degree in computer science. Francisco went on to earn a bachelor's degree in the same field from Northern Arizona University (NAU) in Yuma, which shares our campus. Now Francisco has two bachelor's degrees and is in charge of the same academic computer lab where six years earlier he had been terrified at having to ask in English how to get an e-mail account.

One student's success, though, belies the tremendous complexities ESL students confront on their way to achievements and defeats: figuring out how to pay for school, gasoline, books, and child care; enrolling in a new, complex, and impersonal educational system; and finding the time and the courage to enter an American classroom full of strangers taught by someone who speaks an even stranger language. On the first day, many of my students literally cannot speak, so scared are they. It is my job to help them discover that the classroom is filled with people who will become their friends, study buddies, and carpool companions. It is also my job to help them understand that learning a language takes more than four hours of class time a week, that explaining to their families why meals will go uncooked and laundry unwashed unofficially accompanies the course's curriculum, and that feeling at ease with my rapid-fire yet clearly enunciated English will materialize over sixteen weeks together.

Establishing Classroom Community

The special experience I bring to teaching on the border is having lived in another country and learned another language. Some master's and doctoral programs require study abroad or immersion programs of their graduate students. The ability to empathize with students who brave immersion in other cultures and languages cannot be underestimated. When faculty members perform in another language the way we require our students to perform, we really discover efficient, interesting, useful methodologies for learning, teaching, and assessing language acquisition.

While living, learning, and teaching in Mexico, I observed that students' classroom participation consists mostly of listening and note taking. My Korean and Japanese students report that this is also the situation for them. To help students get used to the more aggressive American style of asking questions, I have created several activities for the first week that help me understand their strengths and weaknesses and that lessen their inhibitions. During our first class meeting, students write anonymous questions concerning the community, school, class, course, or me on index cards. After five minutes, I collect the cards, read through them, and answer them aloud on the spot. Here are a few examples of the questions students write on the first day of a second-semester writing class: "Why you teach?" "You like you job?" "How many time you teach?" "How many years have you?" "Are children?" "Is hard the class?" The answers lead to a review of the syllabus, course outline, and my background. Openness to students' questions introduces them to the power they have in determining their levels of participation (and learning) in the class. Students love to hear the answers to the anonymous questions. They take more risks. From the very first day, I encourage students to ask questions without fear so that when they have questions during an exercise or class period, they are already comfortable raising their hands.

Immediate and continuous language-assessment activities play vital roles in establishing community in the classroom. Because placement tests do not often cover oral, written, grammatical, and lexical skills, students in a given class may speak well but not write well, and vice versa. Teachers must immediately assess students' skill levels by creating classroom materials that stimulate their affective, behavioral, and cognitive processes. Designing language exercises that allow students to relate the content to their everyday lives while providing structured opportunities for them to copy, combine, and create helps students readily see how much they can control and contribute to their language-acquisition progress.

On our first or second day of class, I project fifteen personal questions on the giant screen at the front of the classroom. Students read them aloud and write their answers, which I read carefully after class and keep private. Their handwriting provides a clue to determining students' levels of formal education, and their answers reveal the students' comprehension, grammar, syntax, vocabulary, spelling, and editing abilities. At this level, I use only present or past tense in the questions, "What is your name?" "Why are you taking ESL classes?" "Where did you study English in the past?" "When did you study English?" "How did you study English?" "What aspects of English are difficult for you?" "What aspects of English are easy for you?" "What are your educational and career plans?" "Do you have difficulty seeing the blackboard, hearing me, or do you have any other concerns I need to know about?" "Do you work?" "When and where do you work?" "Do you take care of other people (parents, spouse, children, siblings)?" "Do you have a car that runs?" "Do you have a phone number or e-mail address?" "Where do you live?" (This last question often concerns students, so I remind them that I am not part of the United States Immigration Service. I only want to determine who can ride with another student if someone's car breaks down or runs out of gas.) I make copies of their answers for my class files and return the originals the next class period with a note of thanks, a welcome to our class, and corrections to the major grammatical and spelling errors. The immediate personal attention and welcome allow students from diverse backgrounds to become members of a special group, our class.

Advising students outside class enhances their sense of community and assists them in growing certain academic skills; making the best use of the school catalog; understanding the admission, placement, and registration procedures; and so forth. Various members of the family usually join these advising sessions in our tiny offices, but faculty members recognize the importance of advising the whole student and the whole family, work inherent in teaching ESL at a community college on the border. Because ESL students are often the translators and transporters for the family, their studies and class attendance can be unexpectedly interrupted. These family responsibilities frequently undermine their success in class. Students learn to communicate with their families about reassigning responsibilities to another family member while class is in session.

How Do ESL Teachers Spend Their Time?

The full-time ESL faculty members at community colleges focus on the students, institution, and community; teaching and learning occupy most of their time. The Faculty Appraisal Guidelines at AWC designate 80% of faculty workload to teaching implementation and 20% to professional development, college service, and community service. Faculty members typically teach 15 to 18 credits a semester and hold a minimum of one office hour for every 3 credits taught. Heavy teaching and office-hour loads keep faculty members on campus and in contact with one another. Since teaching involves so much more than showing up with an assignment for the students, the creative energy informing classroom practices more often than not stems from discussions with ESL colleagues and observations about our students.

Those discussions, however, can only take place in a community, one that offers continuous opportunities for shaping the institution's goals and for creating innovative and responsive curricula. To have a say about what, where, when, how, and whom we teach, faculty members must participate in the design and implementation of departmental assessment processes and program reviews. The results of shared fact-finding endeavors help us design departmental and curricular goals that match the needs and resources of the students and the institution. They help us choose and design placement tests, texts and software, delivery systems (face-to-face, interactive television, online, or video courses), as well as come to consensus with colleagues on the specific objectives and student learning outcomes for each course in the program. All full-time ESL faculty members help carry the load of analyzing competencies, designing courses, teaching, recruiting, and advising students. Without their complete participation, consensus cannot be reached, and students, the members of our community most affected by admissions and scheduling policies and procedures, stand to lose their voice.

Under What Conditions Is ESL Taught?

Both professionals and untrained volunteers teach English as a second language in for-profit and not-for-profit venues. In the rural district that Arizona Western College serves (roughly 10,000 square miles), a person wanting to learn English has several options. The county and Chicanos por la Causa offer free literacy, adult basic education, ESL, and citizenship classes. AWC offers adult basic education and ESL, but these courses are not free. In 2004–05, each credit cost $34, plus fees and textbooks. During a typical sixteen-week semester, 300 students choose to study during the day at our main campus on the mesa, 10 miles east of the city of Yuma. Because our community of over 100,000 residents does not have a comprehensive public transit system and taxis are generally out of our ESL population's price range, everyone needs access to a car. Another 200 students choose to study at night at our smaller satellite centers, leased or borrowed classrooms in local elementary and middle schools.

The ESL department at Arizona Western College is part of the modern languages division, although many other community colleges group ESL with developmental (remedial) reading and math, literacy and citizenship classes, or adult basic education. At AWC, the ESL department helps other college personnel understand the similarities between methods we use to teach English as a second language and those we use to teach students Japanese, for example. As such, ESL is not a remedial course. In 2004–05, the ESL department consisted of 9 full-time faculty members, 3 of whom taught only 3 to 6 credits each semester because they held other instructional or administrative positions, and more than 30 adjunct faculty members. Most ESL adjunct faculty members teach language arts in the local elementary, middle, and high schools during the day and an AWC adult ESL class or two at night. The biggest problem they have, aside from battling sheer exhaustion from teaching kids and teenagers all day in overcrowded and over-mandated schools, is making the transition to teaching adults. It takes a few class meetings and several gentle reminders for them to treat our ESL students as adults—adults who have very little time or patience for condescending attitudes or tones of voice, uninformed teachers, or assignments that are not immediately returned with specific feedback. Adult ESL students need content and methods that help them navigate their busy lives in a foreign culture. Many times the adults are the parents of the same students the adjunct faculty members teach during the day. Adjunct faculty members in our department are not required to have a master's degree in ESL because AWC's ESL courses fall outside transfer status. Adjunct faculty members can teach from 1 to 18 credits a year, and they are not required to participate in any college activities except classroom teaching and semester orientation. Full- and part-time ESL faculty members cover a total of 1,900 credits each semester at AWC.

How Do the Students' Goals and the College's Mission Affect Curricular Decisions?

The English we teach results from assessing the ultimate goals of our students. Matching an educational institution's mission to its students' goals helps ensure that resource allocation ultimately benefits the students: that's the bottom line. Since students' goals change over time, what, how, and for whom, to whom, and with whom we teach also change. Teachers maintain a flexible curriculum and prepare for a variety of teaching circumstances. When I arrived at AWC in 1988, I taught night classes in the satellite center three blocks from the Arizona-Sonora border, a converted gas station equipped with a tape recorder and a chalk board. The air conditioner failed when a swarm of yellow jackets clogged its air intake, and the August temperature topped 100 degrees. Policy dictated that classes would be canceled only in an emergency, but only true desert rats would soldier on in that heat. We continued class.

This type of dedication, characteristic of our students and faculty members alike, lent itself to our ESL program design: ESL for survival, ESL for the workplace, and ESL for academic purposes. Most of the students in 1988 simply wanted to communicate with doctors, their kids' teachers, and their bosses. A smaller fraction worked packing vegetables or cleaning hotels, restaurants, and schools, and this population required additional workplace vocabulary and orientation to workplace behaviors. An even smaller fraction wanted to earn an occupational or transfer degree from the local community college. Today the majority of our ESL students want to pursue a certificate or degree to find employment that will help them sustain their families at a level beyond simple survival.

A portrait of a recent graduating class can help readers see how our ESL program figures prominently into the academic life at a border college such as AWC. Of the 450 AWC graduates in May 2004, 57 had taken one of our ESL classes. Of those 57, 93% had received financial aid, 21% were under twenty-five, 32% were between twenty-six and thirty-five, and 47% were over thirty-six. Of the 57 former ESL students, 29% had started at AWC in or after 2000, 38% between 1994 and 2000, and 33% before 1993. One-third of this cohort had persevered for more than ten years to complete ESL courses and an associate's degree. I advised, counseled, and taught over 2,500 ESL students at AWC during the course of my career, and tears of pride and joy got caught in my ear-to-ear grin when students crossed the stage to receive diplomas.

A few years ago, I had the honor of reading all the graduates' names as they received their diplomas. In the interest of shaving off a few minutes of the already three-hour graduation ceremony, I was instructed to read quickly and seriously names and degrees earned. When former ESL students walked the line and passed by the podium where I announced their names, many spontaneous hugs and kisses as well as cries of "Miss Ellen, I did it!" slowed the ceremony. Those students clearly defined their goals and accomplished their missions, making their dreams a reality.

How Do Government Policies Affect College Policies?

ESL community college teachers spend a great deal of time advising students and helping them establish a workable plan to complete their educational sequence, be it a course cluster, certificate, or degree, all of which represent dreams and hopes. Faculty members need to keep abreast of the current federal, state, and local immigration, education, tax, health, and insurance laws. We need to be aware of the web of job, legal, medical, financial, and other educational resources in the community where we teach in order to direct our students and their families to them.

In the late 1980s, students could qualify for a Pell Grant simply by showing economic need based on tax returns and the ability to benefit from the course of study. They had only to be legal residents, not American citizens. To demonstrate ability to benefit from educational programs, AWC administered its own paper-and-pencil placement test. Today, only a few government-approved tests are allowed, such as the Combined English Language Skills Assessment (CELSA). We struggled to get a complete copy of CELSA, which impeded evaluating its relation to the parameters of AWC's ESL program. To retain the financial aid award, students had to earn at least a C in every class. Once students accomplished their stated goals, they could not receive more Pell Grant monies. These last two conditions are still in effect.

Another effect of the Pell Grant conditions was that we canceled our Certificate in ESL ceremonies, where the teachers and families rejoiced in each student's accomplishments, to avoid foreclosing students from future aid. We also refrained from calling our ESL program a program so that it would not appear as a completion of a major; we now call it a course cluster. In this way, students can complete our five-semester ESL cluster and then continue to pursue an occupational certificate or degree or a transfer degree and retain eligibility for Pell Grants. One semester, 23 of 30 students in my structure class received financial aid in the form of Pell Grants.

Students must understand the necessity of making time for practice outside the classroom and for study at home so they can pass courses with a C or better. A person can live in the Yuma area without ever speaking English, so faculty members arrange opportunities for our students to speak English outside the classroom, coordinating conversation exchanges between ESL and Spanish students.

"Just Teaching?"

The community college movement's explicit focus on teaching provides faculty members almost limitless opportunities for professional growth. Each of us brings a special experience, talent, focus, or passion to our classes. My colleagues have developed textbooks, unique learning activities, and online courses rooted in their classroom work. Several have participated in teacher exchanges. We all conduct teacher training through college in-services and local, state, and national TESOL (Teachers of English to Speakers of Other Languages) events. AWC and NAU, Yuma, host the state conference every other year and grant a discount to participants who come from Sonora and Baja California del Norte. We often arrange visits to schools in San Luis Rio Colorado, Sonora, as part of the conference program.

For twenty-five years, the TESOL organization has had the greatest influence on my professional development, providing me with countless teaching tips to round out my classroom repertoire, as well as with many occasions to lead workshops and make long-lasting friendships. The language professionals who gather for any TESOL event share the purposes of establishing connections with one another and improving oral and written communication for their students. Its members come from almost every country and represent every type of public or private scholastic endeavor in the United States and abroad. TESOL members are language students and teachers, researchers, authors, publishers, lawmakers, college presidents, and high school principals. Some are affiliated with programs such as the Peace Corps, Volunteers in Service to America, and Fulbright exchanges. Some are volunteers in Head Start and literacy programs. We teach under trees, in tents and tenements, in living rooms and cafés, on the front stoop, at charter schools, community centers, community colleges, and universities. We are interested in language acquisition and development from infancy to old age. Whatever our passion or perspective, we share our ideas, time, and energy to make learning a language less cumbersome and political and more unifying for students.

Do ESL Teachers Ever Rest?

In second-semester ESL classes, students write a descriptive paragraph titled "Someone I Admire." I often model with Francisco's story. My students' courage and perseverance amaze and motivate me, and I tell them so. When the routine sets in, it's 110 degrees, and I'm trying to muster the energy to teach the last classes of the spring semester, I remember my students and the consistent and incredible effort they make to get to class and participate. I realize how lucky I am to do what I love every day. We work hard, learn English, and explore firsthand the variety of people and paths in life. The special communities created among colleagues and students across the globe and in the classroom sustain us. We can rest later.

NANCY J. BROWN

IT'S ABOUT LIFESTYLE
Reflections on Teaching at a Small Catholic College

Know that an active, joyous, and multifaceted professional
life is possible at a teaching institution.
— Donald E. Hall —

At a small college, academic life has its own rhythm; at a small Catholic college, not only the academic calendar but also saints' days and the church calendar mark the rhythms of the seasons. A certain sense of reverence, enhanced by celebrations with the sisters of the founding order, accompanies holy days. A certain dignity underwrites all that we do, which is both a result of and the cause for enjoying the freedom to be religious and to work broadly, sharing an ethic that holds respect for the individual as a core value. The campus buildings and grounds of Lourdes College serve as a visual metaphor, and the art-rich intimate environment never ceases to soothe. Religious art collected from all over the world lines the walls, halls, and ceilings of our buildings; images of Saint Francis and the people and events of his life adorn the campus in the forms of murals and statuary. Impeccably maintained gardens and pathways invite meditation. The physical environment serves as an outward expression of the inward spiritual ecology of this small Catholic college in Sylvania, Ohio. As a longtime laborer in the vineyard of this liberal arts college environment, I argue that a less elite, small, religiously affiliated college can be a comfortable, happy place to build a successful and satisfying academic career of teaching, service, and scholarship. As Nona Feinberg suggests, "All academics need to learn about the diversity of academic cultures as well as of ethnic cultures" (77).

Feinberg, David Evans, and Donald Hall, all of whom have worked in teaching-intensive schools, write convincingly about enjoying deeply gratifying careers at colleges and small universities, where teaching receives more institutional value than research. In his essay "Small Departments and Professional Desires," Evans reassures readers that "small, unglamorously located, and modestly endowed institutions . . . are genuinely able to compete with any institution in the country for the best candidates" (205–06). The best small-college faculty members choose such institutions for reasons of compatibility; the community atmosphere nurtures them.

For faculty members at Lourdes College, community means a great deal. Who you are and what you do matter. You are known. A bulletin board in the conference room becomes a message center. Thank-you notes, prayer requests, and announcements of births, deaths, resignations, and new replacements help us feel connected to one another, more like a family than an educational corporation. College personnel adopt the mission statement for themselves as well as for the students. Regular face-to-face contact with the president and the vice presidents fosters a sense of shared responsibility for the college's successes and challenges. In addition to having a strong sense of a common mission, workers at a small college uphold a spirit of accommodation and good will; collaboration is the favored way to make change, and the size of the college means that everyone works with everyone else over and over. Therefore one must maintain a respect for individual goals and an unshakable commitment to students.

Respect and concern for students and for one another are hallmarks of small religious college cultures, and they strengthen the core sense of community. Everyone shares, in the good times and the bad. The tight-knit nature of faculty work ensures our connection to all aspects of the institution, financial included. Nonelite tuition-driven institutions feel immediate effects from any turn in the economy. Without heavy endowments, enrollment declines of just a few students can have financial implications for all departments. In addition, as for many private colleges founded by a religious congregation, the amount of financial support coming from the sponsoring organization may fluctuate.

Graduate students considering employment at such institutions should know this economic reality up front, since it affects faculty life and the community to which faculty members belong. Because the financial health of such an institution depends on tuition, salary raises may not be automatic, and health and retirement benefits may be average or below average. Yearly fund drives encourage faculty and staff members to donate a portion of their salary to the college, thus demonstrating commitment to the institution's mission. On a positive note, our community culture demands open sharing of financial information among the board of trustees, the faculty senate, the staff, and the administration of the institution, so there are few surprises. Together, we take economic trends in stride. As the years have gone by, I have come to see economic fluctuations as cyclical and to value other enduring factors that contribute to the quality of life at a small college: the spiritual center, the lifelong friendships forged with colleagues, and the opportunity to teach a broad range of courses.

Graduate students should also know about the joys of the egalitarian ethos at a small religious college, something salary levels and economic fluctuations cannot erode. In whatever capacity a person serves a small college, concern for students permeates the mission. My college insists that excellent teaching be the highest priority for faculty members. Evans contends that at small institutions "various cohorts view their roles as teachers [as] a topic of regular, not to say obsessive, concern" (207). Thus faculty members must have an informed pedagogy. Lourdes's focus on graduating well-prepared citizens promotes in-service efforts that develop new pedagogies aimed at achieving this end. A recent grant-funded study of learning-style theories, technology, and pedagogy brought about a collaboration of faculty members paid by the grant and other faculty members from every department of the college. Concern for excellent teaching does not stop there: classroom management techniques—how best to motivate students and to deal with problem students—frequently dominate discussions in department meetings and in college-wide meetings, just as they inform conversations in the cafeteria and at the photocopier.

For the right candidate, a small college offers the opportunity to teach a variety of courses. Many of our faculty members develop interests outside their areas of specialization. English faculty members at a liberal arts college usually identify as generalists, "well-informed readers facilitating student encounters with various texts in order to inculcate a love of reading and language, and a care for culture, that will persist throughout students' lives" (Evans 208). An applicant who is interested in teaching many different courses in literature and composition, while inculcating "a love of reading and language" in students, impresses our faculty more than a record of publication. In a college where general education requirements may drive department offerings, half to three-quarters of a four-course load may be some combination of lower-division general education classes. In our English department all five full-time faculty members share the load of five sections of Composition 1, four sections of Composition 2, five sections of Introduction to Literature, and a range of upper-division courses. Because more than half the courses students are required to take are liberal arts general education requirements, faculty members are able to draw connections for their students between their courses and those taught in other disciplines.

I consider this variety of course preparations a great advantage to employment at a small college. I came to Lourdes with a specialty in American Romanticism, but in the past fifteen years, I have taught early British and late British literatures, enabling me to indulge my taste for *Beowulf*, Chaucer, and Milton, without slighting my interest in Thoreau or Hawthorne. By teaching Studies in the Novel, I renewed my acquaintance with Moll Flanders and Balzac. In Studies in Poetry, I caught up with contemporary poetics and students' original work. Literature by Women offered me the perfect opportunity to bring Dickinson and Morrison into the dialogue. I have worked with English majors interested in going to graduate school and with English majors wanting to teach junior high school. As I have continued to grow intellectually, I have pursued my latest passion: community literacy. Being someone who thrives on variety, I have reveled in this teaching environment.

Teaching, consuming as it is, fulfills but one part of any professor's tripartite commitment to an institution of higher education. Service and scholarship are also expected. At a religiously affiliated institution, the opportunity for service can overshadow the expectation for scholarship. In keeping with the prevailing teaching-intensive academic culture, the *Lourdes College's Faculty Handbook* says that faculty members should devote seventy percent of their time to teaching-related activity and that they may devote the remaining thirty percent of their time to service and scholarship in any proportion they choose. The emphasis on service can surprise junior faculty members. Because Lourdes has only around sixty faculty members, the business of running the academic arm of the college requires them to serve in several capacities. Shared governance can mean that faculty members oversee the orderly management of curriculum development, the quality of faculty and student life, admission requirements, library services, and graduation preparations. Although their contracts may require service on one or two committees that carry out this work, many faculty members serve on five or six because of their strong sense of institutional loyalty. Given the diversity of work to choose from, a faculty member may be called on to lead one committee and to follow on others; sometimes the shift from leader to follower can happen two or three times in a single day. In addition to the regular faculty committees, task forces studying specific issues, department subcommittees exploring possible new programs, social committees, book clubs, lectures, athletic events, and student organizations depend on faculty involvement, promotion, and attendance.

Such a dependence on faculty leadership in the community means that opportunities to do good work abound, and at a small school, the product of the work is clear and present. Innovation serves the institution as much as committee and social work do. New majors can develop quickly, since administrators receive innovative ideas with interest and enthusiasm. At my college, I have created courses, majors, and student activities, as well as developed new programs across disciplinary boundaries.[1]

Augmenting the formal structures of shared governance—committees, commissions, task forces, and councils—are occasional addresses to faculty and staff on issues such as the importance of the liberal arts to an informed citizenry and to freedom of the mind, the importance and use of instructional technology in teaching, and methods of working with challenged students in the classroom. I routinely attend national conferences as a college representative, and I advocate for literacy and language arts to my state legislature.

As a service to the institution, literature and language professors' writing competencies come to bear on all kinds of draft documents and reports. I have written and managed grants, edited colleagues' papers and memos, written and reviewed catalog revisions, proofread letters, answered hundreds of punctuation questions, edited the literary magazine, and helped draft the student government constitution. Involvement in publications and documents leads to a broad institutional familiarity, thus enhancing my understanding of the college as a whole and permitting me to make even greater contributions to its culture. Being a part of so many dimensions of the institution makes me feel integral to it—the service contributes to the family feeling.

What I do affects the well-being of the college community, so I know I matter.

Service, however, is not confined to serving the needs of the college; many faculty members prefer involvement in community service. Whether participating in Habitat for Humanity projects, giving blood, tutoring in schools, volunteering at soup kitchens, serving their religious parishes, or collecting books, clothing, or school supplies for missions in other countries, Lourdes College faculty members maintain a visible presence in enhancing the quality of life of the city, thereby keeping the college in the public eye.

The third part of the professor's life is scholarship. Not all faculty members find extensive service fulfilling. Those who do not can use their time away from teaching activities to pursue their scholarly interests. Indeed, faculty members can find some time to read, write, think, and publish regularly, and the attention they receive from the college community is flattering. Scholars share their work not only nationally with colleagues in their disciplines but also locally at department gatherings, faculty meetings, and sometimes in their classrooms. Publish a book, and the college will prominently display it in the showcase people pass daily. Have a paper accepted for publication or presentation at a conference, and the scholar will get a congratulatory phone call or a note from the president, who will read the faculty member's work and share the news with the board of trustees.[2] These publications reflect the variety of scholarly interests that can enhance the reputation of the college at a more global level. Scholars are visible at a small college, and what they do matters.

Whether engaged in scholarship, service, or teaching, a small-college professor is busy all the time. The small-college professors Lisa Botshon and Siobhan Senier explain their surprise when confronted with the amount of time they were expected to spend working. I suspect all of us in the profession can share a little bit of guilt for their unknowing. We recognize that class contact time constitutes just a small fraction of our duties, the fraction most students see, but faculty members need to publicize all the rest that they do. At some campuses, that entails being present forty hours a week. At others, being on campus for a few office hours in addition to attending committee meetings and classes suffices, and the professor is free to work from home. Whatever the institution's culture expects, being a professor, like any other profession, is a full-time job. Forty- to sixty-hour work weeks are not an unfair expectation. Perhaps publishing a log that aspiring professors could examine would help them see the rhythm and demands of faculty work. Such a log would show those early breakfast meetings with donors, the hours of preparation for teaching, and the even more numerous hours invested in writing carefully crafted notes to first-year students about their compositions. It would record meetings scheduled for one hour that take two, as well as the number of meetings attended, sometimes three or four in a single day. And it would indicate the time spent on campus greeting new students, attending talent shows, advising student organizations, and talking with prospective students and bringing their families to performances and recitals, homecomings, sporting events, and all-campus picnics. We should not allow our undergraduate or graduate students to think articles flow fully written from mind to publisher; we should tell them about our essays that we thought were perfect until they came back from our editors with requirements for extensive revision. We should alert them to funding fluctuations, to the conference we had been counting on attending until the governor (or the board of trustees) slashed our funding. At a small college, the life of the institution becomes the center of a committed professor's world.

Viewed as a log, the work seems daunting, but the log cannot show the immense pleasure that accompanies faculty obligations and duties—the pride a professor feels at graduation when students who have worked long and hard get hugs from the president when presented with their diplomas. When you are deeply invested in the growth of students, unparalleled satisfaction and contentment come when alumni seek you out in the crowd to introduce their families to you. Of course, the workload is heavy at a small college, but for a devoted teacher, the return is joy—the joy of loving the work. It is about lifestyle.

When work has a sense of ministry, the lifestyle at a religious institution reflects it. Being Catholic has not been a requirement to teach at my institution, but most faculty members who stay share a dedication to serving students spiritually. Rather than restrict intellectual pursuit, my college, in its mission statement, encourages a "dynamic search for truth," in which faith, tradition, and reason are inseparable; the tensions are dialectic, each one informing the others in vibrant and interesting ways. Faculty members, instead of feeling repressed by the openly declared religious values of the institution, enjoy a freedom they believe would be restricted by a secular ecology. God talk, church activities, masses, and prayer permeate the college's culture. Religious faculty members recognize a presence of the sacred, and visitors comment on the quiet or the serenity of the campus. Faculty and staff members talk openly about their faith, comfortably bringing God into conversation or the classroom. Their conscious commitment to living in a faith-centered community provides an atmosphere that nurtures intellects and souls. Faith and intellectual discovery complement each other, bringing balance to both in open dialogue. And in times of crisis, there is no question about where to go or what to do. On 9/11, for instance, everyone on campus headed for the vice president of ministry's office. Then, as now, spontaneous prayer holds us together: personal prayer keeps us mindful of our mission, communal prayer sustains us, and ceremonial prayer reminds us we are but conduits of the culture and the Word.

When teaching is a ministry, ceremonies take on import. The fall convocation includes prayerful affirmation of the mission:

> Lourdes College, a Catholic liberal arts institution of higher education in the Franciscan tradition, serves men and women by providing continuing opportunities for intellectual discovery, accentuating both liberal learning and integrated professional education. It is the mission of the College to stimulate the growth of integrated persons; to engage them in an honest and dynamic search for truth; to encourage them to incorporate sound religious and philosophical values in their learning and in their interpersonal relationships; to challenge them to develop and deepen personal and social responsibility; to inspire in them a commitment to community service; and to provide an atmosphere that nurtures a holistic approach to learning within a caring, supportive, faith community.

Christmas brings shared prayer and mealtime with students. Baccalaureate, at which the graduates are blessed, precedes graduation ceremonies, where the bishop may greet each graduate crossing the stage. Students matriculate into and commence an educational experience that wraps them in religious values.

I have seen many changes in the college and in myself over my nineteen years at Lourdes College, but a strong sense of stability pulls me back semester after semester. The serene beauty of the grounds and buildings reminds me of the overarching eternal; the four-story mural of Saint Francis glistening in the sun reminds me to be an instrument of peace; the carillon's hymns at noon remind me of "the common cords of community" sung about in Lourdes's alma mater (Currie and Gregor); and the posted notices of service opportunities remind me that if I want peace, I must work for justice. Although the faculty and staff members' faces have changed over the years, the college's mission has remained the same. Our small college exists to educate our students for careers and lives of service. Each fall, with our opening faculty meeting, we affirm our mission and our responsibility to the students. Faculty and staff members adopt this mission for themselves as well as for their students, and living the mission has consistently and richly rewarded me.

The difference between work in religiously affiliated liberal arts schools and large universities is a matter of degree, not kind; in either place, the pace is fast, the challenges are large, and the rewards are fulfilling. PhD-granting departments can assist prospective faculty members by providing exposure to a variety of teaching situations while they are in graduate school. Future faculty members should discover themselves and their professional interests before entering the job market and getting on the tenure track. Internships that provide teaching opportunities to interested teaching assistants could go a long way in helping reveal the rewards and challenges of teaching in small colleges. Regional and national forums about various educational settings and issues can open spaces for honest inquiry, where graduate students can ask frank questions of practicing professionals. Fully informed graduate students can better select the kinds of teaching environments that will suit their needs and thus become empowered to focus a career search accordingly. When a small college is a first choice, not a last resort, the professor, the college, and the students will be happier and richer for it.

NOTES

1. For example, over the years I have served as chairperson of the Division of Fine Arts, chair of the Assessment Committee, member of the Undergraduate Curriculum and Policies Review Committee (chair for one semester), member of the School of Graduate and Professional Studies Council, cochair of the Self-Study for Accreditation (and report writer), member of

the Multicultural Subcommittee of the Curriculum Committee, chair of the Placement Testing Committee, member of the Americans with Disabilities Act Committee, chair of the Developmental Education Committee, member of the Women's Studies Advisory Council, member of the Student Life Committee, and chair of the Student Government Association Task Force.

2. A glance at the Lourdes College faculty showcase reveals a pleasing assortment of publications: the textbooks *One Voice: Music and Stories for the Classroom*, by Barbara Britsch and Amy Dennison-Tansey, and *The Ohio Adventure*, by Mary Stockwell; the articles "The Use of Laboratory Animals: An Ethical Balancing Act," by Mark Christiansen, and "The Founding and Early History of Chicago's Newberry Library: Free to Whom?" by Thomas Kaufman; the books *Save the Date: A Spirituality of Dating, Love, Dinner and the Divine*, by Jason King and Donna Freitas, *Quilting and Braiding: The Feminist Christology of Sallie McFague and Elizabeth A. Johnson*, by Shannon Schrein, and *Using Medical Terminology: A Practical Approach*, by Judi L. Nath, and a conference paper titled "Judith: Cheated Out of Fame," by Nancy J. Brown.

WORKS CITED

Botshon, Lisa, and Siobhan Senier. "The 'How-to' and Its Hazards in a Moment of Institutional Change." *Profession 2000*. New York: MLA, 2000. 164–72.

Currie, Randolph, and Joyce Gregor. "Song of Lourdes College." 1989.

Evans, David R. "Small Departments and Professional Desires." *Profession 1999*. New York: MLA, 1999. 204–13.

Feinberg, Nona. " 'The Most of It': Hiring at a Nonelite College." *Profession 1996*. New York: MLA, 1996. 73–78.

Hall, Donald E. "Professional Life (and Death) under a Four-Four Teaching Load." *Profession 1999*. New York: MLA, 1999. 193–203.

"Mission Statement." *Lourdes College*. 12 July 2007 <http://www.lourdes.edu/why-lourdes/?s=72&c=89>.

MARK C. LONG

READING, WRITING, AND TEACHING IN CONTEXT

It is Monday morning, and my first-year students have gathered to discuss an essay by the Pulitzer Prize–winning science writer Natalie
Angier. When I ask for a description of Angier's argument, they are
silent. Wondering whether the essay moves too quickly for the students, I change the question. "What position is Angier arguing against?"
I glance down at the sentence that begins the fourth paragraph: "The
cardinal premises of evolutionary psychology of interest to this discussion are. . . ." Silence. When I ask one student where in the essay we
might begin our discussion, she asks me, unabashedly, why I am calling on *her*. When I call on another student, he speaks vaguely about an
essay he has at best skimmed. I can almost hear the class's collective
groan of, "Get real. Why is this stuff important? What does this have to
do with me?"

These twenty college students, enrolled in my first-year writing
course, are mostly products of New England schools. Approximately
forty-five percent are residents of New Hampshire. Forty percent are
first-generation college students. I'm the newest of twelve full-time
members of the English department at Keene State, a public liberal
arts college in southwestern New Hampshire.[1] This semester, in addition to first-year writing, I am teaching two general education literature courses and one upper-level survey of American poetry for majors.
I'm also selecting books for spring semester courses, completing a
book review, drafting a conference presentation, and reviewing the proofs
for my second peer-reviewed journal article. At home, our two-year-old
son Nathaniel demands most of our attention as we adjust to the move

from an urban bungalow in Seattle to a nineteenth-century farm-house in rural New England. And if all this were not enough, in early October Rebecca and I rushed to the hospital to greet our new daughter, Ellinore.

As first semesters go, this story is not exceptional. In fact, I have yet to meet an untenured faculty member who does not claim a comparable past. Whether one is teaching two or four courses each semester, working with first-year writers or graduate students, writing an essay or a book, or juggling professional and family commitments, the demands on junior faculty members are acute and unrelenting. No matter where we end up, we struggle to manage the roles and responsibilities of faculty life. Why, then, does the profession systematically value the mostly individual work of scholarship and publication over the relational work of teaching and service? Why do we routinely de-emphasize the many commitments of faculty members—to students, the discipline, the department, the college, and the local or regional community? What are the costs of isolating the activities of reading and writing and teaching from the intellectual communities in which we work?

The promotion and tenure process these past two years has prompted me to reconstruct my professional development, and I have found myself repeatedly returning to these questions. When I graduated from the University of Washington, in spring 1996, I had produced an interesting dissertation, presented my work at local and national conferences, even published an article in a peer-reviewed journal. In addition, I worked for one year as assistant director of the writing center and for three years as an assistant director of the university's expository writing program. In my subsequent two-year appointment as postdoctoral instructor, I taught lower- and upper-division courses, including expository writing, surveys of fiction, and a seminar on poetics and pragmatist philosophy.

At the time, with the market in crisis, the job search was unsettling at best. Between preparing letters of application, arranging dossiers, and traveling to interviews, job candidates read John Guillory's description and critique of the current mode of professional preparation, Nona Feinberg's explanation of the risk for graduate students who expect "that their careers will be played on the same chessboard that they have been making moves on for their undergraduate and graduate careers" (75), and the MLA Commission on Professional

Service's proposal to change "the terms of the conversation" about the quality, significance, and impact of faculty work (162). Yet despite the bourgeoning literature on professional preparation, the job market, and faculty work, most new hires lamented the disconnect between the professional life they aspired to and the conditions in which they actually worked.

Like me, most job candidates accepted without question the distinction between the research-intensive university and the teaching-oriented college. (I interviewed at both.) Yet the more I read college mission statements, learned the differences between unionized and nonunionized faculties, and considered in a more systematic way the organization of curricula, the more I found a wide range of working conditions—even among institutions of the same type. In fact, when I accepted an offer from Keene State College, I first discovered (and have since confirmed) that while there is a difference between teaching two or four courses each semester,[2] a relatively high teaching load can be a positive indicator of an institution's commitment to teaching undergraduate students. More important, as I would learn, such teaching-intensive positions are often in departments whose members have created a culture that both acknowledges and values the multifaceted work faculty members perform.

My first year confirmed the axiom that we always learn the most important lessons too late. Soon after my arrival at Keene State, I was treated to frank assessment of faculty attitudes toward the institution. There were people who had clearly settled for jobs for which they were temperamentally as well as intellectually unsuited. Others, not surprisingly, appeared perfectly content to expend their time and energy dismissing students, other faculty members, and the administration in allegiance to what were, I must confess, an admirable set of principles. Because I was determined to establish a constructive contrary to these approaches, I began to pay much closer attention to those colleagues at the college who spoke more genuinely and progressively about their work, thus confirming another axiom: Stick with the winners. In addition, I began to consider how my professional life might be shaped by joining a unionized faculty. The collective bargaining unit, after all, defined minimum rank salaries, contractual obligations, benefits, and other conditions of employment. Perhaps more important, my own department's procedures for evaluation and its guidelines for tenure and promotion were consistent with college-wide guidelines. As it turns out, such transparency proved extraordinarily useful: it relieved many of my anxieties regarding college and departmental procedures, and it helped me consider more carefully how best to work with students and colleagues in the department and college.

By my second year—now well aware of the manner in which professional identities are locally defined and shaped over time—I became more confident in the advantages of my position in the profession at large. At professional conferences, always an occasion to listen to people expound on their work, I talked with faculty members still struggling mightily with the gap between their professional desires and the institutional realities of their schools. Many complained, sometimes bitterly, about not receiving the support and time necessary to achieve a balance in their research and teaching activities. Surely teaching less creates the time to publish more, yet the timeline for scholarly production forced untenured faculty members to make difficult choices about their teaching. Listening to them, I called to mind Parker Palmer's comments on the costs of doing work that is not one's own: "How many teachers inflict their own pain on their students, the pain that comes from doing work that never was, or no longer is, their true work?" (30). Indeed, even people I admired would talk about students and classroom work in ways that often revealed a lack of engagement and interest in the labor of teaching. When I raised this issue, I was rightly reminded that in the end teaching would not form the basis of a tenure decision.

These attitudes suggest that faculty members imagine their professional identity before actually arriving at the institutions in which they are fortunate enough to find work.[3] When talking with second- and third-year faculty members about the demands of keeping office hours, taking on advisees and conferencing, as well as building supportive and ongoing relationships with students—activities central to the work of most faculty members—resentful remarks reinforced this conclusion. And from those working in teaching-intensive institutions like mine, I heard more than once the dream of more congenial working conditions elsewhere. This dream had taken on some semblance of reality, I was told, through the voices of those senior colleagues who had determined, with remarkable certainty, that the college (whether students, staff, faculty, administration, system, trustees, state legislators, take your pick) was hostile to anything resembling genuine intellectual work.

According to conventional wisdom, success in the profession requires a certain number of publications as a condition for promotion and tenure; so it is no accident that most new faculty members simply accepted that the path to professional success "leads through the library, through the word processor, and through professional conventions" (Bromell 107). Once I had settled into my position at Keene State, however, I realized that my colleagues questioned the restrictive meaning of the term *scholarship* as the material fact of publication or the so-called activity of research. They described the scholarly activities of reading and writing—measured not simply by publication but by deliberate interpretation and sustained reflection—as a part of the work of English faculty members. The written guidelines for promotion and tenure maintained rigorous professional standards, responded to the different ways that faculty members contributed to ongoing scholarly conversations, and acknowledged the exciting ways faculty members participated in shaping the public perception of and access to the humanities.[4]

In their response to the current "crisis in scholarly publishing," Jennifer Holberg and Marcy Taylor sensibly call for an open discussion of both preserving scholarly integrity and challenging prevailing assumptions about scholarship. "What do we value?" they ask. "Is it actually the book/article or the *action* that each produces—the intellectual effort, the possible effects in terms of teaching and learning, the way in which 'scholarship' can hope to change the minds and hearts of institutions for the better?" (5). Keene State faculty members and administrators highly value book-length projects, but all parties have acknowledged other ways faculty members demonstrate serious and meaningful scholarship. Recent faculty accomplishments include receiving travel and research grants; editing editions, anthologies, and collections of essays on teaching; and publishing books and peer-reviewed journal articles, creative nonfiction and journalism, as well as book chapters, reviews, and encyclopedia entries. The ongoing scholarly activity of members of my department has, out of necessity, evolved in relation to their teaching responsibilities and service activities at the college. Seeing this synergy in the work of many of my colleagues, I reconsidered my plan to revise my dissertation into a book on theories of reading. To my surprise, I also began to feel reservations about the book I had set forth to write on William Carlos Williams and the tradition of American poetry. At the time, it was apparent that either project would have negatively affected my teaching, widened the gap between my scholarship and my course development, and taken precious time away from my two young children.

The freedom to determine my own intellectual development and priorities was, I must confess, an unexpected gift. The department and college developed promotion and tenure guidelines not predicated on quantitative and external comparative measures of scholarly activity. More significant, the faculty refused to equate research with the material fact of publication. Acknowledging various forms of scholarly activity and recognizing the multiple audiences for intellectual work, the promotion and tenure guidelines fostered a culture less focused on production and more engaged in the mutually reinforcing work of reading, writing, and teaching. Freed from the one-size-fits-all timeline of promotion and tenure, I have maintained an active life as a reader and writer in more than one field. My writing projects have included journal articles, book chapters, review essays, and, more recently, biographical and critical reference essays. One of my goals has been to write sophisticated and theoretically informed prose accessible to a wide range of readers. Without the pressure to produce a book for tenure, I have been able to allow my reading and writing to follow a path that has led me to consider a more developed, and substantive, book-length manuscript. But this project will likely not be concluded until after I complete work on a special journal issue for which I am guest editor, wrap up a collection of essays on teaching that I am coediting, and rotate out of my current position as department chair.

In addition to redefining my scholarly agenda in the light of my career trajectory and teaching commitments, I have been able to dedicate more time to changing the institution. My colleagues Kirsti Sandy and Phyllis Benay, other members of the interdisciplinary task force on writing, and I have begun to transform the culture of writing at Keene State. We have set out to move communally from a culture of complaint through a culture of conversation to a culture of commitment. Our most ambitious project has been to design and coteach an annual program, the Summer Institute on the Teaching of Writing. Our goals for the week-long institute are to bring eight Keene State College faculty members together each summer to examine the ways they use writing in their courses, the effectiveness of those practices, and the development of new strategies. Our premise is that to improve student writing, faculty members need to approach the teaching of writing differently in their disciplines. The institute begins with intensive discussions about what we value in our own writing and what we expect from our students. We examine what we know about students as writers and about the relation between writing and cognitive development. As the differences between faculty perceptions of student writing and student writers become visible, we negotiate those differences in our courses. Participants then work individually and collaboratively to transform their writing assignments, methods of evaluation, and course designs.

My teaching has benefited, as well, from the greater degree of freedom Keene State accords faculty members to define their intellectual development. I've been fortunate to continue teaching writing, schedule permitting. When not designing and teaching new versions of our general education literature course, I have taught courses in American poetry and environmental writing as well as seminars on major American authors. In my third year, I successfully petitioned for one course of reassigned time to expand and publicize some of the pedagogical ideas I had been considering since my arrival at Keene State. New courses and innovative ideas about the content of and teaching in the disciplines circulated among the faculty members who had arrived with me at the college, too, and by my third year, scarce resources were reallocated to promote a number of new projects, including my own department's idea to create a common reading program for first-year students.

As my notions of scholarship broadened, I found the time to pursue the intellectual work of curriculum development. Our department's most recent curricular revision, introduced the year before I arrived at Keene State, added to the English major a required introductory writing and criticism course, a multicultural requirement, and a broader theory requirement. This new course sequence explicitly articulated the writing and critical demands made of students at each level of the curriculum. The department, however, came to see the need for additional writing, critical thinking, and reading in all our courses, and we were increasingly concerned with developing and reinforcing competencies in our first-year writing and required general education literature courses.

The ongoing curricular conversation in the English department resulted in a proposal to change from a program of three-credit courses to a program of four-credit courses. We decided, first, that the quality of student education would be improved by faculty members' teaching three courses each semester and students taking four. By providing more intensive instruction in the process of writing and more substantive, extensive study of literature, we envisioned our new program as a keystone in the college's mission to create an intellectual environment grounded in the liberal arts that fosters both the personal and professional growth of our students. At the level of the department, our interests centered on developing a greater self-awareness of how we approach writing, critical thinking, documentation, and close reading at each level.

This major curriculum revision is but one example of an English faculty deeply committed to college-wide and community activities. Department members routinely participate in the first-year experience (in summer orientation activities, coordinating and teaching in the first-year writing program, developing and promoting Keene State College's signature Summer Reading Program); we actively advise in the college's general education program, teach required literature courses, and participate in the general education revision process. We teach in the interdisciplinary programs of American studies, Holocaust studies, and women's studies. We work together to promote diversity and multiculturalism through the development of new courses (lesbian and gay writers, Pacific Rim literature, women's writing, Native American writers) and author readings, such as the Summer Reading Program authors Sherman Alexie and Gish Jen. And we take our work out into the local community and region, regularly participating in New Hampshire Humanities Council programs and serving as members of task forces, committees, and executive councils. In all this effort, although we fight the budgetary constraints of a small state-funded institution, we have craftily, if not deviously, transformed our place of work.

Yet when I talk with those outside the department and college—with colleagues from graduate school, with academic peers at professional conferences, and with job candidates in interviews—I am continually surprised by their responses to the teaching-intensive mission that guides most professors. If I describe the rewards of working with academically and developmentally challenged students, someone will invariably change the subject. "What about scholarship?" I am asked. "How do you find the time to write?" And if I talk about curriculum work, first-year student orientation, or the Summer Institute on the Teaching of Writing, I receive gentle sympathy and have even been advised (more than once) to avoid cluttering my valuable time with too much committee work. It follows that I am stuck in a less desirable situation, doomed to struggle with an excessive teaching load, lower-level courses, and unmotivated students, while others in more desirable situations enjoy course releases, research funding, upper-level seminars, and graduate students.

As my students often say, "Get real." At the very least, such perceptions underscore a narrative of professional success and failure that simply cannot account for the scholarly and cultural work of reading, writing, and teaching in context. Unable to situate the work of faculty members in particular institutions, we have obscured the multiplicity of institutional conditions in which they build professional lives. Michael Bérubé observes that despite the differing configuration of course work at large research institutions, most faculty members spend most of their class time teaching undergraduates. The University of Illinois, Urbana, he writes, is not "a utopian society composed of magnanimous, well-adjusted faculty members. It is merely an ordinary place from which a great number of the standard in-house complaints about the profession sound either weird or irrelevant" (7). In this respect, Bérubé continues, it is not different from where he teaches, Penn State University, "where senior faculty in English teach 'first-year seminars' and every faculty member is required to teach a Monday-Wednesday-Friday schedule once a year" (7). The point, once again, is simply that particular institutions and their needs influence the nature of faculty work and the accepted definitions of scholarship.

So why is the profession reluctant to redefine scholarship? The philosopher Alasdair MacIntyre explains that we often fall back on conventional narratives although we suspect their validity:

> [W]e are never more (and sometimes less) than co-authors of our own narratives. Only in fantasy do we live the story we please. . . . [W]e enter upon a stage we did not design and find ourselves part of an action that was not our making.   (199)

MacIntyre's words allow us to acknowledge the difficulty of changing conventional attitudes and practices in the profession. So while it is imperative to provide more comprehensive graduate training in preparing future faculty members, we cannot presume that graduate students imagine the varied conditions of the profession during their university years. After all, how does one know where one is going while developing a sense of where one is?

We can, however, encourage graduate students to see the landscape of the profession as broader and more diverse than they might imagine it. First, graduate students (and faculty members) need to know that working conditions vary not only across but also within institutional types and commonplaces about teaching and research are difficult to sustain when the conversation shifts from generalization to the specific things faculty members spend their time doing at institutions that value teaching and research. Second, faculty members (at research- and teaching-oriented schools) would do well to consider the increasing evidence that changing economics and demographics of higher education will reshape the reward system that privileges research over teaching. The forecast is clear: teaching undergraduates has been, and will increasingly be, at the center of faculty work in English and the humanities.

What will follow is up to us. On the future of English studies, George Levine wonders "whether the profession and the institutions in which it professes can sufficiently re-imagine themselves so that teaching courses at the freshman and sophomore level might be intellectually interesting to faculty" and might even be consistent with one's intellectual preoccupations as a scholar (13). As I have attempted to demonstrate in this essay, many of us who profess are already there. We have reimagined our work and our professional identities to meet our students at all levels of the curriculum with the challenging work of reading, writing, and thinking. We have managed to make satisfying professional lives in less than ideal circumstances by setting aside the conventional narrative of the profession, by accepting the fact that we read and write and teach where we are. In acknowledging that these fundamental activities of the profession are institutional activities, we unsettle the narrative of the profession that still determines what graduate students and newly minted PhDs define as desirable and less desirable positions. We can then begin to understand the culture shock first-year faculty members experience as a necessary stage through which people begin healing the division between individual expectations of the profession and the actual situations in which we profess.

NOTES

1. Keene State College (KSC) is a public liberal arts institution, one of three campuses of the University of New Hampshire system. KSC enrolls approx-

imately 3,900 full-time undergraduate students and 1,000 part-time undergraduate and graduate students. First organized as a normal school in 1909, KSC is a Carnegie master's institution and a founding member of the Council of Public Liberal Arts Colleges, or COPLAC. Member colleges are predominately undergraduate public institutions of moderate size with strong liberal arts curricula that offer at least half of their degrees in liberal arts fields. Current member institutions are the College of Charleston (SC); the Evergreen State College (WA); Fort Lewis College (CO); Henderson State University (AR); Mary Washington College (VA); Ramapo College of New Jersey; St. Mary's College of Maryland; State University of New York, Geneseo; Truman State University (MO), formerly known as Northeast Missouri State University; University of Maine, Farmington; University of Minnesota, Morris; University of Montavello (AL); and the University of North Carolina, Asheville. The alliance of public colleges and universities seeks to provide a high quality liberal arts education in the public sector for students who would not otherwise have that opportunity.

2. Donald E. Hall offers a more extended discussion of the way this conversation about teaching loads distorts the actual working conditions of faculty members, especially at nonelite institutions. See *Academic Self* 22–32.

3. See Lisa Botshon and Siobhan Senier's "The 'How-to' and Its Hazards in a Moment of Institutional Change." While I admire and agree with most of Botshon and Seiner's account of the disparity between faculty members and their schools and the limits of hard work and perseverance, I am less confident in their call for a "radical redistribution of resources" (171). The only radical redistribution I am familiar with in the state of New Hampshire is continued funneling of money away from educational institutions. Also see Hall's "Response to Lisa Botshon and Siobhan Senier."

4. I include here the relevant sections of the definition from the English department's promotion and tenure guidelines. "Scholarship . . . is here defined as research, critical writing, or creative work that is intended to reach a professional audience. Research and critical writing may be published as essays, reviews, or monographs, or may be presented orally at conferences. Creative work may include poetry, fiction, drama, creative nonfiction, and the screenplay, and may be published in journals or books or be performed. It may also include the production of films or videos. Related activities (also considered scholarship) may include refereeing articles for scholarly journals, editing scholarly or creative journals, consulting or advising in film or video production, acting as respondents on panels, or organizing and chairing sessions at professional conferences. . . . Work accepted must be broadly related to the applicant's professional field. Though work completed over the entire course of the applicant's career will be considered, evidence of recent (since previous promotion) and ongoing scholarship is required. This is not meant to be an exclusive definition of scholarship and obviously does not include everything that might be defined as 'related professional activities.' Candidates may propose whatever they feel is appropriate, but they will be expected to explain how their activities fit either the department's definition of scholarship or the

college's definition of 'scholarship and related professional activities' "
(rev. 15 May 2003).

WORKS CITED

Angier, Natalie. "Men, Women, Sex and Darwin." *New York Times* 21 Feb. 1999, late ed., sec. 6: 48.

Bérubé, Michael. "Teaching to the Six." *Pedagogy: Critical Approaches to Teaching Literature, Language, Composition, and Culture* 2.1 (2002): 3–15.

Botshon, Lisa, and Siobhan Senier. "The 'How-to' and Its Hazards in a Moment of Institutional Change." *Profession 2000.* New York: MLA, 2000. 164–72.

Bromell, Nicholas. "What Next? Thought and Action in Intellectual Work." *American Quarterly* 47.1 (1995): 102–15.

Feinberg, Nona. " 'The Most of It': Hiring at a Nonelite College." *Profession 1996.* New York: MLA, 1996. 73–78.

Guillory, John. "Preprofessionalism: What Graduate Students Want." *Profession 1996.* New York: MLA, 1996. 91–99.

Hall, Donald E. *The Academic Self: An Owner's Manual.* Columbus: Ohio State UP, 2002.

———. "Response to Lisa Botshon and Siobhan Senier." *Profession 2000.* New York: MLA, 2000. 172–75.

Holberg, Jennifer L., and Marcy Taylor. "Editor's Introduction: Getting the Profession We Want; or, A Few Thoughts on the Crisis in Scholarly Publishing." *Pedagogy: Critical Approaches to Teaching Literature, Language, Composition, and Culture* 4.1 (2004): 1–5.

Levine, George. "The Two Nations." *Pedagogy: Critical Approaches to Teaching Literature, Language, Composition, and Culture* 1.1 (2001): 7–19.

MacIntyre, Alasdair. *After Virtue.* Notre Dame: Notre Dame UP, 1981.

MLA Commission on Professional Service. "Making Faculty Work Visible: Reinterpreting Professional Service, Teaching, and Research in the Fields of Language and Literature." *Profession 1996.* New York: MLA, 1996. 161–216.

Palmer, Parker J. *The Courage to Teach: Exploring the Inner Landscape of a Teacher's Life.* San Francisco: Jossey-Bass, 1998.

ANN E. GREEN

LOCAL POLITICS AND VOICE
Speaking to Be Heard during the Pretenure Years

My father, a dairy farmer for most of his life, explained to me once the goals of unionizing for farmers. He said, "Imagine, would you, what would happen if everyone dumped their milk for three days. Imagine the smell of all that sour milk. Imagine New York City with no available milk." His argument was that a milk strike would immediately drive home the point that farmers—not middle men—needed more money for their product, but he invariably followed this talk with this observation: "But it will never happen. The reason farmers are farmers is that they don't want to listen to anyone else. They want to set their own hours and be their own boss. We'll never unionize."

My early training as a farmer's daughter is surprisingly similar to my current work as a professor of English. Like the farmers my father described, most academics want to do their own thing, determine their own work schedules, set their own priorities for research, and establish their own goals and standards for teaching. Paradoxically, faculty members experience a great deal of fear and paranoia about letting colleagues know what they're doing, about sharing ideas or strategies, and about developing common goals. This sense of paranoia pervades the ranks of untenured faculty members, a population often encouraged to stay silent, do research, and come up for tenure without participating in local politics, the part of faculty work that runs the university.

Shared Governance (for All)

I have begun to think more and more about why candidates we interview for jobs often possess neither a sense of institutional service and shared governance nor an understanding of the ways both contribute to the life of an institution. Shared governance involves faculty members in decision making on curriculum, tenure, scholarship, and teaching. Systems of peer review and evaluation combined with broadly based faculty participation on various campus committees—from personnel committees that make rank and tenure decisions to curricular and sometimes admissions decisions—work against trends toward a more corporate university, where teachers, operating with compromised academic freedom, become instruments to deliver preplanned instructional units to "customers." Since shared governance requires professors to voice their concerns and since it protects academic freedom and tenure, any reticence among untenured faculty members and job candidates reflects a kind of willful underpreparedness. Graduate students and junior faculty members routinely receive advice from people like Ms. Mentor (Emily Toth) to "be silent; find stress-reduction exercises; do the best . . . to make friends." Rather than suggest cooperative faculty efforts for systemic change, Ms. Mentor advocates for traditional power structures by suggesting that junior faculty members remain silent unless there's "[m]assive dishonesty, sexual harassment, racism, and homophobia." This seems a disservice to both the institution and the candidate. Ms. Mentor further writes, "But a sword is only useful when there is a genuine battle, and where the sword wielder has some hope of winning." In battles in the contemporary university, however, if aggrieved teachers wait until an occasion of "[m]assive dishonesty" to wield a sword, they are guaranteed to lose.

I am also suspicious of didactic advice, mantras untenured faculty members and graduate students repeat to order the chaos of our job market. While an MA student, I heard a number of ridiculous presumptions about professional expectations. Some of my peers believed that publishing anything outside one's field would mark a scholar as an academic dilettante; only the narrowest of research specializations increased one's marketability. Others arrived at the strange calculation that presenting ten conference papers and publishing one article would produce one job offer. Many feared that unless they were hired by a research-intensive institution, they would write very little, save for internal memos about curriculum. Other graduate students were told that the best time to have a baby is between the third and fourth chapters of the dissertation and that they should never accept any food or drink during a job interview because there might not be enough to go around. While some of this advice is downright wrong, much of it vitiates work at a small institution, where faculty members often teach outside their areas of specialization, both junior and senior faculty members publish and research, and a wide range of interests keeps them active and engaged. Despite the landmark status accorded Ernest L. Boyer's *Scholarship Reconsidered: Priorities of the Professoriate* and despite the appearance of other writing about the state of the profession, graduate students still mistake the research-intensive university as the model for higher education, an umbrella term covering a tremendously diverse and remarkably effective range of colleges and universities, each with distinctive academic cultures.

Tenure decisions, curriculum development, and faculty and student awards are part of the shared governance common to faculty work at small and large institutions, whether teaching- or research-intensive. Shared governance is, in fact, the glue that keeps the system of tenure and academic freedom together. Unaccustomed to thinking in institutional terms and generally lacking formal study in the history of higher education, many junior colleagues overlook the link between tenure and academic freedom. The paradox of a collective and collaborative system in place to preserve the individual's academic freedom in teaching and research becomes invisible when junior faculty members invest in two faulty assumptions: that academic freedom means doing whatever they want and that academic freedom becomes a faculty right only after a positive tenure decision. To the contrary, the American Association of University Professors (AAUP) clearly defines academic freedom in their "1940 Statement on the Principles of Academic Freedom and Tenure":

> Institutions of higher education are conducted for the common good and not to further the interest of either the individual teacher or the institution as a whole. The common good depends upon the free search for truth and its free exposition.
>
> Academic freedom is essential to these purposes and applies to both teaching and research. Freedom in research is fundamental to the advancement of truth. Academic freedom in its teaching aspect is fundamental for the protection of the rights

of the teacher in teaching and of the student to freedom in learning. It carries with it duties correlative with rights.

Systems of shared governance protect academic freedom, the freedom to define a research agenda, even if it might be controversial. Aside from the uncomplicated assumption of universal truth, the 1940 statement (and its 1970 annotations) is amazingly current. But what does this definition mean for junior colleagues in English and foreign language departments? How can we mitigate a pervasive atmosphere of paranoia concerning untenured faculty members' teaching and research?

I write from the perspective of a recently tenured faculty member in English, hired in 1998 to start a writing center. Early in my career, I decided that important issues (diversity, the university's family medical leave policy, and writing) required my advocacy, even if my advocacy would ultimately result in a negative tenure decision. I thought about tenure the way someone had advised me to think about the job search itself—as a mutual process between the institution and the candidate. Instead of conceiving of tenure as something done to me, I preferred to see it as a collaborative process, a marriage of sorts. If being tenured is like marrying the institution and if the three topics one should discuss before marriage are sex, money, and children, then the three topics candidates need to consider before tenure are curriculum, salary, and governance. Just as people attempt to know their significant others before marrying or committing to them, I wanted to know my institution and to place local history in the context of national debates before the tenure decision. Seeing tenure decisions more broadly better positions candidates to enter into discussions with other members of the university community.

Institutions of higher education depend heavily on faculty talents apart from teaching acumen and so need to hear every voice, not just the tenured voices. And for the untenured, silence, as Audre Lorde articulates it, does not protect. In fact, silence can damage junior faculty members personally and professionally, since people do not magically find their voices after tenure if they avoided speaking regularly and rhetorically all along. Junior faculty members, particularly members of marginalized groups, must find ways of speaking within the context of the larger institution. Listeners hear voices differently depending on a speaker's race, class, gender, and sexual orientation. Consequently, everyone in an academic community should consider subject position, timing, and priorities when speaking. By balancing these rhetorical concerns, junior faculty members can participate in local politics, thus promoting their own professional standing as well as the welfare of the institution that hired them. Indeed, if new hires avoid participating in university politics before a tenure decision, senior faculty members may misread their reticence and may encounter tenure narratives rife with poor rhetorical choices. To speak rhetorically is to understand local politics and to know rhetorical situations when speaking. Participating in local politics not only assures faculty members of a voice in the institution but also prepares untenured professors to better present their fit in a department (see Newman).

STARTING A WRITING CENTER: LOCAL HISTORY

The arguments I make here owe a debt to feminist theory; to my graduate training in the experimental writing, teaching, and criticism PhD program at the State University of New York, Albany; and to my experiences from the last six years as assistant professor of English and director of the Writing Center at a small comprehensive university. In addition to directing the Writing Center, I created it, a situation that certainly posed problems for a new rhetoric and composition specialist. Yet I believe new faculty members can undertake administrative work and can engage with the university community in productive ways. Regardless of specialty, people from traditionally marginalized groups must obtain power in academic hierarchies so that in the long run they might collectively change the current power structure. Before assuming power, though, all junior faculty members should learn the local history of their institutions and build coalitions in them. By learning local history and lore and by building coalitions, faculty members work against the traditional academic model of individual success and toward systemic, institutional change through rhetorical speech.

Before accepting the offer from Saint Joseph's University (SJU), I received sage advice from a faculty member at Albany: Listen to people. She said everyone at SJU would have a story about how they came to the university, and these stories would give me a sense of the local history, a sense crucial to the process of positioning myself rhetorically in the institution's stated and unstated missions. Since

I would create a writing center for the university, a political and research-orientated task, listening to the university's lore helped me frame the design of a materially and ideologically responsive writing center.

Starting a writing center involves what Boyer calls "scholarship of integration," scholarship that illuminates "connections across disciplines, placing the specialties in larger contexts, illuminating data in a revealing way, often educating nonspecialists, too" (18; see also Roen). In addition to enacting "scholarship of integration," starting a writing center made me think about institutional culture and the relationships among faculty members and among departments. I entered an institutional context in which a conversation about the university's mission statement was ending. While mission statements, as another colleague often reminds me, can say little about what an institution actually does (show me a budget, and I'll show you the institution's mission), SJU's mission informed the Writing Center mission and assisted me in promoting the Writing Center in line with the institution's mission. In this way, the work of the Writing Center reaffirms the story the institution tells about itself. The university mission statement advocates a "transforming commitment to social justice," for instance; the Writing Center can enact this commitment through community-based tutoring services, activism concerning diversity and language on campus, and support for increasing racial diversity on an overwhelmingly homogeneous campus.

On a larger scale, writing centers could focus on diversifying. Most writing center directors are female, and writing centers are notoriously feminized spaces where tutors supposedly clean up the bad student papers. According to Nancy Grimm:

> Writing Centers are marked by the same traditional notions of what women provide—refuge, nurturance, emotional support, personal guidance—qualities that generally are not integrated theoretically or structurally into the teaching and or research mission of the university.   (82)

I found that Grimm's assertion came true when I began and administered a new writing center. Often, colleagues assumed the center's tutors would correct the grammar in student papers and return them error-free. Other times, I received various complaints from teachers about students who had visited the center but whose papers were not fixed during their visits. These sorts of complaints have been well documented by other writing center theorists (see, e.g., North; Grimm; Nelson and Evertz).

In working against the common assumptions about writing-center work manifested in discourses on the SJU campus, I found it useful to articulate the center's connection to the university's mission. I wanted the writing center at Saint Joseph's to create spaces for writers of all abilities from all stakeholder groups (faculty, staff, students) to write creatively as well as critically. During the first two years, students formed weekly poetry-writing groups open to anyone in the institution, the writing fellows course began to include a service-learning component with literacy tutoring in the community, and staff members began to mull over ways to link the Writing Center to other campus offices and groups to cosponsor readings and events around writing and social justice. Each aspect of this work indebted the SJU Writing Center more deeply to the university's mission. An additional aspect of the Jesuit mission is *cura personalis*, roughly translated as care for the individual student. In speaking publicly about the Writing Center, I found it useful to conceptualize our effort in the *cura personalis* ideology—we addressed individual student writing, worked toward social justice, and highlighted the beauty of language and poetics, all hallmarks of Jesuit intellectual life and important parts of our work as a writing center.

My own scholarship addresses systemic social change through feminist and antiracist ideas of writing. Diversity work is my life's work, and relating this focus to the Writing Center and the Jesuit mission gave me a strong theoretical position from which to speak. I could, for example, develop alliances with the Gender Studies Committee, the Diversity Commission, and the Office of Multicultural Life. While the process of connecting the Writing Center to diversity and the Jesuit mission is long and ongoing, establishing the SJU Writing Center as something beyond a grammar "fix-it" shop broadened its practical and intellectual scope and established the center as a visible entity on campus that was central to the institution's ethos. My pretenure lesson was this: If I wanted to build a writing center based on theoretically sound principles drawn from the field of rhetoric and composition, I could not represent the Writing Center according to faculty desires for "fixed" writing and then change my arguments after tenure; I could not follow the common advice of being quiet until tenure. Instead, I would have to articulate the Writing Center as a place that addressed students' varied needs and ally discussions of the Writing Center with other campus conversations. By openly defining the work of the Writing Center director as teaching and research, I avoided the administration's impulse to categorize such labor as service. In addition to speaking about the Writing Center's achievements, I documented its progress in annual reports to my department chair (in addition to the annual faculty work reports) and publicized the center through the annual Writing Center newsletter, a brief affair containing articles on writing and pedagogy. The documentation of the center's activities proved valuable during my third-year review and tenure decision (see Harris; Gebhardt and Gebhardt).

Since the Writing Center started, it has made many small gains: it sponsors a regular scholarship for a student of color who majors in English or serves as a writing fellow, it employs a diverse (for this institution) group of writing fellows, and it received a $30,000 grant to start a writing center in a stressed and underfunded Philadelphia public middle school. As a member of the Diversity Commission and the Gender Studies Committee, I have spoken about the connections among the Writing Center's work, diversity, and the Jesuit mission of social justice in ways that—at least partly—are successful in getting heard. If I had waited to speak about diversity until tenured and safe, I would probably have done so at a high cost to my sanity and emotional life, as well as a high cost to my scholarly life; listening to an institutional context and figuring out ways to express positions in that context have been empowering as well as productive.

COALITION BUILDING

Small institutions offer possibilities for cross-disciplinary collaboration that foster coalition building. The opportunity to work with colleagues from a variety of different disciplinary backgrounds stands out as one of the challenges and joys of serving as a writing center director at a small institution. My cohort of untenured friends, for example, included women from philosophy, theology, and chemistry with whom I often conversed about the institution, tenure, and local politics. In an academic institution, information is often power, and understanding the location of various initiatives, and the stories behind these initiatives, helps faculty members better negotiate them. Although untenured, we had some institutional power in advocating for one another and in supporting one another, personally and professionally. At SJU, as at most universities, women faculty members populate the associate and full ranks in smaller numbers than men, so they often serve on more committees than their male counterparts (Kolodny 86). While true of my cohort, this situation did not deter us from using our participation in committees to educate one another about the university's inner workings. Sharing information and talking across disciplines increased our cognizance of ways our disciplines function differently in the university and of ways the institution responds to junior faculty members, particularly women. Our conversations helped us understand local culture and form a consensus about the institutional issues most important to our cohort. Such talk helped us build coalitions, think about our long-term goals for the institution, and plan for collective action. Men have worked this way for years, but in contrast with the stereotype of the old boys' network, this loose coalition of women professors shared information and insight.

I am using the word *coalition* as Bernice Johnson Reagon does in "Coalition Politics: Turning the Century." She describes coalition work as "not work done in your home. Coalition work has to be done in the streets. And it is some of the most dangerous work you can do. And you shouldn't look for comfort" (359). Indeed, those of us who have built coalitions together do not always find this work comfortable, since disciplinary differences and differences in social class, sexual orientation, religion, and age can separate us. Our differences, however, can also enrich our work together and assist us in speaking rhetorically to the wider university. Conversations within the relatively safe group of untenured colleagues open up spaces for us to rehearse the rhetorical speech we use in wider circles, whether in our home departments or outside them.

Talking across disciplines can build the kinds of coalitions that lead to institutional and systemic change. When a seat became available on the Advisory Board for Faculty Compensation, the Faculty Senate Executive Committee appointed me to this position, an appointment resulting, in part, from previous coalition-building efforts. This position has led to some of the most enlightening committee work that I have done. As director of the Writing Center, I control an $18,000 annual budget, but seeing how the Writing Center budget compares with other budgets across the institution, understanding what percentage of an institution's finances go toward faculty salary, and learning how a 5% tuition increase produces X number of dollars that could be applied to faculty salaries or benefits are important and pragmatic feminist work. Too often women, particularly women in the humanities, fear budgetary work, and this fear, based mostly on lack of information, prevents us from effectively moving into administrative posts where budgets define a large part of the job. It also prevents us from applying for grants and participating in difficult institutional decision-making processes (see Kolodny).[1]

By becoming more savvy about university politics, feminists can effect meaningful change in an institution, but only if they are supported by motivated colleagues, especially those who make their beliefs public by teaching in women and gender studies programs. Collections like this volume might also be able to address another silence—the silence that those who teach at nonelite institutions experience in the profession at large.

LOCAL POLITICS

In *Failing the Future: A Dean Looks at Higher Education*, Annette Kolodny asks:

> Who, as a graduate student, was encouraged to think about committee obligations, administration, departmental management, scheduling, curricular reform, or any of the other details that make up the dailiness of university life? And how many graduate students learn anything about the history of higher education in this country or understand the distinctions between different types of higher educational institutions? (192)

Kolodny's remarks may ring true for most graduate students in most places, but not all. The University at Albany, State University of New York, where I was a graduate student, addresses the concerns Kolodny and others outline through course work and through the teaching and administrative experiences students obtain during graduate school. The Albany program requires students to take the courses The History of English Studies and The Teaching of Writing and Literature, which orient them to the evolution of English studies over the last one hundred twenty years. The program was designed to "develop politically reflective scholar-teachers while establishing graduate study in English as an appropriate site for the scrutiny of educational life" (Knoblauch 19). Eight years after C. H. Knoblauch's explanation, Judith Fetterley describes the program as "designed to make students politically sophisticated" and argues that it "makes possible, indeed invites, a feminist analysis" (706). What I learned at Albany, however, was not so much through the content of the course work as through the practice of the faculty. By and large, faculty members were willing, and some of them eager, to discuss with students the politics of the department and the manner in which these politics reflected the larger schisms in English studies over theory and practice, teaching and research.

As graduate students, we participated in various departmental committees. While certain faculty members viewed graduate student committee positions somewhat ambivalently, I learned a great deal about department politics from debating issues relevant to graduate students and to undergraduate teaching. Learning about the strategic value of minutes and about *Robert's Rules of Order* helped prepare me for my very first bit of departmental service in the English department at SJU—my role as department minute taker. After recovering from the initial shock that I, the most junior member of the department, would be recording department minutes (and after matching faces to names in a department of three Franks, two Joes, and two Richards), I appreciated the preparation I received by observing and participating in department meetings at Albany. While my Albany experience made me slightly paranoid about my ability to take minutes (I tended to omit detail in favor of the overall sense of the meeting, because minutes could be so politically fraught), at the very least, I recognized that even a small aspect of department life—minutes at department meetings—could become an important subject for hours of debate. Everyone who graduates with a PhD in English should recognize the political importance of language; many, however, do not realize what this means in terms of local politics. As department minute taker, I had to record minutes—in its own way, a kind of speaking back to what happens in a discussion—but I was aware of the potential consequences of minutes and meetings.

———

Rather than try to model teaching-intensive institutional practices after PhD-granting institutions, research institutions should replicate many teaching-intensive colleges' practices. PhD-granting institutions should also consider ways they can build coalitions with nonelite schools in their area. It would be easy enough in educationally rich cities for research-intensive institutions to initiate conversations about faculty life in the academic cultures of comprehensive universities and colleges. Research universities could create links with smaller institutions through teaching-exchange opportunities, colloquiums, or shared conferences, and graduate students could then talk with faculty members from nonelite places, where they are most likely to build satisfying careers. Instead of positioning research institutions as always central to the conversation (with those of us at nonelite institutions often placed as an audience listening to those from the elites), we might think about how research institutions could really listen to what faculty members at nonelite institutions describe and hear what's going on in most small universities. And those of us at small institutions can begin defining some of the professional conversation. While it will take a great deal of time to undo the privileging of research and the research institution in discourses about and practices of higher education, those at nonelite institutions can speak rhetorically to make public the rich teaching and intellectual work of our professional lives.

Faculty members, including adjunct and part-time teachers from community colleges, comprehensive universities, and small liberal arts colleges, could share their experiences in graduate seminars, and we could indicate to candidates the tips for a successful interview at the MLA Annual Convention with a diverse range of colleges. This exchange would help prepare graduate students for the working conditions that they will typically encounter. I am thinking here of one of my new colleagues who attempted—as she had done in graduate school—to read and respond to multiple drafts of every student paper. While this was an admirable goal, what was possible with twenty students as a teaching assistant was not possible with one hundred students as a junior faculty member. She asked, "So what I was taught in graduate school isn't possible?" I replied, "Not if you want a life." It would be useful for research universities to recognize that a typical faculty load is likely to be at least sixty students a semester, and possibly one hundred or even two hundred.

To compensate us for this work, research institutions could offer us access to their libraries (without any annual fees) or access to other resources that we need but that our smaller institutions cannot afford (perhaps cosponsoring speakers and readings or other shared events). None of these changes costs much, but they could potentially create a better understanding of faculty work across institutions. Cross-institutional collaboration in the training of graduate students would at least prevent the shock and surprise of candidates when encountering the teaching load at our institutions for the first time. Rather than wonder what nonelite institutions want, those at PhD-granting institutions might begin to think about ways that they could share their power with nonelite institutions and encourage us to participate more actively in the training of new faculty members for our profession. The graduate programs that take some of these steps will certainly begin to place more of their graduate students, and, more important, those graduate students will be better trained to be colleagues and to have successful, joyful careers at small colleges and comprehensive universities.

NOTE

1. The Advisory Board on Faculty Compensation (since we are not unionized, this committee serves as our salary negotiating committee) has recently advocated for a paid family medical leave benefit for faculty. The resulting complicated series of negotiations has involved research of different policy documents and studies of the budgetary and institutional effects of family medical leave. While this issue remains unresolved, I hope dialogues with other faculty will produce strategies for creating a policy that would provide all faculty with a semester of leave at two-thirds pay to care for a family member or to adopt or give birth to a child. That this particular policy has been under negotiation for the last ten years indicates not only the viability of systemic change but also that such change is long-term. Junior faculty members, armed with such knowledge, can consider speaking as a way to achieve long-term change.

WORKS CITED

American Association of University Professors. "1940 Statement of Principles on Academic Freedom and Tenure, with 1970 Interpretive Comments." 17 July 2007 <http://www.aaup.org/AAUP/pubsres/policydocs/1940statement.htm>.

Boyer, Ernest L. *Scholarship Reconsidered: Priorities of the Professoriate.* San Francisco: Jossey-Bass, 1990.

Fetterley, Judith. "Symposium: English 1999: Dreaming the Future of English." *College English* 61 (1999): 702–11.

Gebhardt, Richard C., and Barbara Genelle Smith Gebhardt, eds. *Academic Advancement in Composition Studies: Scholarship, Publication, Promotion, Tenure.* Mahwah: Erlbaum, 1997.

Grimm, Nancy Maloney. *Good Intentions: Writing Center Work for Postmodern Times.* Portsmouth: Boynton, 1999.

Harris, Muriel. "Presenting Writing Center Scholarship: Issues for Faculty and Personnel Committees." Gebhardt and Gebhardt 87–102.

Knoblauch, C. H. "The Albany Graduate English Curriculum." *ADE Bulletin* 98 (1991): 19–21.

Kolodny, Annette. *Failing the Future: A Dean Looks at Higher Education.* Durham: Duke UP, 1998.

Lorde, Audre. *Sister/Outsider.* Freedom: Crossing, 1984.

"Mission Statement." *Saint Joseph's University.* 17 July 2007 <http://www.sju.edu/sju/mission_statement.html>.

Nelson, Jane, and Kathy Evertz, eds. *The Politics of Writing Centers.* Portsmouth: Boynton, 2001.

Newman, Kathy. "Junior Professor: Nice Work If We Can Keep It." *Academe* 85.3 (1999): 29–33.

North, Stephen M. "The Idea of a Writing Center." *The Allyn and Bacon Guide to Writing Center Theory and Practice.* Ed. Robert W. Barnett and Jacob S. Blumner. Needham Heights: Allyn, 2001. 63–78.

Reagon, Bernice Johnson. "Coalition Politics: Turning the Century." *Home Girls: A Black Feminist Anthology.* Ed. Barbara Smith. New York: Kitchen Table, 1983. 356–68.

Roen, Duane H. "Writing Administration as Scholarship and Teaching." Gebhardt and Gebhardt 43–55.

Toth, Emily. "When Should You Grab a Sword?" *Chronicle of Higher Education* 29 Sept. 2000. 17 July 2007 <http://chronicle.com/jobs/2000/09/2000092901c.htm>.

Part III

PREPARING FUTURE FACULTY MEMBERS

CAROL RUTZ

COMING HOME SURPRISED
Indirect Paths to the Professoriat

Graduate students in English studies often view their work as dues paying on the way to their true calling as esteemed professionals. In this
version of the Oz fantasy the work awaiting transformed graduate students over the rainbow is serenely intellectual, infinitely satisfying, and
supremely relaxed, accomplished with the benefits of civilized amenities. These amenities typically include spacious offices with leather
armchairs, miles of bookshelves covered with autographed first editions
bearing intimate personal dedications, windows that look out on a campus quad dotted with sweet-faced students lounging under trees and en-
grossed in books or laptops, and gently chiming Old World clocks that
call faculty members to tea or sherry with their colleagues. Confining
classroom teaching to a few hours on Tuesdays and Thursdays leaves the
rest of the week for the pleasures of research and writing.

I exaggerate, of course. I find it difficult, however, to exaggerate in
the other direction, to make the realistic cultural work of full-time faculty members more complex, consuming, and political than the professional lives most of us experience. Even those who have written
about the absurdities of academic life (David Lodge, Randall Jarrell,
Richard Russo, and Kingsley Amis, to name a few) have not attempted
to magnify the demands on faculty members. The academic status quo
provides plenty of material for satirists as they play on the dreams and
vanities of professors who imagine academic lives different from the
ones they inhabit.

Graduate students' fantasies chart dissimilar territories. For graduate students in the humanities, hours spent in research on a scholarly

problem worthy of a dissertation represent a valuable and terrifying rite of passage that results in admission to the ranks of the professoriat. While the serious pursuit of a research question has much value, I argue that graduate programs can do more for candidates than train them to conduct scholarship and research, narrowly defined. Graduate students who leave degree programs with scholarly credentials alone have missed out on important instruction for assuming the responsibilities dominating professional life, responsibilities that can produce the satisfaction of making a difference to institutions and students, as well as to individual professional standing.

The complexity of academic life should inform the graduate school experience at every level. Currently, the material conditions for attaining the professional goal can vary, especially in the kind of work required of the degree candidate. Graduate students who support themselves with teaching assistantships understand in some measure that scholarly research (isolated, individual, library-centered) will always compete with classroom responsibilities. They may even appreciate the intricacies of scheduling a group of people to cover a range of courses in a given department over several semesters. In contrast, fellowship students may be oblivious to these realities, having received institutional support for scholarship without the distraction of teaching (Lovitts and Nelson). If graduate students expect the ascension to the professoriat to result in a relaxed schedule that allows for a focus on scholarship, they will encounter serious disappointment (Nyquist, Austin, Sprague, and Wulff).

Those disappointed expectations begin in incomplete understandings of faculty work, which are unwittingly facilitated by uneven assistantship and fellowship duties. Misunderstandings conspire to affect formulations of professional goals that omit entire categories of the job, omissions that enable graduate students to define their goals in naive and unrealistic terms (e.g., "When I am a professor, I can do my own work"). All of us must do more to help future faculty members recognize the many forms good work takes in the academy, from teaching and scholarship to administration and community outreach, not to mention undergraduate advising, departmental meetings, search committees and other short-term task forces, college- or university-wide committees, grant writing for scholarly work, community outreach, and various student activities. Add to the faculty workload the inevitable requests for independent studies, recommendation letters, and supervision of undergraduate capstone projects and graduate theses and dissertations, and that civilized scholarly life begins to look like a time-management nightmare to uninformed and ill-prepared graduate students.

To learn about faculty life at research-intensive universities, graduate students should shadow their advisers for a few days during each regular school term. Even with that enviable Tuesday-Thursday schedule, the so-called conveniences of electronic mail, the Internet, and voice mail ensure a full integration of teaching and administration into a professor's time at home as well as in the office. Well-organized professors may schedule for themselves a regular, sanctified period of time for research, because they know how easily their time will disappear into work and family responsibilities. I do not raise this point to claim that family life intrudes on scholarly work or teaching. Life is more than work, and workers of all kinds find themselves in families. For balance to develop, working adults learn to manage multitasking lives that imitate those of our ancestors, even if the circumstances are different. Rather than plow fields with an ox, grind grain to bake our own bread, haul water, chop firewood, tend livestock, and raise a large garden, we face different tasks. Nevertheless, the busyness of adult professional life combined with family life requires stamina and organization. Especially for the student who attends graduate school immediately after receiving an undergraduate degree, shadowing graduate faculty members can provide a clear-eyed view of professional life and the mentoring needed to prepare for that life.

The Accidental Training

My story of graduate study may be useful in illustrating the point that we need to inform graduate students of the variety of expectations in English departments. The job I hold today at a small, selective liberal arts college combines teaching, research, and administration in creative ways, and, remarkably, the work I did as a graduate student prepared me for this job through practical experience. First, the inevitable disclaimer: I cannot exhort applicants to graduate programs in English studies to follow my example in detail. Nevertheless, my experience demonstrates that graduate school can offer far more in the way of professional preparation than courses and a dissertation.

I may have had too much information about the scholarly life before graduate school. My father was a biology professor at a small liberal arts college, and I learned early that the flexibility of a professor's teaching schedule was offset by long laboratory sessions, summer research, supervision of student research, preparation of manuscripts, class preparation—lectures, labs, exams—and professional meetings, departmental meetings, committee meetings, and faculty meetings. And there was grading—everything from scoring multiple-choice exams for large lecture sections to evaluating insect collections in a senior entomology seminar or individual field research projects. Every advisee who went on to graduate or professional school—and there were many of them—represented a living investment of my father's time and professionalism. The recommendations he wrote, the calls he made, and the buttonholing he did at meetings acted out his belief in students who would become his professional peers. He loved his job, and he was valued by the institution, his colleagues, and his students.

As a kid, I was unreflective about all this. From the perspective of my tiny slice of the world, my father's work life was typical of adult experience. He seemed to have plenty of time to help out around the house, cook a mean stew, and hang out with my brother and me. But as I approached the end of my college years, I simply could not stomach the idea of graduate school. I told myself at the time that my field was the problem, weary as I was with the New Criticism that dominated inquiry in English studies in the 1970s. I could not imagine choosing something to study in enough depth to justify a dissertation. That lack of imagination about graduate school combined with a too-familiar view of life as a full-time faculty member. I saw myself as lacking the intellectual heft—not to mention the energy—to manage an academic career. Spooked, I started looking for other ways to support myself.

For a good twenty years, I took jobs with little direct connections to my education, telling myself I was employable only because I could type and spell, the skills that got me interviews and jobs. Of course, that thought was ridiculous. Once in a job, my liberal arts education helped me learn relevant terminology, procedures, and names and put the new material into context. In jobs ranging from the circulation desk of a university library to a medical records office in a private psychiatric facility, I learned a great deal about administration, hierarchy, budgets, business etiquette, and more. Within a few years, I could organize a meeting, take efficient minutes, assign work to others, meet deadlines, account for my time and other resources, prepare a budget, design forms, write memos and reports for specific audiences, and work collaboratively with colleagues on projects. Yet I overlooked my newly acquired and worthwhile knowledge. I was working, and my work required me to perform tasks that others expected me to perform. None of that seemed the least bit remarkable.

Even so, the aggregate of my education and skills led me to accept enjoyable staff positions at Carleton College, a small liberal arts college in Minnesota. After about five years in the dean of students office and a year in the publications office, I began to understand why I enjoyed the work so much: I resonated with the institution itself and the values its people embodied. Daily contact with students and faculty members forced the recognition that I knew the academic life well and once tentatively aspired to it as a career. Without necessarily intending to resume an educational path abandoned nearly twenty years earlier, I enrolled in an MA program designed for working adults at Hamline University, in Saint Paul, a school within driving distance of my home. Three years later, I had more administrative work experience, plus I had recovered my studying and writing acumen and had an advanced degree to show for my trouble. My Hamline thesis committee members strongly urged me to pursue a doctorate, based on their sense of my potential as an academic.

I appreciated their confidence but remained wary of attempting a doctoral program with the expectation of a tenure-track appointment. Even if I were an outstanding graduate student, I would be substantially older than my cohort and would face a tough job market, especially for jobs at schools like Carleton or Hamline, the kind of working environment I knew and loved. I resolved to apply to graduate programs in composition and rhetoric—a specialty not even recognized at Carleton—and to fashion flexible post-PhD goals. In so doing, I intentionally set aside the cherished ideal of a tenure-track appointment at a small liberal arts college and sought other possibilities. I knew universities and community colleges always needed writing teachers, and I was excited enough about working with students to consider combining adjunct teaching with other kinds of employment. After years as an office worker, business writing came easily to me, and I daydreamed about consulting or training situations in the corporate world. After all, something good might come of my work in the publications office at Carleton, where I learned basic principles of document design and production, served as the project manager for multiple campus clients and outside vendors, and became a good copyeditor. Of course, editorial jobs were no more plentiful than tenure-track faculty jobs, but freelance work was abundant. The more I thought about it, the more I reasoned that I could combine a PhD with my existing skills in a number of productive ways.

Some of this reasoning slanted toward wishful thinking, but without these little delusions, I could not in good conscience abandon a full-time job with benefits to tackle a doctoral program at the University of Minnesota, where I would earn about $3,000 per quarter teaching first-year composition. In addition to the loss of colleagues, earning power, and a retirement plan, I traded a fifteen-minute commute and free parking a few yards from my office for an hour in heavy traffic and paid parking in a lot five blocks from my attic cubicle. When I left Carleton and became a full-time graduate student, my husband was self-employed and our children were in middle school. Somehow I had to cover my own expenses and earn enough to pay for groceries. Fortunately for me, the composition program's teaching assistantship at the University of Minnesota included a tuition waiver, or the whole plan would have fallen apart. The family felt the loss of my former income, but we garnered some unexpected benefits from my new status as a doctoral student. For instance, I planned my graduate classes and my teaching around my sons' school schedules. We all did homework together, which both amused and challenged the boys. More important to their overall education and quality of life, I could attend the parent-teacher conferences, games, concerts, and other activities I missed as a full-time staff member at Carleton. Although entirely unexpected, the graduate program provided me with a schedule that promoted a close connection to my children at key times in all our lives.

My schedule was complex outside graduate school, and the work—teaching and taking courses—was intellectually demanding and physically tiring. Having arrived at graduate school resistant to a narrow view of possible outcomes, however, I embraced opportunities to prepare myself broadly as a scholar, teacher, editor, consultant, or whatever might turn up. At that time (early 1990s) the University of Minnesota's composition program was known for a rich curriculum and strong TA training (Anson and Rutz). As soon as I could, I started teaching advanced courses in business and science writing to strengthen my teaching repertoire, and I also applied for TA-training roles and other administrative positions available to graduate students in the program. Whenever possible, I took on freelance editorial work (both for the cash and to maintain my skills), and I taught summer school every year I was eligible.

I left the University of Minnesota after five years. During that time, I completed courses and preliminary exams for my doctoral program; taught twenty courses at both introductory and advanced levels; earned a teaching award; worked as the program director's assistant to help hire, train, and schedule TAs from all over the university to teach in the program; wrote a successful curriculum-development grant; assisted in administering a dual-enrollment program serving dozens of area high schools through faculty development; and delivered papers at several national and regional conferences.

Coming Home Surprised

All this experience paid off in the short run when I developed an on-campus professional community in which I conducted a classroom-based study for my dissertation research. In the longer run, my experience specifically prepared me—to my everlasting surprise—to come home to Carleton in a new role as the director of the writing program, a non-tenure-track position that combines teaching and faculty development, as well as the hiring and training of student writing tutors. Initially a part-time, temporary position, the opportunity at Carleton became the perfect place to finish my dissertation and collect more experience for a job search. The dissertation is long finished, and my annual assessment of the job market has yet to yield a better situation than the one that has developed for me at Carleton. To my great delight, I have resumed relationships with colleagues who are glad to see me back in a new role, my teaching is appreciated by students, and my scholarship flourishes. Plus, parking is still free.

Where once I served on the staff in largely clerical jobs, my current responsibilities include teaching two or three writing courses a year, advising undergraduates, administering the writing-across-the-curriculum program, planning and leading workshops and other faculty development activities, conducting individual and program assessments, and writing grant proposals to support many administrative programs. In addition to offering me a rich theoretical background, graduate school gave me experience in teaching at all levels (writing courses for first-year and upper-division students), faculty development (TA training and workshops for high school teachers), and grant writing—not to mention the opportunity to teach hundreds of preprofessional students to do the same. Although I learned little about assessment in graduate school, attendance at conferences put me in touch with the people in my field who could help us at Carleton understand writing assessment. Finally, having established a foothold in a professional community has made it possible for me to bring composition and rhetoric experts to campus to interact with undergraduate tutors, attend classes, confer with faculty members, lead specialized workshops, and participate in our Learning and Teaching Center's speaker series.

SUGGESTIONS FOR GRADUATE STUDENTS

The skills I acquired and, in some cases, polished in graduate school would serve a tenure-track faculty member as well. Knowing how to approach a committee assignment, a faculty search, an advising situation, or the intricacies of local accounting practices helps anyone survive the nonteaching, nonscholarly segments of faculty life. Given that many faculty members can expect to chair a department, lead the faculty senate, or serve a stint as an associate dean or in some other administrative role, practice at the graduate school level, no matter how limited, is never wasted. Furthermore, the satisfaction of developing new curricula, solving budgetary problems, obtaining external funding for a new program, and so much more enhances the pleasures and richness of faculty life.

Having come home surprised, I offer some suggestions for graduate students with broad career goals and for those who might consider broadening their career goals. Granted, my circumstances as a nontraditional graduate student with a considerable work history color my advice; however, students of varied demographics can take positive steps in their graduate programs to create connections between the preprofessional and professional worlds of academia. Even in a program that does not offer graduate students paid nonteaching duties, resourceful students of any age can participate in useful activities to enhance marketability and open attitudes toward worthwhile work.

Get involved in the graduate student organization. These organizations vary in their composition, but someone will have to take minutes at meetings and distribute them, and someone will serve as president or convener—the person who organizes the meetings, sets the agenda, and follows up with members and others. Running this kind of committee offers practice for the inevitable committee work required of faculty members.

Mentor new people. New graduate students appreciate having a contact person who helps them learn the ropes. Furthermore, explaining an academic environment to a new person helps the old-timer identify important features of that environment at all levels.

Get involved in TA training. Doctoral programs vary considerably in their approach to preparation of teachers. Some require specific courses, team-teaching with a faculty member, observation of a faculty member or an experienced TA, intensive presemester training seminars, or some other form of training. Coordinators often appreciate the involvement of graduate students who have experienced the training themselves.

Serve on a departmental committee. Most graduate programs have graduate student representation on one or more committees. The meetings alone offer graduate students a primer on the workings of an academic department away from the classroom setting.

Serve on search committees. At many universities, at least one graduate student will serve on every departmental hiring committee. Reviewing files, contributing to the discussion about candidates, and participating in interviews help prepare graduate students for their own job searches. In addition, graduate students often host job candidates and other visiting speakers, spending significant amounts of time with them. Many a professional collaboration has been born en route to an airport.

Get acquainted with the department office staff. All academic departments function with the help and support of the nonteaching staff. Graduate students do well to befriend office staff members and learn how they do their work. Secretaries and program assistants may be willing to teach graduate students spreadsheet and Web page software in exchange for help on projects. A little volunteered time can produce invaluable insights into the labor required for reports, curricular scheduling, the politics of office assignments, and more. In many departments, particularly at public universities, the budget is public. Office

staff members can explain where funds originate and how the departmental budget fits into the university as a whole. Graduate students
who understand one budgeting system can apply that knowledge to
their postgraduate situations.

Explore professional activities. In consultation with an adviser or
other mentor, graduate students should begin to establish themselves
as professionals. Among the possibilities: participation in professional
electronic discussion lists (choosing judiciously to avoid being over-
whelmed by the volume of reading), membership in professional organizations and subscription to publications at the lower graduate student
rates, attendance and presentations at professional conferences, and the
identification of potential collaborators.

Few of the activities described above can be accommodated by the
ideal Tuesday-Thursday schedule. Such a schedule represents a fantasy
that excludes much of the real work academics do, whether in their offices and classrooms or at home. To ignore the work that solves department problems, brings new people into the community, allocates
resources, trains teachers, and promotes scholarly activity is to strip
academic life of much of its richness. Graduate programs owe their
doctoral candidates clear information about the professional lives ahead
of them—including the realities of the job market. They also should
provide candidates reasonable opportunities to practice the administrative skills they will need after they graduate, whether they become
professors, department chairs, writing center directors, faculty development personnel, editors, high school teachers, journalists, MLA
staff members, or something else. Scholarly work occurs in a complex
context, and graduate study offers an efficient, sensible means of revealing that context to graduate students.

WORKS CITED

Amis, Kingsley. *Lucky Jim.* New York: Viking, 1953.

Anson, Chris M., and Carol Rutz. "Graduate Students, Writing Programs, and
    Consensus-Based Management: Collaboration in the Face of Disciplinary
    Ideology." *Writing Program Administration* 21.2-3 (1998): 106–20.

Jarrell, Randall. *Pictures from an Institution: A Comedy.* New York: Farrar,
    1954.

Lodge, David. *Changing Places: A Tale of Two Campuses*. London: Secker, 1975.

Lovitts, Barbara, and Cary Nelson. "The Hidden Crisis in Graduate Education: Attrition from Ph.D. Programs." *Academe* 86.6 (2000): 44–50.

Nyquist, Jody, Ann Austin, Jo Sprague, and Donald Wulff. *The Development of Graduate Students as Teaching Scholars: A Four-Year Longitudinal Study, Final Report*. Seattle: U of Washington, 2001.

Russo, Richard. *Straight Man*. New York: Random, 1997.

ANNE PASERO

A STUDY-ABROAD GUIDE FOR FOREIGN LANGUAGE FACULTY MEMBERS

Some twenty-five years ago I applied for a Spanish professorship at Marquette University because, among other reasons, the position carried with it the opportunity to direct the university's undergraduate study-abroad program in Madrid. That I never had the chance to study overseas as an undergraduate made the idea of doing so as a professor appealing. Soon after my arrival at Marquette, the opportunity to spend time in Madrid materialized, so I cast aside warnings from colleagues about delays to my tenure process and packed my bags. I have never looked back, nor have I regretted that decision. To this day, I find study abroad one of the most fulfilling and satisfying aspects of the academic experience for faculty members as well as for students, one that makes culture a tangible object of intellectual reflection in the frame of lived everyday experience. As a means of discussing ways faculty members from diverse academic cultures can build bridges between American and overseas institutions, I orient this essay in two directions, addressing the advantages and challenges of study abroad first for faculty members—especially for those at teaching-intensive institutions—and then for students, for whom study abroad often transforms their lives.

I begin by outlining my own study-abroad experience and the opportunities it provided for me. I directed the Marquette in Madrid program three times and during three different periods, 1982–85, 1993–95, and 2001–03. I was the director of the PRESHCO consortium of colleges (Programa de Estudios Hispánicos en Córdoba), made up of Oberlin, Smith, Trinity, Wellesley, Wheaton, and Wooster and based in Córdoba, Spain, for the academic year 1999–2000. Most recently (2004–05), I served as director of the Vanderbilt in Spain program, located in Madrid. I have also served as president of the American Association of Programs in Spain. Most of my experience is Madrid-related, but with PRESHCO I had the chance to adapt to a whole new program site, staff, working environment, and students.

Each of the five times I served as director in Spain, I found new challenges in working with students to enhance their cultural knowledge, overall adaptation, and personal development; in administering programs and helping bring fresh vision and ideas to their development; and in deriving benefits for myself from the cultural exposure and professional environment. Although I never had unfettered research time available to me because of the many and diverse demands of the position, I nonetheless furthered my research agenda on contemporary Spanish women's poetry by gathering relevant source materials, meeting with and interviewing women poets, conferring with potential publishers, and even working regularly with a specific poet to collaborate on a translation or bring to culmination a long-term book project. This personal collaboration with authors has proved to be of great value to my professional scholarly development, thus challenging the status of study-abroad directorships as distractions for pre- or posttenure faculty members.

The concept of study abroad has changed dramatically, from an outlet for language majors of means to a popular line item on the résumés of college juniors. Commenting on this broadening appeal of study-abroad programs, Sharon Wilkinson writes:

> The internationalization of American curricula is quickly becoming a national priority. . . . Study abroad, long recognized as the quintessential global learning experience, was traditionally reserved for an elite few, usually the brightest and most financially able, and destinations were heavily concentrated in Europe. The concept of inclusiveness in overseas education is only now beginning to impact study abroad recruitment and program design. (81)

As a witness to study-abroad programs' growing inclusiveness and intellectual expansion since the 1980s and during the nine years I served as a program director, I must note that study-abroad faculty leaders still work to dispel certain unfortunate stereotypical notions about directorships and directors or advisers, primary among them the idea

that the position of accompanying students to other countries quali-
fies as a faculty vacation of sorts, that the professor has little else to do
but enjoy the sights and the pleasures of being abroad. Nothing could
be further from the truth. As I have learned over the years, serious involvement in study abroad with students requires of faculty members
a full-time, all-encompassing devotion. Never completely predictable,
study-abroad programs demand adaptable and flexible faculty leaders,
people willing to attend fully to students' needs, whether academic,
psychological, medical, or legal.

In general, study-abroad positions offer faculty members positive
possibilities for growth; directors live and work abroad and benefit
from extended interaction with students outside the classroom, thereby
getting to know them on a level usually not possible on the home campus. I count as the highlight of my career the chances to know students in different contexts and to witness their adaptation to and
maturation in a new culture.

While twenty-five years ago a faculty member's preparation for assuming a challenging overseas administrative task received scant attention, today universities and departments are much more aware that
directing a program abroad represents a serious undertaking, one requiring the designated study-abroad faculty director to develop certain
skills such as a potential for administrative work, the ability to function well in dual cultures and diverse roles (teacher, adviser, program
supervisor, surrogate parent, counselor), the ability to sustain one's research program while making the transition between places and positions, and the energy and enthusiasm to bring to life the assignment
abroad. Ideally, faculty members ought to be tenured, but advanced assistant professors can perform well overseas, if confident in the support of their institutions.

Study-abroad directorships offer foreign language faculty members
truly remarkable opportunities for intellectual and personal growth.
As cultural ambassadors, directors and their students can expand provin-
cial academic cultures and personal mindsets during the course of
their time overseas and when sharing their insights with others once
back home. First and foremost, of course, such positions enable faculty
members to live abroad and experience full immersion in the language
and culture of choice, an attractive perk after all those years of stateside graduate study. Faculty members who conduct research in an area
related to the study program enjoy access to unparalleled resources in

another country, even if most directors find little free time away from administering their programs to carry out extensive projects. Regardless, being abroad undeniably allows directors occasion to collect source material in their fields and to attend lectures, readings, expositions, and exhibits. In addition, the collegial atmosphere American faculty members share with faculty members and administrators from foreign universities sometimes yields long-term connections and joint projects. Working abroad for a year or two affords faculty members a break from their home campus routines and allows them time to gain a new perspective on their career development. Lastly, directors acquire administrative experience, cultivating leadership skills and autonomous decision-making abilities, all of which may be valuable preparation for college or university administrative positions on their home campuses.

With the relative autonomy of study-abroad directorships comes weighty responsibility. Support staff members and resources ease the overall burden placed on directors, but the ultimate responsibility for students' welfare rests with them. In a litigious society, the college or university's liability for all aspects of its study-abroad programs endows directors' decisions with legal implications. Action (or non-action) could result in charges of negligence on the part of the college or university in preserving the welfare of its student body, so directors need assistance in assessing student welfare. In addition to the home campus study-abroad office, almost all programs have at least one on-site secretary or administrator who can assist with arranging housing and medical, legal, religious, recreational, and tourism options for students. During rare times of crisis, assistants can also provide support and backup information for directors.

Concerning safety abroad, contemporary political realities have heightened program participants' anxieties about terrorism. Directors always connect with the proper United States Embassy and with the State Department to identify any potential threats unique to the region and to devise detailed plans for responses to incidents of terrorism directed against Americans, should they occur. This issue, probably more than any other, alarms parents and loved ones, some of whom need directors to calmly reassure them of the students' probable safety. Students, once they become familiar with their host country, tend to be the least concerned about safety, so they need periodic reminders about the ramifications of a sometimes threatening global era.

Globalism, however, can also help American students realize they are not the center of the universe. Students need explicit instruction in behaving as representatives of the United States while abroad and should remember that they are guests of a nation and do not enjoy more privileges than their hosts. I cannot stress enough the importance of good study-abroad orientations, both on campus and abroad, in helping make students aware of their attitudes toward diverse cultures, the consequences of their actions, and the importance of safety during their stay.

Just as some students enroll in college by default, so certain students join study-abroad programs by default, choosing an overseas program only because their friends do, their parents think they should, they have heard the parties are good, or they view study abroad as a fine thing to have on their résumé. In short, directors should be prepared to deal not only with the serious, academically motivated, linguistically prepared students but also with those students who come along for specious reasons not necessarily evident at the outset of a term or semester. To complicate matters further, sometimes the most academically gifted students may adjust poorly to a new cultural environment. The responsibility of caring for all students, regardless of their motivation and maturity, can overwhelm directors. According to Richard Williamson, "The responsibility of directing a study-abroad program is so great that some American institutions now hire only resident directors with a lot of experience" managing students holistically. He goes on to indicate that the "time may fast be approaching when universities and departments hire professional directors to run programs abroad . . ." (14).

Until that time arrives, full-time tenure-track or tenured faculty members fill directorships and subject themselves to deans' and colleagues' misguided assumptions about study-abroad positions—namely, that faculty directors have garnered nice vacations overseas with responsibilities incomparable to the more onerous and time-consuming committee tasks and departmental or college obligations shouldered by home campus colleagues. Those who have participated actively in study abroad can bring back to their campuses clear reports of the numerous and substantial responsibilities associated with their positions. This record is especially important because usually the director overseas does not teach, and both students and colleagues need to understand the rationale for this exemption from the classroom.

Lack of clarity regarding study-abroad director positions can influence the evaluation of faculty members' progress toward promotion and tenure. Some colleges or universities have policies prohibiting nontenured faculty members from participating in study-abroad programs, whereas others simply discourage pretenure faculty members from study-abroad distractions. To allow more time for research, Marquette University has in the past frozen the tenure clock for pretenure study-abroad faculty members, resuming the tenure process once faculty members return to campus. This practice is slowly changing, and directors prefer not to stop the clock while abroad. In general, the service performed by faculty members overseas simply is not given its due. In addition, overseas directors know that the near impossibility of finding undisturbed research time while abroad is another obstacle for pretenure study-abroad faculty members. It would behoove colleges and universities to recognize the importance of study-abroad positions to the development of faculty members, to consider them appropriately when evaluating the progress of candidates toward promotion and tenure, and to determine legitimate ways to reward study-abroad service on the merit scale. I do not yet know of any university that will substitute overseas administrative experience for research production when assessing a faculty member for tenure, but this policy might be useful for administrators in the future, especially to encourage broader faculty participation in study-abroad programs and to facilitate the intellectual work necessary for movement from assistant to associate rank.

Students' intellectual work benefits from study abroad as well. This experience is transformative, for both director and students, and can change the direction of one's career path or life development. In years past, language learning dominated study-abroad programs' rationales, but students today gain more than linguistic competency from their immersion in other cultures. While a year abroad is ideal, clearly not every student has the financial, academic, or familial resources necessary to support a full year of study abroad. Generally speaking, students who study in a host country for a year become more fully integrated into the culture of the host country than their half-year counterparts do and master the target language by the end of their stay. As Barbara Burn verifies in her assessment studies, "Language acquisition is far less when study abroad is only a semester rather than a full academic year or more" (183). Nevertheless, undergraduates most commonly study abroad for the duration of one semester or quarter; some colleges and universities even offer midyear or interim period programs. There are also summer programs, varying in length but usually lasting six weeks, a period of time less satisfying for language learning but still long enough to provide valuable cultural exposure to students.

Some schools, my own included, strongly recommend or require participation in the equivalent of one semester (during the academic year or the summer) in a program abroad for Spanish teaching majors and international business students. Other colleges, such as Goucher College, require some form of study abroad for all students, citing as a reason for this curricular change the obvious benefits of cross-cultural dialogue. I am so convinced of the advantages of sending American students abroad that I recommend considering requiring such a semester for degree completion. The Goucher president Sanford Ungar confirms, "The overriding principle is that young Americans be introduced to the idea that other people have important things to contribute to societies" (qtd. in Chmela). When enough young people have developed a greater awareness of the world around them, they unlock real possibilities for creating positive change in their own society. For many of them, study abroad means really moving away from home and experiencing culture shock and alienation. After the initial period of shock, students are forced to develop high degrees of tolerance and flexibility, since they learn that studying abroad means living abroad, at least for a time, and that difference in style, manner, and substance inheres in other cultures and nations. When students return home most can assess the implications of the end to provincialism that residing abroad has prompted. Years later I often hear from former study-abroad students who regard their time in Spain as the most meaningful and transforming experience of their college careers.

Advantages for students who study abroad extend well beyond language fluency to include personal growth and increased maturity. Young study-abroad participants adapt to changing circumstances, develop interest in their host cultures, muster willingness to meet people and cultivate those relationships, and gain confidence in themselves when functioning outside their comfort zones. In addition, study-abroad students see themselves as contributing to a larger purpose, whether to the study-abroad group or to their own sense of the United States in a global context. American students in Europe find themselves uncomfortable when confronted with pointed historical or political questions, discovering that young Europeans often have much stronger backgrounds in and knowledge of world affairs in general, and of United States history in particular, than their American counterparts. Students who share a period of time overseas develop a bond forged from the common expression of a kind of freedom, intellectual and otherwise, which they are unlikely to have again.

The ideal way for students to become integrated into the university setting of their host country is through direct matriculation, a system whereby American students enroll in classes with students from the host country and conform to the academic standards and requirements of the host country's higher education authority. Programs such as Georgetown University's favor this kind of setting. Most students, however, find this approach too demanding and scary and consequently shy away from committing to a semester of hard work that will be judged according to sometimes far more rigorous standards than those of the American college or university. From a practical standpoint, I recognize that most American students abroad are busy discovering themselves, traveling, and enjoying the advantages of world cultures. For many, it can be the only semester of their academic career that provides any kind of relief from work and family obligations.

While students may not consider their overseas academic settings the most critical component of their experience, such settings should nevertheless offer students the opportunity to become engaged in the target language and culture. More often than not, students need to seek ways to become integrated into their host cultures, quite apart from the classroom, primarily through making foreign friends and becoming involved in their activities. The same holds true for housing arrangements. A family situation is ideal, when there is some semblance of a family life in the home and where the student can feel a sense of comfort and security.

Another viable housing option, especially for more mature and independent students, involves finding housing with young people who are citizens of the host country. Adjusting to the new culture and lifestyle is rarely easy. In fact, students often arrive with rather grandiose expectations, fostered by their own illusions, only to find that functioning well abroad can be arduous, demanding, and sometimes alienating. Students who come with personal problems often experience such problems more acutely in a foreign setting. Students who have always found adjusting easy may also be caught off guard, finding for the first time that they have to work at the simplest of tasks. Obviously, if directors observe students suffering from severe cultural or psychological shock, they should consult with resident experts to help provide guidance. Common psychological problems both at home and abroad include eating disorders, substance abuse, depression, and peer conflict. While most physical problems are minor, involving common colds and flu, emergencies arise (severe illness, serious accidents, serious crime incidents), demanding directors' organized access to medical resources, insurance information, and the means by which to keep the parents and home institutions informed. In a time of emergency at the hospital, the directors may be responsible for accepting or refusing treatment on students' behalf. As I indicated earlier, close contact with both the program assistant and the home campus administrator are essential and will aid the director in the decision-making process.

Despite its problems and complications, the study-abroad experience is one of the most exciting, rewarding, demanding, and satisfying prospects available to academics and students. Serving as a director is quite different from teaching in the classroom, and the position allows faculty members and students to share an adventure they will remember fondly for years to come.

> [W]hen confronted with real challenges, such as communication barriers and lack of familiarity with regional customs, students quickly become active learners—mirroring the experiential learning theory of Outward Bound. . . . In this post–September 11 climate, this type of experiential learning will serve them well.   (Gray, Murdock, and Stebbins 51)

I value my study-abroad experiences, even if they did delay my tenure. Such a delay pales in comparison with the immediate and long-term enrichment my directorships have contributed to my personal life and teaching career.

WORKS CITED

Burn, Barbara B. "Study Abroad and Foreign Language Programs." *Changing Perspectives on International Education*. Ed. Patrick O'Meara, Howard D. Mehlinger, and Roxana Ma Newman. Bloomington: Indiana UP, 2001. 178–89.

Chmela, Holli. "Foreign Detour en Route to a College Degree." *New York Times* 19 Oct. 2005: A21.

Gray, Kimberly S., Gwendolyn K. Murdock, and Chad D. Stebbins. "Assessing Study Abroad's Effect on an International Mission." *Change: The Magazine of Higher Learning* 34.3 (2002): 44–51.

Wilkinson, Sharon. "Beyond Classroom Boundaries: The Changing Nature of Study Abroad." *Beyond the Boundaries: Changing Contexts in Language Learning.* Ed. Roberta Z. Lavine. Boston: McGraw, 2001. 81–105.

Williamson, Richard C. "The Quintessence of a Study-Abroad Program: The Director." *ADFL Bulletin* 13.4 (1982): 12–15.

JO ANN BUCK AND MACGREGOR FRANK

FACULTY-IN-TRAINING PROGRAM
Preparing Future Community College Faculty Members

A BRIEF HISTORY

The 1970s saw the rapid growth of two-year colleges in America, new institutions offering transfer and vocational opportunities to a diverse student population. Existing in local communities, these "community colleges" (Fitzgerald et al. 6) enrolled students of diverse ages, socio-economic levels, and racial and ethnic backgrounds. In just two decades, community colleges became the schools of choice for students who had been previously foreclosed from higher education. According to a United States Department of Education survey in 1997, nontraditional students (older than twenty-two) made up nearly 60% of all students enrolled in two-year colleges, and minority groups accounted for roughly 32% (Woodard). These demographics still apply, and many first-generation college students and students who lack knowledge of college-level expectations seek entrance through community colleges' open-door admission policy.

The demands of the local communities required the new college movement to offer a variety of programs. When local furniture manufacturing became a significant economic factor in Guilford County, North Carolina, Guilford Technical Community College (GTCC) responded to the demands of this local industry by creating a one-year upholstery diploma and a two-year applied business degree.

The broad range of students who choose to study at GTCC and the expansiveness of the technical, vocational, and college transfer programs we offer require faculty members with specialized skills. Historically, however, graduate-level preparation for community college teaching has been deficient. According to Florence Brawer, faculty preparation for community college teaching in the early 1970s had three tracks: academic preparation and experience teaching in secondary schools; graduate programs yielding traditional master's degrees; and work experience in technical and vocational fields with little, if any, pedagogical training. Although community colleges have grown exponentially, faculty preparation programs have not kept pace. Jamilah Evelyn notes that "[g]raduate schools generally don't supply teachers-in-training with the tools they'll need to succeed in the two-year college world. And they don't show any signs of doing so in the near future." Without explicit study of community colleges' specific mission, student diversity, open-door admissions policies, and variety of curricula, traditional graduate students exit their programs with discipline-specific content but with little understanding of two-year colleges.

The obvious inadequacies of faculty training combined with a hiring boom at the two-year level did inspire certain universities to create specialized community college faculty preparation programs during the early 1970s:

> the doctor of arts, the master of philosophy, the educational
> specialist, the diplomate in college teaching, the master of arts
> in college teaching degrees. . . . Congress encourage[d] such ac-
> tivity through Part E of the Education Professions Develop-
> ment Act.   (Reese 27)

Programs flourished at a variety of graduate degree–granting institutions: Boston University; University of Colorado; Tufts University; State University of New York, Fredonia; University of Michigan, Ann Arbor; University of Virginia; Appalachian State University; and Rochester Institute of Technology. These universities developed specific programs with off-campus internships for prospective community college teachers (Reese 28). The best programs of the time required a teaching internship, an occasion for those preparing for faculty roles to take their subject matter training from their graduate schools to real learners at community colleges (28).

With attention paid in the 1970s to training a specialized faculty for two-year colleges and with periodic sparks of interest in the community college over the following decades, we might assume that by 2008 all two-year college instructors have received specialty training.

According to Arthur Cohen and Brawer, between 1965 and 1980, "the number of public two-year institutions nearly doubled, and their enrollments increased tenfold" (xv). Graduate school–based programs for preparing community college instructors declined, however; they simply "never became a major source of two-year college teachers" (72). Once the expansion of the 1960s and 1970s ceased, "institutional expansion subsided, and relatively few new staff members were employed," and by the "start of the 1980s new, full-time positions were scarce" (72, 86). Since little demand existed for two-year college faculty training programs when full-time teaching positions became unavailable, most specialized programs withered away. With the notable exception of George Mason University's National Center for Community College Education, which continues to offer a thriving two-year college preparation program, and a few consortia and initiatives developed by national academic associations (Rifkin), Brawer's summary of faculty preparation remains as relevant to today's graduate students as it was when she bemoaned faculty members' lack of training in 1973.

RATIONALE FOR THE GTCC FACULTY-IN-TRAINING PROGRAM

The English department of Guilford Technical Community College, like so many other English departments at two-year institutions, relies heavily on adjunct faculty members to support its course offerings. In a typical semester, nearly half the department's courses are taught by adjuncts. Each year, this dependency becomes more difficult to sustain because local competition for effective instructors is fierce. Add to that a limited part-time budget that results in relatively meager per-course salaries, and the pool of qualified adjuncts shrinks further. At GTCC, as well as at other community colleges in the state, increased enrollments force the addition of more composition sections—the courses adjuncts typically teach—since all degree programs at GTCC require two composition courses and diploma programs require one. Never able to staff all the English classes with full-time faculty members, we face a rising need for qualified adjuncts.

Nationwide, in fact, the number of full-time faculty members available to teach increasingly popular composition courses is dwindling. According to an April 1997 issue of *Community College Week*, nearly 65% of full-time community college faculty members were forty-five or older at the time of the survey (Wright). These instructors will retire in large numbers by 2015, leaving their departments with vacancies. In fact, a 2004 survey indicated that at least 80% of the "graying faculty" will retire within twenty to twenty-five years (Rifkin 2). A clear need for quality replacements exists, but the inadequacy of typical graduate school curricula and the dearth of training programs for teaching at community colleges raises the question, From where will these faculty members come?

Not only will retiring faculty members need replacing, but community colleges will require more faculty members to meet the demands of the growing student enrollment. College enrollment of traditional-age students is expected to increase by 13% from 2000 to 2015 ("Postsecondary Issues"), and community colleges will surely provide space for some of them. As budgets tighten and enrollment demands increase, public senior colleges in North Carolina are compensating by raising admission requirements to route some students to community colleges. These students will make up identified academic deficiencies to become eligible for transfer admission (Fitzgerald et al. 2).

As anyone who has devoted a career to community college teaching will attest, community college students constitute a population distinctly different from typical four-year students. In addition, community colleges have a mission-driven relation with and specific obligations to the communities that support them. Such factors justify the need for specialized training for a distinct teaching niche in the profession. It is time to dispel the common myth that those who teach at community colleges just wound up there, either tired of the hassles of contemporary high schools or unable to conduct scholarly research at four-year colleges and universities. The hiring of community college faculty members with doctorates has increased in recent years, partly because the expected flood of faculty retirements has begun, creating a relative boom in community college positions at the same time that four-year colleges have struggled to secure new faculty lines. One study indicates that in 1973 13.9% of community college English faculty members held doctorates, whereas 22.7% held doctorates in 1993–94 (Debard). The respondents to the 1993–94 survey revealed that efforts to hire PhDs in English have increased as the market allows.

Job searches during the past decade at GTCC corroborate this trend. Search committee members typically review over ninety applications for each advertised English faculty position and have consistently considered applicants with PhDs as finalists for interviews. Yet an applicant with a PhD who lacks commitment to and teaching experience at community colleges will not fare as well as a candidate with an MA and community college teaching experience. When considering two applicants with equal community college experience, one holding the MA and the other a PhD, the GTCC search committee recommends the PhD for hire.

The literature shows, however, that having the terminal degree alone is not sufficient preparation for community college teaching. Instructors must also understand and appreciate the community college educational milieu. According to the Two-Year College Association's *Guidelines for the Academic Preparation of English Faculty at Two-Year Colleges*, "to prevent the 'open door' from becoming a 'revolving door,' two year college teacher-scholars have to know their students at least as well as they know their field of study and be prepared to adapt instruction accordingly" (Fitzgerald et al. 8; see also Evelyn; Murray; Fugate and Amey; Haworth; Gibson-Harman et al.). In short, there is a need for community college faculty members who have both academic credentials and community college experience and who intentionally select the community college as the venue for their professional lives.

A Solution to Benefit All

Creating the Faculty-in-Training Program (FIT), a specialized community college preparation program for future faculty members, involved convincing faculty members and administrative stakeholders of the obvious advantages this program could bring to GTCC and its English department: fewer adjunct faculty members and less turnover; a different pool of teachers, some typically ineligible to teach at universities; a steady supply of available teaching assistants; a chance to mentor faculty members in GTCC English classrooms; cost effectiveness, since GTCC could designate the same payment for teaching assistants as they did for adjunct faculty members; opportunities to develop working relationships with university English colleagues; opportunities for professional development for participating department members; possibilities for scholarship and publication for participants; and recognition of innovation from the GTCC administration and community college colleagues.

We wondered what would be the draw for another group of stakeholders, the potential TAs. Graduate students with MAs could teach their own classes, an opportunity not available to them, if, as is common, their home colleges used only doctoral students as TAs. In addition to the per-course stipend that other adjuncts earn, we could offer TAs training for the profession, specialized community college training that graduate English departments would not offer their students. Moreover, with the community college emphasis on workplace readiness, we could offer instruction on integrating specific, career-related soft skills into composition assignments. Often people with advanced academic degrees become content experts without having practiced developing course objectives or devising effective strategies for teaching skills such as adaptability, information processing, teamwork, responsibility, and problem solving. Other advantages for TAs would include mentoring and formal written evaluations, participation in professional networks, and enhancements to their résumés, all of which would make them more competitive when applying for community college faculty openings.

Thinking more broadly, we recognized a need to open lines of communication between community college and university faculty members, especially since a scarcity of cross-institutional dialogue has left university faculty members with little knowledge of community colleges. For example, when one applicant to the FIT program requested a recommendation from a graduate school professor, the professor wondered aloud why the applicant would want to consider community college work, where "the students are mediocre and [the applicant's] colleagues would be uninteresting." While we recognize that such an uninformed attitude may not be typical, our experience has convinced us that often enough, what our university colleagues know about community college life has been based more on misinformation than on actual contact with community college students, faculty members, administrators, or staff members.

Yet studies focusing on community college issues generally originate at the university level, programs for training community college administrators always reside in university graduate schools, and the few community college faculty training programs that do exist normally reside in universities. Our program represents a paradigm shift in the domain of community college faculty preparation. Designed, administered, and based at the community college, it seeks not just to train instructors in a particular discipline but to provide a full community college experience for future faculty members by immersing them in a community college culture. Rather than rely on the perspectives of university faculty members, community college experts need to assume responsibility for the training of their own faculty members. Despite heavy teaching loads, community college faculty members must embrace this new paradigm to ensure the competence of their future colleagues. To date, two programs have made progress in this new direction: the one established at the College of Lake County, Illinois, which provides teaching internships for graduate students in English (Murphy 259), and the GTCC FIT program.

Data gathered from newly hired faculty members at four-year colleges and universities suggest the importance of community college training programs. Recent studies of PhD programs find a higher percentage of degree completion among students who worked as teaching and research assistants than among those who enjoyed graduate fellowships because, as Barbara Lovitts and Cary Nelson speculate, they are more integrated into their programs. Another study casts light on the plight of newly hired PhDs, who "found life stressful with heavy teaching loads, new course preparations, getting to know colleagues, adjusting to a new organization, and handling requests to serve on committees or assist on departmental tasks" (Trower). The gap between preparation for and occupation of the teaching life inspired us to design our program as a means of giving potential community college instructors a chance to experience faculty life firsthand. In so doing, they might better discern whether their particular personalities, abilities, and goals fit in the two-year college setting.

GTCC Approval and University Contacts

Although we could pay teaching assistants what we paid our adjunct faculty members for teaching courses, if the program were to provide the kind of preparation we envisioned, TAs would have to commit to additional working hours for more extensive training. Furthermore, to comply with the Southern Association of Colleges and Schools guidelines and to have the program function as we wanted, the director of the program would require reassigned time to develop materials, serve as administrator of the program, and become the lead teacher for the TAs. These requirements would mean additional dollars to support the program. Instead of the originally intended departmental per-course adjunct rate, we determined to pay TAs an increased per-course rate that would reflect the additional duties required of them, such as teaching four courses over two semesters, tutoring in the Writing Center, attending seminars as well as required college and departmental meetings, and interacting with mentors. The administration allocated funds to reassign the director from two classes each semester. With both philosophical and budgetary support secured, the department was ready to contact graduate school colleagues.

After our initial meeting with faculty members from the graduate English program at the University of North Carolina, Greensboro (UNCG), they not only supported the idea and benefits of the FIT program but readily supplied advice and sample TA materials from their own program. They also agreed to support our new program in their department, to publicize it, to serve as contacts and distribute applications, to identify and contact qualified applicants, and to maintain informal contact with us. Together we prepared recruitment materials, examined the files of enrolled MA students, identified eligible applicants, and informed them of the TA opportunity. When applications were submitted, our GTCC screening committee reviewed them, interviewed candidates, created appropriate correspondence, and accepted three TAs to begin in August 1999.

IMPLEMENTING THE PROGRAM

To embrace the paradigm shift from university to community college responsibility for preparing future faculty members, we designed the FIT program around three main elements: the mentors, the program director, and the teaching assistants. Now in its ninth year, the program has adjusted according to the learning curve all new programs experience, although three components—the mentors' role, the director's role, and the TAs' duties—remain foundational and can help other university–community college partnerships develop.

The Mentors' Role

In the first year of the program, three mentors, all experienced full-time GTCC English department faculty members, worked with the three graduate TAs. Mentors provided their teaching assistants with advice, teaching materials, and pedagogical strategies and acted as sounding boards for them and as their faculty liaison—half teacher, half cheerleader. They also served as teaching models, observing teaching assistants' classes twice each semester, conferring with them both pre- and postobservation, and contributing in annual performance evaluation. Finally, mentors helped the director identify FIT program needs and develop appropriate program materials.

The Director's Role

The program director, granted reassigned time for two courses each semester from the normal six-course semester teaching load, had a threefold role. First, he served as a liaison between the GTCC English department and the graduate program directors at UNCG. His teaching experience at UNCG and his expertise in composition and rhetoric allowed UNCG to include him as a member of its adjunct graduate faculty. His second role, contact for the GTCC English department's three formal mentors, positioned him to receive feedback from them about individual TAs and to consider suggestions concerning program changes or refinements. The director convened regular planning and assessment meetings with mentors and other interested faculty members, and he arranged for department members with expertise in particular areas to meet with the TAs for professional development activities. Third, he handled the program's administrative functions, from screening applications to conducting ongoing assessments to writing the final evaluation of each assistant's teaching performance. As the main seminar instructor, he assumed responsibility for their training in the discipline, and he tracked their development as teachers.

Teaching Assistants' (Teaching Associates') Duties

The teaching assistants taught two first-semester composition classes (one preparation). In their second semester, contingent on successful performance in the first semester, they could either teach that same first-semester course again or teach one of the next courses in the sequence, depending on departmental need and the mentors' assessment of ability.

Because the FIT program intended to facilitate the development of fully functioning community college professionals, the teaching assistants served the department and the college in other ways. First, they worked as tutors in the Writing Center for six hours a week. In the second semester of their appointment, these hours were reduced to three a week so that the TAs could assist their mentors or other faculty members in one of our distance learning formats, either online courses or telecourses. Thus the assistants learned firsthand about the responsibilities and challenges of teaching in these environments, evaluating student assignments in online and telecourse composition courses, responding with critical feedback to their authors, posting responses in the discussion forum, composing topics for discussion, and even responding to student concerns, thereby gaining experience in the politics of student–faculty member interactions. When opportunities arose, TAs team-taught critical thinking courses with their mentors.

In addition to their instructional duties, TAs attended all departmental and college meetings, maintained regular office hours, joined the National Conference of Teachers of English and appropriate constituent or related organizations (Two-Year College Association Southeast and the North Carolina Conference of English Instructors), and networked with other teaching faculty members. All the teaching assistants presented at regional conferences their first year, and they maintained reflective teaching journals that provided the basis for a published journal article (see Cowan, Traver, and Riddle).

We required the TAs to take part not only in the regular college-wide and departmental in-service training but also in professional training in weekly seminars. Most of the seminar involved discussions of composition theories and pedagogies, but some of the sessions entertained special topics (e.g., exploring cooperative learning, integrating GTCC's employability skills into the curriculum, teaching with technology enhancements, understanding professionalism, and demystifying the job search process). Including as many other members of the department as possible helped guarantee the program's broad-based support.

KEY PROGRAM CHANGES

As the FIT program enters its tenth year, the experiences of a variety of stakeholders have contributed to its evolution. Below is a brief summary of key adjustments made to the program in an attempt at continuous improvement. University and community college faculty members who begin similar partnerships can benefit from our insights.

1. Because some TA applicants achieve distinction on paper and in an interview but still lack classroom presence, the application process now requires a fifteen-minute teaching presentation so that representative departmental faculty members can judge candidates' probable classroom competence.

2. Since the FIT program aims to simulate the lives of full-time faculty members for TAs, their title was changed from teaching assistant (implies preparation in teaching only) to teaching associate (captures a broader range of responsibilities).

3. After FIT program representatives negotiated with UNCG, the university agreed to award three hours of graduate credit to graduate students in the FIT program.

4. Rather than assign a permanent mentor to an incoming teaching associate, we assign a faculty member to serve as a primary contact for TAs. Early activities for TAs include journal responses in which they explain an ideal mentor-mentee relationship. Primary contacts also share their mentoring styles. After six weeks, primary contacts typically become mentors to their assigned TAs, but switches and substitutions can ensure a worthwhile experience for both TA and mentor.

5. To alleviate some of the stress of formal observation, TAs observe their mentors before being observed themselves. Mentors complete the process, including a preconference, observation, and postconference, using the language of observation and critiquing their own teaching with their TAs. Since TAs view their mentors' teaching and can explore their mentors' reflections on their teaching, TAs are better prepared for their observations.

6. TAs benefit from their close proximity in shared office space. Journal entries note the support and insights TAs receive from one another, so offices house at least two and at most four TAs.

7. Informality has become the mainstay of the weekly seminars. Coffee, juice, and food appear each week, as TAs grow

together, becoming family members of sorts. This casual atmosphere nurtures risk taking, and TAs have readily shared their insecurities, teaching successes, and classroom challenges. The casual ambiance also encourages mentors, as well as other department members, to drop in and participate in discussions.

8. Involving members of the department beyond those serving as mentors has been invaluable to all. Not only have faculty members shared their disciplinary and pedagogical expertise, they have experienced a renewed sense of pride in their daily professional practice. Since TAs partake of departmental meetings, service, and professional development, department members strive to model professional and collegial behaviors for our TAs to take to other departments when hired as full-time faculty members.

9. A competency-based assessment model has been designed, with program outcomes for TAs. Each TA completes a teaching portfolio that documents the outcomes identified, something useful for the job search.

10. An FIT advisory committee has been established. Committee members consist of former TAs, university faculty members, and the department and division chairs who hire instructors. The committee meets biannually to review program components, program outcomes, and professional progress of TAs, as well as to recommend changes based on their experiences with the program.

11. The orientation of incoming TAs now occurs during a two-week period in July before their first fall semester. It includes a discussion of the philosophy and history of the community college movement and a review of institutional policies and procedures. Primary contacts meet with the TAs and plan some time with them to answer questions about courses, assignments, and fall start-up.

TAKING STOCK

Nine years of anecdotal and statistical evidence suggest that our program has been remarkably successful. This success allows us to admit into the FIT program graduate students enrolled at UNCG and applicants with completed graduate degrees from other universities. Since we began the program, we have expanded it to include TAs in history, religion, philosophy, graphic arts, and computer information systems, and we will include other disciplines as we grow. While we have made a number of important adjustments to the program and assessment models, the basics remain unchanged. Once teaching associates augment their skills during their year with us, they seem ready to assume faculty roles in community colleges. Mentors and the FIT program director have grown professionally as they nurture the TAs' development. Student evaluations of teaching effectiveness suggest that GTCC students are highly satisfied with the TAs' instruction. When key items on the evaluations were compared for TAs and adjunct faculty members, our students consistently rated the TAs higher.

The reactions of college administrators at regional and national conferences are gratifying, especially when they urge the TAs to apply for faculty openings at their institutions. Our first vision has become a reality, but the proof of the program's effectiveness will be the TAs' successes as full-time contributing members in regional two-year college departments.

WORKS CITED

Brawer, Florence B. "Community College Teacher Preparation: Past, Present, Future." Amer. Assn. for Higher Educ. Conf. Chicago. 13 Mar. 1973. ERIC. 23 July 2007 <http://www.eric.ed.gov>.

Cohen, Arthur M., and Florence B. Brawer. *The American Community College*. 2nd ed. San Francisco: Jossey-Bass, 1989.

Cowan, Toni, Joyce Traver, and Thomas H. Riddle. "A TA Perspective of a Community College Faculty-in-Training Program." *Teaching English in the Two-Year College* 28 (2001): 251–58.

Debard, Robert. "Preferred Education and Experience of Community College English Faculty: Twenty Years Later." *Community College Review* 23.1 (1995): 33–51. *Academic Search Premier*. EBSCO. Guilford Technical Community Coll., Learning Resources Center. 1 Nov. 2007 <http://www.epnet.com/>.

Evelyn, Jamilah. "The Hiring Boom at Two-Year Colleges." *Chronicle of Higher Education* 15 June 2001: A8.

Fitzgerald, Sallyanne H., et al. *Guidelines for the Academic Preparation of English Faculty at Two-Year Colleges*. Urbana: Two-Year Coll. Assn. of the Natl. Council of Teachers of English, 2005.

Fugate, Amy, and Marilyn J. Amey. "Career Stages of Community College Faculty: A Qualitative Analysis of Their Career Paths, Roles, and Development." *Community College Review* 28.1 (2000): 1–22.

Gibson-Harman, Kim, et al. "Community College Faculty and Professional Staff: The Human Resource Challenge." *New Directions for Community Colleges* 117 (2002): 77–90.

Haworth, Karla. "More Community Colleges Push to Hire PhD's as Professors." *Chronicle of Higher Education* 8 Jan. 1999: A12–14.

Lovitts, Barbara, and Cary Nelson. "The Hidden Crisis in Graduate Education: Attrition from Ph.D. Programs." *Academe* 86.6 (2000). 29 Nov. 2007 <http://www.aaup.org/AAUP/pubres/academe/2000/ND/>.

Murphy, Sean P. "Improving Two-Year College Teacher Preparation: Graduate Student Internships." *Teaching English in the Two-Year College* 28 (2001): 259–64.

Murray, John P. "Interviewing to Hire Competent Community College Faculty." *Community College Review* 27.1 (1999): 41. *One File*. InfoTrac. Guilford Tech. Community Coll. Lib., Jamestown. 9 Aug. 2004 <http://www.infotrac.galegroup.com>.

"Postsecondary Issues." *Education Commission of the States*. 15 June 2004 <http://www.ecs.org>.

Reese, Jack E. "Structuring the Teaching Internship." *Junior College Journal* 42.8 (1972): 27–31. ERIC. 23 July 2007 <http://www.eric.ed.gov>.

Rifkin, Tronie. "Public Community College Faculty." *American Association of Community Colleges*. 15 June 2004 <http://www.aacc.nche.edu>. Path: Resource Center; Projects/Partnerships; Current; New Expeditions; Issue Papers.

Trower, C. A. "Paradise Lost: How the Academy Converts Enthusiastic Recruits into Early-Career Doubters." AAHE Conference on Faculty Roles and Rewards. Tampa. 1–4 Feb. 2001.

Woodard, Colin. "At Community Colleges, Foreign Students Discover Affordable Degree Programs." *Chronicle of Higher Education* 17 Nov. 2000: A77–78.

Wright, Scott W. "A Graying Movement Ponders How to Cope with Mass Retirements." *Community College Week* Apr. 1997: 14.

VICTORIA N. SALMON

PREPARING FUTURE
TEACHER-SCHOLARS

Well over fifteen years ago, George Mason University (GMU) established an innovative graduate program that focused on teaching and
scholarship. This program, the Doctor of Arts in Community College
Education (DACCE), recently underwent serious revision and transformation to meet the needs of two-year and four-year undergraduate education in the twenty-first century. In addition to the doctoral degree,
the Higher Education Program (HEP) offers the Master of Arts in Interdisciplinary Studies / Community College Teaching; the Master of
Arts in Interdisciplinary Studies / Higher Education, Administration
or Student Services; and the College Teaching Certificate.[1] All programs concentrate on developing good practices for teaching in two-
and four-year colleges. Although substantial curricular changes have
marked the relatively short history of GMU's higher education degree
programs, the philosophy remains unchanged: to combine academic
discipline knowledge with professional education scholarship and
practical teaching experience. Integrating this philosophy into the architecture of the doctoral degree means candidates select a knowledge
area (e.g., history, English, psychology, information systems); complete an education scholarship core, an internship, and comprehensive
examinations in both their knowledge areas and the education core;
and defend dissertations that further the scholarship of teaching.
These requirements demand close partnerships between the GMU faculty and advisers as well as with the area's two- and four-year colleges,
so that doctoral students can fulfill their course work at George Mason

University and complete internships at one of the higher education institutions in the metropolitan area.

THE SIGNIFICANCE OF THE TEACHER-SCHOLAR MODEL TO THE PROFESSORIAT

Many professors do not identify professionally as teachers, an identifier conventionally at odds with the scholarly attributes of the professoriat. Through the scholarship of thinkers such as Kenneth Eble and Ernest L. Boyer, however, and through the leadership offered by institutions such as the Carnegie Foundation for the Advancement of Teaching, two- and four-year college faculty members have begun to consider the teacher-scholar model's significance to the professoriat. Universities and most colleges value research, whereas community colleges value teaching. These two elements of the academy need not be separate, as research that centers on theory and praxis in the undergraduate classroom has gained greater attention across the disciplines, thereby legitimizing the reciprocity of teaching and scholarship, scholarship and teaching. Boyer encourages his audience to eliminate a "restricted view of scholarship" by confronting ways that "[t]heory . . . leads to practice. But practice also leads to theory" (15, 16). Following this logic, the college classroom serves as a laboratory, and scholarship can elaborate all that occurs in a classroom-laboratory. Boyer trusts scholarship founded on teaching, and generous scholars who practice this type of research share their experiences with other practitioners. Lauding the principle of sharing pedagogical ideas and classroom-based research, Boyer maintains that "the work of the professor becomes consequential only as it is understood by others" (23). Professors who respect the work of the classroom know they have a responsibility to share their efforts rather than hide their work by closing the classroom door. Teacher-scholars, especially, know that observing others, and being observed, improves their research for in-class activities and for public distribution.

The openness of the scholarship of teaching and learning may confuse many novices, for "there is no single best method or approach for conducting [this type of] scholarship" (Hutchings 1). Teacher-scholars who participate in the Carnegie Foundation for the Advancement of

Teaching share their individual experiences—joys and frustrations—as members of the undergraduate teaching community. Rising above anecdotal gab session, though, the participants apply traditional requirements of research to investigating the practice of teaching: they shape questions to examine, review documents and texts, and develop hypotheses and theories. In the foundation's *Opening Lines: Approaches to the Scholarship of Teaching and Learning,* each contributor demonstrates a personal commitment to teaching-centered scholarship (Hutchings 3). These professors indicate their concerns regarding some of their colleagues' lack of understanding of—or maybe even respect for—their work. Despite resistance to pedagogical research from within the academic hierarchy, Carnegie researchers explain best practices and offer theories about why certain teaching designs work, grounding their theories in rich intellectual histories and various disciplinary epistemologies.

Although definitions of scholarship change over the years, dominant definitions of *scholar* and *scholarship* persist. They often slight community college faculty members, since these members of the academy rarely embrace the title "professor," a title that seems to ignore teaching, the central responsibility of two-year college faculty members. Were community college faculty members to adopt the professional identifier "teacher," as many do, they would, in a sense, co-opt a term traditionally associated with primary and secondary educators, thus absenting themselves from discourses about higher education. Perhaps community college faculty members are reacting to a historical marginalization within higher education when they reject "professor" in favor of "teacher." University researchers have used "instructor" to identify two-year college faculty members, a term that itself locates them on the margins of higher education. The *Oxford English Dictionary* defines *instructor* thus: "in American colleges: A college teacher inferior in rank to a professor." In an effort to redefine the role of faculty members across sectors of higher education, GMU's Higher Education Program embraces "teacher-scholar." Combining the elements of "scholar" (researcher, intellectual, discipline-specific expert) with the elements of "teacher" (practitioner, communicator of research), "teacher-scholar" removes community college faculty members from the margins of higher education, accepting and recognizing them as valuable participants in the scholarship of teaching and learning.

The DACCE program opens up a space wherein practitioners create interdisciplinary dialogue about the feature of faculty life common to everyone in the professoriat—teaching. While Elaine Showalter contends that teaching is "intellectual work, which can be discussed, reviewed, critiqued, adapted, and built upon by peers," those in higher education are more inclined to look at "the *way* people teach" and how it "is related to *what* they teach" (B7). She maintains in her essay "What Teaching Literature Should Really Mean" that pedagogical scholarship "has to be discipline specific," which is precisely the idea guiding the work of the GMU program. Various disciplines have particular pedagogical needs, and students in the program make connections between pedagogy and knowledge through papers, presentations, and collaborative projects. The education core courses bring together students from multiple disciplines so that someone from history can share discipline-specific teaching strategies with others from chemistry, music, or information systems, thus making possible new and interdisciplinary pedagogical formulations. Students learn firsthand the historical and intellectual relations among the disciplines and often overcome the common "ambivalence among academics about the scholarly status of teaching" (Huber and Morreale).

Although teaching occurs behind closed doors and in isolation, teacher-scholars necessarily take cues from the classroom experiences of professors across disciplines to improve their instruction. Future faculty members in the HEP might study the work of Angela Provitera-McGlynn, a psychology professor at Mercer County Community College for thirty years. She discusses her classroom experiences in *Successful Beginnings for College Teaching: Engaging Your Students from the First Day*, stating outright, "I believe that teaching is an art. As in any art, it takes plenty of practice to hone your skills as a teacher" (11). In *The Craft of Teaching* Eble shows that faculty members can learn these skills. Thus our students hone their pedagogical skills through course work and internships and discover that teaching is a process, one constantly subject to review and change. Teaching the same course repeatedly may characterize professorial life at teaching-intensive colleges, but teaching the same course the same way each semester is a choice. The Higher Education Program includes works by Boyer, Eble, and the Carnegie Foundation in its syllabi so that future faculty members can place pedagogical ideas in the context of the teacher-scholar model for the professoriat and thus prepare for vital careers at teaching-intensive colleges. DACCE professors incorporate other well-known texts, Web sites, and other electronic sources about pedagogy into the curriculum to encourage students to practice Boyer's scholarship of integration and to recognize that sometimes "traditional . . . categories prove [to be] confining, forcing new topologies of knowledge" (19).

THE MISSION OF THE DOCTOR OF ARTS IN COMMUNITY COLLEGE EDUCATION

George Mason University responds to the call for excellence in interdisciplinary research and teaching, not simply by adding programs, but by rethinking the traditional structure of the academy.

The university offers more than 100 degree programs, including many innovative interdisciplinary programs that allow students to design personalized courses of study with faculty guidance.   ("Academics")

The DACCE program prepares students to be leaders in undergraduate education, adhering to the focus of the program since its inception in 1988. In addition to gaining expertise in selected disciplinary or interdisciplinary knowledge areas, graduates of the program become proficient in four core cognates: scholarly activity related to teaching and learning; technology for the teaching and learning processes; discipline-specific pedagogy; and program and curriculum design, development, and assessment. All courses emphasize leadership, ethics, and diversity in higher education. The background in course work and the guided practical expertise provided by the internship prepare students of the program to lead their institutions in various ways.

Given the dynamic nature of a college education and the growth of programs in nontraditional fields, GMU students develop their academic interests with an eye toward educational leadership. While many DACCE students take their twenty-four knowledge-area credits exclusively in one discipline, they are encouraged to think broadly and to work with their advisers to select appropriate courses from more than one discipline. In fact, over twenty disciplines across the university participate in the doctoral program as knowledge areas. Advisers,

or liaisons, attend DACCE program meetings about various requirements and student issues. E-mail conversations and other electronic
methods of communication keep students, knowledge-area advisers,
and program faculty members in continual contact. An External Advisory Committee, which consists of academic and government leaders
from across the country, offers the program director support and guidance for such issues as potential academic changes, financial and grant
support, and policies.

CURRENT STUDENTS AND GRADUATES

The students in our HEP degree programs already work in community
college systems or in noneducation jobs while completing a degree
program that can lead to a second career. Community college professionals enter the program to earn advancement as faculty members or
to become administrators. Graduates hold full-time positions at community colleges in the Washington, DC, metropolitan area and at two-
and four-year colleges across the country. The current student population is 56% male and 44% female, 72.5% Caucasian, 15.1% African
American, 3.3% Asian and Pacific Islander, 2.5% Hispanic, and 6.6%
other. The DACCE program and its diverse graduates respond to the
objections "that most doctorate holders have been prepared as researchers not teachers" by completing courses in college teaching, curriculum development, and assessment (Cohen and Brawer 78).

All students in the Higher Education Program must complete an
internship; doctoral students complete two internships, of which at
least one must be a teaching internship, even if candidates have prior
teaching experience. The internship provides an important complement to students' formal academic training as teacher-scholars. To reg-
ister for the internship, a form of independent study, students secure a
position and a mentor, who allows students to attend, observe, and assist in assigned undergraduate courses. Even though the students teach
several of the semester's classes under the guidance of a mentor, internships are not adjunct faculty positions. After the students complete the internship, their mentors write reviews and submit them to
the program administration. While working as interns, students attend
at least two seminars each semester so they can reflect critically on
their experiences and on the relations between theory and practice.

Reflection and discussion inform the contents of students' internship portfolios (weekly journals, syllabi, tests, reports, policy memos, and a research essay concerning classroom techniques, pedagogical theory, and classroom effectiveness). Students apply texts and theories from their courses College Teaching, Scholarship of Teaching, and Curriculum Design to their semester's projects, producing a body of work about praxis or the manners in which theory informs practice and practice informs theory.

After completing the knowledge-area and education core course work, the internship, and the comprehensive examinations, students in the doctoral program write a dissertation to demonstrate expertise in both their knowledge area and instructional practice. This dissertation reflects the unique nature of the program: students, themselves teacher-scholars, create original scholarship that speaks to various discourse communities. Researchers interested in particular disciplines and in the pedagogical practices unique to their disciplines find the dissertation a useful tool for inquiry. Since the DACCE program and its dissertation are interdisciplinary, committee members represent various aspects of students' academic careers: the chair and one committee member represent the knowledge area, and the third committee member represents the program's faculty. These members work in concert to ensure that students' research accurately reflects all segments of the academic curriculum.

Faculty members and graduates of the HEP regularly publish their findings in a range of venues. The program's Web site (http://dacce .gmu.edu) includes a link to Community College Research Abstracts, a service that publishes summaries of our students' and faculty members' scholarship. Although most institutions do not associate community college educators with research and scholarship, a large body of work has been developed in the last several years, and the DACCE program has contributed significantly to that body of scholarship. George Vaughan, the first director of this doctoral program and a prolific community college scholar, called for research based on praxis for many years. Adhering to his vision, the HEP contributes to the scholarship, academic conversations, and discourse communities of over twenty disciplines. The program participates in the Association of American Colleges and Universities, the American Association of Community Colleges, the League for Innovation, Black Issues in Higher Education, the National Community College Hispanic Council, the

Council for the Study of Community Colleges, and the Council for Resource Development.

———

As the demographics of undergraduate students change, so must scholarship and teaching. These two essential elements of higher education underwrite the teacher-scholar identity. At most four-year colleges and research universities, professors generally excel at contributing to their disciplines by publishing multiple texts in their fields of expertise. Many faculty members, though, still lack the necessary skills and tools to teach well at the undergraduate level and to invite undergraduate students into academic discourse communities. Often professors do not think of themselves as teachers, because they labor in the academy, a forum for demonstrating rather than teaching knowledge.

On the other hand, community college faculty members teach as many as five or six courses a semester, and they infrequently participate in traditional research and scholarship. These educators focus on practice, and the time constraints associated therewith often preclude their participation in national dialogues concerning the underlying theories that guide their work. GMU's Higher Education Program bridges these gaps in higher education and strives for excellence in teaching in the disciplines through academic advancement and pedagogical expertise. A cultural shift can occur in the professoriat only when faculty members from across the academy reflect on their professional identities (teachers, scholars, teacher-scholars, professors) and on their interdependence. This cultural shift has begun to occur in academic programs such as the one outlined in this essay, but completion of the shift requires current and future faculty members to invest in, rather than shy away from, the diversity of higher education.

NOTE

1. The Master of Arts in Interdisciplinary Studies / Community College Teaching combines the eighteen-credit education core with eighteen credits of graduate work in one of the following knowledge areas: computer science, English, mathematics, psychology, or teaching English as a second language. These concentrations qualify students to teach entry-level courses in rapidly growing fields at the two-year college level. Community college instructors who teach in technical-occupational or career program

courses are encouraged to explore the Master of Arts in Interdisciplinary Studies / Community College Teaching for growth and development.

In spring 2004, GMU's graduate council approved an additional degree: the Master of Arts in Interdisciplinary Studies / Higher Education, Administration or Student Services. GMU and local community college faculty members designed this concentration to train students for administration leadership positions in colleges and universities, associations, and government agencies whose activities affect higher education. This program prepares graduates for such positions as academic advisers, admissions professionals, continuing education coordinators, financial aid administrators, minority student services employees, and student activities directors.

WORKS CITED

"Academics." *George Mason University.* 1 June 2004 <http://www.gmu.edu/acadexcel/>.

Boyer, Ernest L. *Scholarship Reconsidered: Priorities of the Professoriate.* San Francisco: Jossey-Bass, 1990.

Cohen, Arthur M., and Florence B. Brawer. *The American Community College.* 4th ed. San Francisco: Jossey-Bass, 2003.

Eble, Kenneth. *The Craft of Teaching: A Guide to Mastering the Professor's Art.* San Francisco: Jossey-Bass, 1988.

Huber, Mary Taylor, and Sherwyn P. Morreale. "Situating the Scholarship of Teaching and Learning: A Cross-Disciplinary Conversation." *Disciplinary Styles in the Scholarship of Teaching and Learning: Exploring Common Ground.* Ed. Huber and Morreale. Washington: Amer. Assn. for Higher Educ. and the Carnegie Foundation for the Advancement of Teaching, 2002. <http://www.carnegiefoundation.org/publications/sub.asp?key=452&subkey=610>.

Hutchings, Pat. "Approaching the Scholarship of Teaching and Learning." *Opening Lines: Approaches to the Scholarship of Teaching and Learning.* Ed. Hutchings. Menlo Park: Carnegie, 2000. 1–10.

"Instructor." *Oxford English Dictionary.* 2nd ed. 1989.

Provitera-McGlynn, Angela. *Successful Beginnings for College Teaching: Engaging Your Students from the First Day.* Madison: Atwood, 2001.

Showalter, Elaine. "What Teaching Literature Should Really Mean." *Chronicle of Higher Education.* 17 Jan. 2003: B7+.

Vaughan, George B. *The Community College Story.* 2nd ed. Washington: Community Coll. P, 2000.

Deborah Gill

FROM GRADUATE STUDENT TO FACULTY MEMBER
Teaching Foreign Languages at Two-Year Colleges

Once candidates complete doctorates in foreign languages, their top priority becomes searching for an intellectual and material place in the academy (or outside it), a search that inevitably inspires vexing questions about relocation, institutional fit, teaching loads, and research possibilities. Such questions closely match a mentality of searching for a dream job somewhere else. I argue that candidates may find more empowerment if they resist passive searches and adopt instead an active mindset (i.e., create a dream job here rather than find one there). Sometimes, as Gertrude Stein noted, "There is no there there." Positions at the two-year level (community colleges, technical colleges, and branch campuses of universities), although often viewed as alternative careers for foreign language PhDs, offer candidates the opportunity to create their own niche, a niche with more than adequate amounts of "there."

CAMPUS CLIMATES AND CULTURE DIFFERENCES WITHIN HIGHER EDUCATION

As a means of assessing variances in campus climates of four- and two-year colleges, I designed two informal surveys, one for faculty members who teach at doctorate-granting institutions and a second for those who teach at two-year colleges (apps. 1 and 2). Sixty-four surveys were distributed to faculty members from the two categories of institutions (32 doctorate-granting and 32 two-year), and 47 were returned (25 doctorate-granting and 22 two-year), a 73% return rate. Although my informal survey cannot be considered statistically significant, the anecdotal evidence I gathered from multiple sources, and the consistency of the responses, allows us to draw some general conclusions about attitudes toward the professional lives circulating in the field of foreign language studies. The surveys included the following key questions related to campus climate:

> Doctorate-granting institutions: Do you believe that there is a difference in the campus climate at a two-year institution compared with that at a four-year or doctorate-granting institution? If so, how are graduate students aware of these differences during their training at the doctorate-granting university?

> Two-year colleges: Do you believe that there is a difference in the campus climate at a two-year institution compared with that at a four-year or doctorate-granting institution? If so, what is the difference, and how is the campus climate different?

All responses affirmatively identified differences in campus climates between the types of institutions that make up higher education. Respondents from doctorate-granting institutions believe graduate students entering a foreign language program do not perceive or comprehend these differences. As they progress through the foreign language program, however, respondents suggest they learn of these differences, albeit in an accidental rather than a planned manner. That is, they become aware of the hierarchy of academic institutions and the range and variety of professional possibilities therein through the grapevine rather than through explicit instruction embedded in foreign language graduate curricula.

The following excerpts from doctorate-granting and two-year institution faculty members represent standard responses to the question about campus climates:

> As [graduate students] are groomed to become the future professoriate, they quickly learn that R-1 [four-year institutions] appointments are the elite positions. Later (after searching), they may consider the less "elite," not R-1, then two-year institutions.

> These [two-year college] students often need much TLC to make the transition to college.

Several respondents revealed that they were unaware of differences between academic cultures, and even between the job duties of professors in those institutions, until after accepting positions in the two-year sector of higher education. One faculty member writes:

> I believed I was hired on the basis of my publication record [as a graduate student]. . . . My field is Latin American literature, not basic language instruction. I didn't find out until after accepting the job what I was going to have to do—i.e., teach beginning language courses.

Clearly candidates must do more to understand the faculty roles associated with institutions from the different sectors of higher education.

Although new faculty members universally must adjust to their roles as assistant professors, faculty members from two-year institutions assert that marked climate dissimilarities between doctorate-granting institutions and their own may complicate the transition from graduate student to assistant professor. One two-year college faculty member notes the shock attending the discovery of variances in student comportment in different academic environments:

> The first day, when I walked into class and saw 35 students sitting in their seats or on top of desks laughing, drinking, and having a good time, I was shocked. When I was a TA . . . , my classes were smaller, and if students were talking when I walked in, it was quietly at their desks.

Candidates should assume the responsibility of investigating thoroughly the colleges to which they apply for professorships, but graduate mentors too can encourage the graduate students' broader understanding of academic cultures.

HIRING PRACTICES

Since budgetary decisions regarding hiring come later in the academic year for two-year colleges than for four-year institutions, announcements of positions in the MLA's *Job Information List* and interviews at the MLA Annual Convention are rare occurrences. Generally, two-year colleges announce positions and accept applications during the spring and sometimes the summer, with the exception of two-year branch campuses whose main campuses make the budgetary and staffing decisions for the entire multicampus system. Many times branch campus faculty positions appear in the *Job Information List*, although telephone interviews frequently replace MLA convention interviews.

To help graduate faculty members and their students better understand hiring practices for two-year foreign language faculty positions, two questions on my informal survey address degree requirements for foreign language positions. Either a master's or a PhD is acceptable for employment as a full-time professor at two-year campuses as well as at some branch campuses. A number of responses indicated that although only a master's degree is required for application to a faculty position, a PhD may be preferred:

> While a Ph.D. is not required, it is certainly looked upon positively. It makes a candidate stand out, especially if the administrator making the final decision has one or is working on one.

> It gave me an edge over my competition.

> It gave me more points when my application was evaluated, putting me in the top percentile of the entire pool of applicants and giving me a shot at an interview.

> There is a sense of elevated status because I have a PhD.

Tenure-track and fixed-term positions are found on all campuses I surveyed, although some two-year colleges have no tenure system and offer no tenure-track positions. The two-year campus responses to my survey suggest that the number of tenure-track positions on any given campus is based on locally determined ratios of full- to part-time faculty. If a department does not have the correct ratio, the opportunity to hire a tenure-track faculty member is much higher than it would be if the ratio were already met. While some fixed-term positions exist at the two-year level, part-time faculty members constitute the largest labor contingent. Of the branch campus respondents, all noted having one tenured or tenure-track faculty member. Other full-time faculty members were on fixed-term, renewable contracts. A number of faculty members mistrust campus administrators' commitment to healthy full-time–part-time faculty ratios:

> I am the only one left, and they're not looking for anyone else. . . . Tenured members of the faculty retire, they are not re-

placed, and adjuncts are hired. I get the impression that they don't even like having promoted anyone to fixed term—they would prefer several adjuncts and phase out all full-time faculty.

Findings in David Laurence's report "The 1999 MLA Survey of Staffing in English and Foreign Language Departments" coincide with this faculty member's observation: 26.2% of the foreign language faculty at associate in arts–granting institutions are classified as tenured or tenure-track; 4.9% were full-time, non-tenure-track; and 68.8% were part-time (213).

PREPARATION AND ADVICE FOR TEACHING AT TWO-YEAR COLLEGES

Given the complex diversity of two-year campuses and academic cultures as well as the institutionally specific idiosyncrasy of academic cultures across the landscape of higher education, the transition from graduate student to full-time foreign language faculty member at a two-year institution can be treacherous. The professorial life of two-year faculty members scarcely resembles the life of graduate faculty members, the mentors who introduce graduate students to the foreign language professoriat. In this section, I provide advice to doctoral faculty members regarding ways to prepare their graduate students to teach in two-year colleges. In addition, I offer graduate students advice about their preparation for the faculty lives that may well differ dramatically from those of their mentors.

When asked, "Do you believe that doctorate-granting institutions prepare graduate students for teaching in the two-year institution?" both four-year and two-year respondents reply with a resounding no. Many graduate programs in foreign languages focus on literature courses and specializations in these fields. From my anecdotal evidence, I extrapolate four ways doctorate-granting institutions can prepare students to teach at the two-year level.

1. *Teach graduate students about pedagogy.* Yanick V. Daniel interviewed four senior two-year faculty members regarding their graduate preparation to teach at two-year colleges, ultimately finding that "they would have preferred training and special course work that directly prepared them to teach language courses or sequences of language

courses" (11). Forty-three of the respondents to my survey also believe that research-intensive institutions need to provide courses specific to teaching content in basic language courses, conversation courses, and writing courses. Although graduate students might complete a semester-long workshop in language teaching or a weeklong seminar on pedagogy, the craft of undergraduate instruction receives short shrift. This structure may stem from budgetary constraints combined with an excessively high professional expectation among graduate students. That is, many graduate programs prepare their students to assume research faculty positions on completion of their degrees. To buck this trend, one respondent suggests helping foreign language graduate students

> by acknowledging that there are more graduating students than research positions at R-1s each year. They should help students to have a plan "b" and a plan "c." These should be viewed as desirable alternatives and not positions for which they have to "settle."

While the number of tenure-track positions outside the doctoral and master's sectors remains relatively small, more foreign language PhDs will be produced each year than the market can bear.

2. *Invite speakers from community colleges to speak with graduate students.* Sixteen of the twenty-two responses from those teaching at two-year colleges include remarks aimed at encouraging graduate faculty members to reach out to their two-year colleagues, thus including them in graduate student training. Two-year college faculty members "can share their personal experiences with graduate students so that they have an idea of the differences between a community college classroom and what they are used to at the PhD-granting institution."

3. *Provide internship opportunities for graduate students.* Some respondents who now teach at two-year institutions recommend internships for graduate students, whereas others from doctorate-granting universities clearly see the benefits afforded to students who "observe faculty [from community colleges] tapped for their teaching excellence." Those who advocate for internships suggest that curricula change to accommodate the experience, giving graduate students credit for serving as TAs or instructors at two-year campuses. Internships are in place at some institutions (e.g., DePaul University, George

Mason University, University of Michigan, Michigan State University, Princeton University), but higher education and future faculty members would benefit from more partnerships between two-year and four-year colleges.

4. *Provide greater guidance to graduate students regarding employment choices and academic cultures.* My survey queried faculty members about graduate students' perceived levels of awareness concerning the roles teaching, service, and scholarship play at two-year colleges. Replies from faculty members at doctorate-granting universities suggest that unless graduate students express an interest in building careers at the two-year level of higher education, this level is "ignored" and considered "unimportant." On the other hand, those currently teaching at two-year colleges see members of the graduate faculty as ethically charged with a duty to inform foreign language graduate students of all career options, including teaching at the two-year level.

If graduate programs are going to help prepare their students to succeed in a diverse job market, the four areas mentioned above deserve careful consideration. To prepare for the professoriat, graduate students and their mentors might resist the seductive yet destructive binary of equating success with research professorship and failure with any position other than a research professorship. The fear of certain intellectual death for faculty members outside research-intensive universities is baseless. Two-year institutions foster generalism and promote intellectual growth outside graduate school specialties among their faculty members. The doctorate, after all, leads to the beginning of a career in academia. Although many graduates from doctoral programs in foreign languages look down on positions at two-year institutions, faculty members who perform such work know its importance and garner deep satisfaction from it. One professor, asked to give advice to a graduate student planning on teaching at the two-year level, stated, "Be proud of the appointment. Recognize that these are important positions; that if one likes teaching, this is a great place to be. More students' lives are changed for the better at two-year institutions than at four-year ones." While two-year colleges do not corner the market on helping students in higher education, the work of two-year college faculty members should not be conflated with the work of their four-year colleagues. By turns exhilarating and confounding, work at the two-year level may coincide perfectly with the political inclinations of many graduate students, so, even without doctorate-granting university support, graduate students can take it on themselves to investigate careers at community colleges by observing classes at one, teaching as an adjunct, or corresponding with exemplary two-year college faculty members. In so doing, they might find two-year colleges that live up to the highest ideals of the community college movement: small class sizes, diverse student bodies (underserved and first-generation students often enter higher education through the community college system), communitarian faculty members, and innovative campus cultures.

What to Expect at a Two-Year College

Rehearsals for the role of full-time tenure-track faculty member during graduate school years run into real limits in terms of effectiveness. Nevertheless, graduate students do well to attend to such rehearsals, especially since they may better balance the three principal areas of two-year college faculty life (teaching, research, and service) only with sustained practice, keeping in mind that teaching excellence is of primary importance at the two-year level.

Community college professors learn to teach students with diverse needs and skill levels in the foreign language classroom. Many returning students will have been away from school for years and may or may not have ever taken language classes; many traditional students may have taken language classes in high school but may not have acquired significant language skills from their experiences. Regardless of students' levels of preparation or educational histories, two-year foreign language faculty members often learn on the job the best ways to make all students feel comfortable in the classroom.

The tall order of addressing individual student needs requires manageable class sizes. Foreign language classes often cohere around a communicative methodology in which students actively use the second language during class rather than passively listen to the teacher's lecture. The more students in a class, the less time for them to practice the target language. Financial, staffing, and enrollment exigencies come to bear on locally determined class sizes, but it's fair to say that two-year colleges attempt to keep class sizes consistent with their missions of open access and individualized instruction. Two respondents to my survey who teach at different branches of the same university testify to different experiences with class size, but both indicate low numbers. At one branch, the registration cap is set at twenty-five, and overrides are allowed in the absence of faculty consent. The professor from the other branch has class limits of twenty students, and overrides are allowed only with faculty consent.

Although professors rarely identify class size as a problem on two-year campuses, teaching loads are another story. Heavy loads can mitigate faculty members' personal commitment to teaching every student, the mandate of the two-year mission. The teaching load of two-year colleges obviously exceeds the load of doctorate-granting universities, since their missions differ. And in two-year institutions, the course loads of community and technical colleges frequently exceed the loads of branch campuses, with community college faculty members usually teaching fifteen credit hours *a semester* and branch faculty teaching fifteen to twenty-four credit hours *a year*. The discrepancy between teaching loads at community colleges and branch campuses results from the research requirements generally required of branch faculty members as part of the tenure process.

Professors at two-year colleges teach 100- and 200-level courses and might offer a survey of literature course or even a special topics course on occasion, but these opportunities depend on enrollments and departmental support. Therefore graduate students who specialize in a particular literary period or genre should not expect to teach courses built around their specialization. Yet teaching at the two-year level is not tantamount to drudgery. Specialists can become generalists who incorporate their knowledge into foreign language courses in ways that help beginning students become more proficient public intellectuals.

As generalists, two-year college faculty members find exhilarating the transition from what Ernest L. Boyer calls the scholarship of knowledge to that of application, using their college settings and heavy teaching loads to the advantage of performing classroom-based research. If students appear to have a hard time comprehending readings from class, and a specific methodology (e.g., Socratic dialogue) leads to hit-and-miss results, faculty members can conduct a pedagogical experiment aimed at raising students' comprehension level from fifty to seventy percent (by using Total Physical Response Storytelling, small group discussions, reading pairs, and so forth). After forming hypotheses about what may increase students' comprehension of reading in the target language, faculty members can administer tests before and after each lesson to assess the effectiveness of their pedagogical approach. Such results lead to significant data collection and, with enough time, data analysis.

The links between content, knowledge production, knowledge application, and technology can also inspire the generalist research agenda of faculty members at two-year colleges. Professors of foreign languages might profitably study uses of technology in teaching culture by using a well-designed virtual learning environment for students to take virtual walking tours, or "culture walks." While on these virtual tours, students read about overseas cities, interact with virtual waiters in virtual bars, and watch videos on the cultural and anthropological traditions of the country wherein the language of study predominates. Again, the use of this technology on cultural competency can be assessed by administering questionnaires and tests. Although I've articulated briefly only two examples of classroom-based research, they reveal to readers the extent to which two-year college foreign language faculty members are uniquely poised to contribute to pedagogical scholarship, since their teaching loads provide ample laboratory time to collect data. Pedagogical research truly meets limits only in one's own imagination, even if I must note the demands heavy teaching loads place on one's time and intellectual space.

For faculty members from two-year colleges, teaching remains primary among the standard professional duties of teaching, research, and service. But two-year college professors still engage in research, which, along with service, enhances teaching. Professors should expect to serve their departments by advising students, sponsoring foreign language events, functioning as a liaison between high schools and the college, and working with part-timers; they should also expect to fulfill division responsibilities by serving on committees and subcommittees (textbook selection, scholarships, benefits, working conditions, to name a few). Faculty members routinely serve the campus as a whole by participating in recruitment and retention activities as well as in shared governance structures (faculty senate, union); by organizing film series, book clubs, open houses, and conversation cafés; and by serving as advisers to clubs (World Cultures Club, Spanish Club, French Club, Theater Club). Since the community college movement seeks to grow dynamic relationships between the college and its community, faculty members pledge their support to the community by delivering talks on cultural experiences from overseas travel or study abroad to local clubs. Sometimes communities rely on foreign language faculty members for translation help, a service that becomes a part of a tenure file. Teaching, research, and service can take up more time than there are hours in a day, so prospective and current community college professors do well to remain focused primarily on their teaching.

———

Teaching foreign languages in two-year colleges can reward newly minted PhDs and veteran professors alike with intellectual opportunities and with motivated, often mature, almost always inspiring students who desire access to the material realities behind democratic ideologies. The keys to success and fulfillment in two-year colleges belong to the faculty members and depend on their willingness to care for students and to use teaching strategies to meet their learning needs.

I leave you with these words from a community college faculty member:

> So, yes, my colleagues at four-year institutions are publishing a lot more than I am. Some of them are even becoming famous or at least well known in their fields. Their paychecks certainly have bigger numbers before the decimal point. But I seriously doubt that their careers—or their lives, for that matter—are any more fulfilling than mine.   (Jenkins, par. 17)

APPENDIX I

FROM GRADUATE STUDENT TO FACULTY MEMBER (FACULTY MEMBERS AT DOCTORATE-GRANTING INSTITUTIONS)

Thank you for agreeing to answer some questions regarding graduate students entering into teaching at the two-year institution. The results of this questionnaire will be compiled and used as part of the study "From Graduate Student to Faculty Member: Teaching Foreign

Languages at Two-Year Colleges." Neither names of individuals nor names of institutions (two-year, four-year, or doctorate-granting) will be used in the final analysis.

Two terms need to be defined before beginning:

> *Two-year institution* refers to all junior colleges, community colleges, and branch campuses of four-year and doctorate-granting institutions.
> *Graduate students entering . . .* refers to graduate students who have been recently hired as ABDs or PhDs.

Please feel free to skip any question(s) that you would prefer not to answer. (Please note: All questions are regarding *foreign language instruction only*.)

1. Do you believe that there is a difference in the campus climate at a two-year institution compared with that at a four-year or doctorate-granting institution? If so, how are graduate students made aware of these differences during their training at the doctorate-granting university?

2. Do you believe that doctorate-granting institutions prepare graduate students for teaching in the two-year institution? Why or why not?

3. How can doctorate-granting institutions help prepare graduate students to teach at the two-year institution?

4. Are graduate students made aware of what to expect regarding teaching, service, and scholarship at the two-year institution? How?

5. What advice would you give to a graduate student who is planning on teaching at the two-year institution?

6. What advice would you give to a graduate student who is considering (or who has accepted a position at) a two-year institution about how to live an intellectually stimulating and pedagogically rewarding life as an academic in the two-year arena?

APPENDIX 2

From Graduate Student to Faculty Member (Faculty Members at Two-Year Institutions)

Thank you for agreeing to answer some questions regarding graduate students entering into teaching at the two-year institution. The results of this questionnaire will be compiled and used as part of the study "From Graduate Student to Faculty Member: Teaching Foreign Language at Two-Year Colleges." Neither names of individuals nor names of institutions (two-year, four-year, or doctorate-granting) will be used in the final analysis.

Two terms need to be defined before beginning:

> *Two-year institution* refers to all junior colleges, community colleges, and branch campuses of four-year and doctorate-granting institutions.
> *Graduate students entering . . .* refers to graduate students who have been recently hired as ABDs or PhDs.

Please feel free to skip any question(s) that you would prefer not to answer. (Please note: All questions are regarding *foreign language instruction only*.)

1. Do you believe that there is a difference in the campus climate at a two-year institution compared with that at a four-year or doctorate-granting institution? If so, what is the difference?
2. Do you believe that doctorate-granting institutions prepare graduate students for teaching in the two-year institution? Why or why not? (If you have a personal experience, please feel free to share it here.)
3. What are the hiring practices for your campus with respect to degree requirements? (Choose one.)
   a. hire faculty members with master's degrees
   b. hire faculty members with doctorates
   c. hire faculty members with master's degrees or doctorates

4. What are the hiring practices for your campus with respect to rank? (Choose one.)
   a. hire only fixed-term (non-tenure-track)
   b. hire only tenure-track
   c. hire both fixed-term and tenure-track
5. How can doctorate-granting institutions help prepare graduate students to teach at the two-year institution or community college?
6. Regarding teaching:
   a. What can graduate students entering foreign language teaching at the two-year institution or community college expect concerning student populations?
   b. What can graduate students entering foreign language teaching at the two-year institution or community college expect concerning class size?
   c. What can graduate students entering foreign language teaching at the two-year institution or community college expect concerning course load?
   d. What can graduate students entering foreign language teaching at the two-year institution or community college expect concerning types of courses they will teach?
7. Regarding research:
   a. What types of research should graduate students entering foreign language teaching at the two-year institution or community college expect to conduct, if any?
   b. What are the possibilities of collaborating with other faculty members for graduate students entering foreign language teaching at the two-year institution or community college?
8. Regarding service:
   a. What types of campus service commitments should a graduate student entering foreign language teaching at the two-year institution or community college expect?
   b. What types of community service commitments should a graduate student entering foreign language teaching at the two-year institution or community college expect?

9. What advice would you give to a graduate student who is planning on teaching at the two-year level?

10. How can a PhD teaching at a two-year institution or community college live an intellectually stimulating and pedagogically rewarding life as an academic?

WORKS CITED

Boyer, Ernest L. *Scholarship Reconsidered: Priorities of the Professoriate.* 1990. San Francisco: Jossey-Bass, 1997.

Daniel, Yanick V. "Foreign Language Instructors at Two-Year Institutions." *ADFL Bulletin* 27.3 (1996): 11–12.

Jenkins, Rob. "Not a Bad Gig." *Chronicle of Higher Education.* 10 Nov. 2003. 27 Nov. 2007 <http://chronicle.com/jobs/2003/11/2003111001c.htm>.

Laurence, David. "The 1999 MLA Survey of Staffing in English and Foreign Language Departments." *Profession 2001.* New York: MLA, 2001. 211–24.

Adrielle Mitchell

CREATIVE PROFESSIONALIZATION
Inculcating Divergent Career Concepts in Doctoral Candidates

Though doctoral candidates in English are considered, and consider themselves, highly intelligent critical thinkers, they show a remarkable group mentality when it comes to fashioning themselves for future employment. Despite recent efforts by the MLA, thoughtful graduate departments, and leaders outside research universities, alternate paths for the English PhD are still seen as clear and utterly divergent choices: you enter either academia or the business, government, and not-for-profit sector (BGN). This binary split reinforces the oral tradition of shelf life and creates a strained, overdelineated division between academics and others. I find this paradigm uncomfortably linear and, finally, dangerous for those who have invested many years, and significant mental energy, taking doctoral degrees.

Unfortunately for aspirants to the professoriat, the market offers tenure-track positions to perhaps only half the holders of recent degrees:

> Our best information suggests that the odds of new PhDs in language and literature finding full-time academic employment in their fields immediately after graduation have been no better than 50-50 and are often lower, while the odds of finding a full-time tenure-track position in the five years after earning the degree have been about two out of three.   (MLA, par. 1)

Thus many recent PhDs face career prospects quite different from the ones they expected as graduate students. They also face the daunting psychological work of reconstituting egos and self-definitions in the light of brutal professional realities. But what if it were possible to position oneself in another way? What if the border between academia and outside academia is more porous, more traversable than we believe?

Although current scholarship in language and literature revels in the fluidity of borders, we are hard-pressed to find the same fluidity in professional constitution. Fluid acts seem reserved for fictional characters, literary theorists, and cultural critics; academics chart straight, linear, and persistent career paths. Implicitly embedded in an institution's ethos, such messages to doctoral candidates can sound terribly like dicta or lectures. One can imagine the university saying, "You're here at the research-intensive institution: we will give you some temporary, ephemeral privileges so you can practice being an academic—extended library privileges, some teaching experience, health benefits, specialization training, quasi-collegiality with faculty members, access to conferences and publication. But hurry! Publish, teach, and build your curriculum vitae here under the safety of our institutional cloak. You can even borrow our letterhead for your job applications. Be timely, efficient, and articulate; leave us soon, but in ways that make us proud of ourselves—seek and attain a tenure-track position in a research university or, if you have to, a four-year college."

The real journey from first-year English doctoral student to employed professional, as we came to understand by the early 1990s, is long, complex, antilinear, and by no means assured. As Maresi Nerad and Joseph Cerny note in their landmark article "From Rumors to Facts: Career Outcomes of English Ph.D.s," the dominant career trajectory of professors looks very much like a two-part process, consisting of a first student stage and a second job-acquisition stage:

> An English doctoral student's journey from the beginning of graduate school to degree completion is long and arduous; for some, equally lengthy is the journey from time of Ph.D. completion to stable employment. This second stage of the journey, the transition from Ph.D. completion to work, left many individuals with hopes unrealized and a need to rethink career aspirations.   (3)

My own career trajectory contained equal stages of professionalization: six years from BA to PhD, six more years from PhD acquisition to stable tenure-track employment. The types of learning, professional experience, employment, and self-fashioning in these two periods were starkly different and equally important. A complex interrelation, or layered professionalization process, emerged from these separate experiences. The professor I am today is an amalgamation of my development as a scholar and teacher of literature and theory (stage 1) and my surprising, but rewarding, transformation into an English educator (stage 2) with primary responsibilities in secondary English teacher preparation.

My case illustrates both a successful revisioning of professional self, as I did ultimately land a tenure-track position, and an unsuccessful professional formation period at the crucial first stage of my career, my graduate education. I experienced a terrible sense of anxiety and failure at the transition point between stages 1 and 2 (solid performance throughout my graduate tenure—conference presentations, excellent teaching, quicker than average completion of degrees, no leaves of absence, community involvement—but no job offer in the degree receipt year, or the next, or the next). Failing to secure a tenure-track position just when one is most competent, ready, and desirous is starkly difficult: one feels stagnant, ashamed, at turns angry at others and oneself, underemployed, confused, you name it. At best, one can retool, but the negative self-assessment lingers:

> Unfortunately, many PhDs begin to explore the full range of employment opportunities available to them only after they have been unable to find a suitable academic position. As a consequence, that decision is usually experienced as one of defeat and personal failure. (MLA, par. 10)

Graduate students would benefit from thinking flexibly and creatively about their careers *before* degree acquisition.

PROFESSIONAL MENTORING

English doctoral students consistently state that though they found their programs solid, enriching, and worthwhile, the amount of professional mentoring in their programs was inadequate: "The recent poll by the National Association of Graduate-Professional Students of current graduate students in English shows that the fostering of professional development in graduate programs received very low approval rates" (MLA, par. 3). This inadequacy, what Nerad and Cerny call a "culture of neglect" (9), significantly hampers the job-acquisition process. It postpones realistic self-assessment, limits professional identity formation, and routinizes graduate education. I believe that mentoring geared to the skills and interests of each graduate student would immensely help this situation. Graduate faculty members should help their doctoral candidates inculcate divergent career concepts as early and as specifically as they can. We in the profession are used to thinking of graduate students en masse (first-years, third-years, those who have completed all but their dissertations), by specializations (the medievalists, the twentieth-century British literatures), and as individuals (for letters of recommendation, for teaching assistantships, for research fellowships). These categories work, for the most part, but they function too generally.

In current and future job markets, strict medievalists or twentieth-century Americanists will rarely secure positions in teaching-intensive colleges. Those candidates who successfully transition from graduate school to professorships at the wide array of teaching-intensive colleges and universities usually hold a set of areas of expertise that they can successfully teach at the undergraduate level. Since the teaching-intensive sector of higher education now needs new faculty members who can teach several intellectual fields, ideal candidates will demonstrate scholarly strengths in two or more traditionally defined scholarly areas; knowledge of several bodies of theory; pedagogical experience in a wide range of course types, including first-year .composition; knowledge and use of technological applications in their field and in the classroom; professional scholarship (an article or two and some regional or national conference presentations); and the beginnings of service work (committee work and national and regional organization leadership).

Graduate faculty members and faculty members from liberal arts, comprehensive, and religious colleges and universities, as well as community colleges, proprietary schools, and technical colleges, can help narrowly focused candidates carve out other academic specialties to fit within the cultures of teaching-intensive institutions of higher learning. All of us who enjoy full-time tenure-track positions in American higher education can collectively help future faculty members with answers to the questions, Which organizations should a candidate join? Who can help a candidate learn and use the newest digital applications and resources in his or her areas? What community service work or service learning can a candidate do to develop skills in this venue? What aspects of part-time work are transferable to a candidate's academic curriculum vitae? What internship might he or she seek out? Faculty advisers should maintain a small number of advisees with whom they meet regularly and often to craft a life (and thereby, a curriculum vitae) that is productive, promising, complex, and marketable to future institutions.

Although all faculty members should join together in the important work of training future faculty members, the responsibility for this training rests mainly with the graduate programs that admit doctoral students. These students have distinguished themselves enough to win the interest of graduate programs, have chosen to pursue the terminal degree in the field, and have envisioned themselves—often with the help of graduate faculty members and the imprimatur of research-intensive institutions—as future colleagues. Current members of the research professoriat, then, have a moral obligation to treat every doctoral student (whose continued academic and pedagogical performance is solid) in this specialized, collegial fashion.

In fashioning preprofessional self-identities during the years of graduate study, students can see themselves as broadly as possible and can consider various venues, areas, and skills they might access, without feeling stigmatized for doing so. Opportunities for finding fulfilling work might surprise graduate students, but recognizing the skills humanities PhDs can offer in different employment situations will enable candidates to carve niches for themselves in this territory, especially candidates offered systematic help. In "A Little Advice from 32,000 Graduate Students," Kimberly Suedkemp Wells and Adam Fagen suggest that students carefully consider their talents, even in ways that are not highlighted in the mentoring they receive from graduate faculty members:

> Don't forget about the "hidden skills" that might not initially come to mind. If you teach, maybe you've also learned how to plan and how to motivate. There are a lot of abilities that you probably take for granted, but potential employers might not: language, communication, analytic and writing skills.   (par. 9)

My experience exemplifies this advice.

Entering from the Side Door:
The English Education Surprise

My story begins like many you have read: I entered the doctoral program in literature at the University of California, Santa Cruz, in 1989 (at age twenty-one), the very year that William Bowen and Julie Ann Sosa confidently but erroneously predicted a radical increase in the projected need for college and university professors beginning in the mid-1990s. I immersed myself in the heady sexual, cultural, and political theory so popular then, taking courses like Medieval Women Writers, and The Gothic Imagination in the literature department and the equally compelling courses Representation, Feminist Theory (with Donna Haraway), and Place, Space, and Subject in the illustrious History of Consciousness Program (which housed its own, more competitive doctoral program but allowed doctoral students from other departments to take its courses). I did well, earning strong course evaluations (Santa Cruz was, at the time, a grade-free institution) and successfully assisting and teaching a number of courses for the literature and philosophy departments. I self-selected a specialty area: British and American modernism, with little comprehension that the job market would ill-support this choice. I carved out twentieth-century poetry (early- to mid-century) as an area I could teach. Despite some personal hardships, I hung on and finished my dissertation in 1995, just shy of my twenty-seventh birthday, a neat, reasonably successful six-year gallop from BA to PhD.

I felt like an overachiever because of my youth and endurance. The job market, however, quickly reduced my stature, yielding no offers in 1994 and in 1995. There is nothing quite like the slow dawning recognition that being an excellent candidate among excellent candidates is not enough. It became apparent that coming from a highly theoretical institution favoring interdisciplinary, meditative courses over genre- or period-based instruction worked against my prospects on the job market. Complicating matters further, I had specialized in an oversubscribed area and had not published yet.

Everything ground to a halt, and I realized that I needed employment. Mercifully, the University of California, Santa Cruz, offered me a one-year lectureship that involved teaching several courses in my field, including Survey of American Poetry, Part B—Late Nineteenth- through Mid-Twentieth Centuries, which allowed me to preserve some self-respect.

The salary—$12,000—was not enough to maintain any sort of life in Central Coast, California, however. Tapping into my undergraduate reserves, I resurrected the fallback high school English teaching certification I had earned in New York and converted it to California certification. This enabled me to take a half-time position teaching in Santa Cruz's Alternative Education Programs (juvenile offenders, expelled students, and pregnant teens), and then the chaotic synergy of my two lives as an adjunct academic and a part-time social service employee began to shake each other up.

For the next five years, I developed these two sides of my professional self, teaching three or four courses each year for the university and working in various capacities for the Alternative Education Department. The money added up nicely, and I developed all kinds of skills. I do not discuss here the jarring incidents of moving back and forth between the two jobs, the stresses inherent in a split professional life, or the profound difficulties of working with at-risk youth. Yet because my enthusiasm for self-fashioning does not deny the very real challenge of such work, I want graduate students reading this to understand that viable, progressive, and ultimately successful career development may entail stress and pain. Recognizing that a doctorate in English (literature) was valuable to my employer, I began to offer my services in grant writing, curriculum development, and professional leadership. I had no background or training in these areas, but I had ample writing and research know-how, which served me well.

Soon, half my half-time job with the Alternative Education Department consisted of administrative and curricular work. The teaching side of the position led me to develop and implement a service-learning partnership between a section of first-year composition at the university and a group of juvenile offenders enrolled at various schools in Alternative Education Programs. The two sections focused on themes related to the juvenile justice system, yielding incredible work from all the students involved as well as an article about the process of teaching these sections from me. All this, in turn, led to a full-time curriculum position in Denver, Colorado. Finally, this experience allowed me to market myself in academia again, but now as something new: a PhD in literature, a five-year adjunct instructor with a wide range of teaching experience at the undergraduate level, and an

English educator with significant experience teaching grades 7–12, administrating, developing curricula, and writing grants.

I cannot mark the exact moment I realized that it might be possible to enter academia through a side door—that is, differently than I had originally expected. One small, targeted job search later (six years after receipt of the doctorate), and it worked: I was offered, and accepted, a tenure-track position as coordinator of English education and assistant professor of English at a small, private, liberal-arts centered, comprehensive institution (Nazareth College of Rochester, New York). In this position, I administrate, supervise student-teachers, and teach English education courses, literature courses, feminist theory, and First-Year College Writing. In one position, I teach in all the fields I had explored since receiving my doctorate.

ENGLISH EDUCATION

Though the central point of my essay is that graduate students must be actively assisted in carving out a professional identity, I say a little more here about the field of English education itself, a field I neither targeted nor trained in, but ended up occupying and enjoying.

English education is a catch-all term for the wide-ranging field of elementary and secondary teacher education and curriculum development in the field of English. In a somewhat unusual situation, English educators exist in both academic and nonacademic (BGN) positions. Curriculum specialists, grant writers, in-service teacher workshop leaders, writers, instructors of methods of teaching English courses, student-teacher supervisors, editors of educational materials (housed at publishing companies), and test writers are all English educators.

If one believes that English language and literature instruction at the precollegiate level is important, then one must consider the work of English educators to be so as well. Unfortunately this work is, for the most part, poorly understood, somewhat hidden, and rarely considered by English department faculty members. Even at institutions that train undergraduates to teach secondary English and graduate students to teach tertiary English, the two programs rarely connect in any meaningful or sustained way. Note English education's omission even from a fairly comprehensive list of important English pathways developed by the MLA Ad Hoc Committee on the Professionalization of PhDs:

> Departments should consider how they reveal, through their practices and policies, the value they place on various professional activities: research and publication; undergraduate teaching and broad humanistic education; *continuing* education of secondary school teachers; new developments and changes in the field; the study of rhetoric and composition, creative and expository writing, and applied linguistics and language-acquisition theory.   (par. 18, emphasis added)

I laud the injunction to curtail the derogation of certain areas of language and literature such as rhetoric and composition, teaching itself (as opposed to research), and language acquisition, but I regret the reduction of English education to only one small component of professional activities ("continuing education of secondary teachers"). Precollegiate instruction should concern us all, as it directly shapes the quality of students we see in our undergraduate and graduate courses. If we want students who demonstrate adequate literacy and critical literacy skills, we should make it our business to create dialogue with K–12 instructors. Training future primary and secondary teachers of English is a job we should not devalue for its inherent pedagogical worth or, more selfishly, for its effect on our college classes.

Furthermore, I believe English doctoral programs offer transferable skills to the field of English education. Most English educators receive their training in education departments, earning social science doctorates (the EdD). The education doctorate usually involves extensive training in pedagogy, giving less attention to the subject area itself—in this case, language and literature. Members of Nazareth's English department, in fact, commented on their disappointment with the finalists for my position who held doctorates in English education rather than English. EdD candidates, though bright and pedagogically savvy, did not study literary analysis or broad humanities scholarship and thus proved ill-suited to an English education position housed in the English department. My application succeeded because of my strong humanities background, not despite it.

In the light of concerns regarding the intersection of disciplinary and pedagogical epistemologies, consider what the National Council of Teachers of English (NCTE) Conference on English Education (CEE) recommends for the future English education professoriat:

> The Commission, meeting over the course of a decade to discuss issues involved in the development of new faculty as English educators, articulate in their report a vision for the type of individuals they hope will complete graduate programs in English education: Self-aware individuals, with a commitment to lifelong learning and ongoing inquiry into practice including their own. Knowledgeable individuals who are well aware of the current research and theory that guides effective practice in the English classroom. Individuals committed to collaboration—in their work with school and university colleagues in their own programs, and in their work with colleagues nationally through their affiliations with professional organizations and other professional networks. Individuals who are astute observers of teaching.
>
> (Smith et al. 7)

As graduate programs in English across the nation shore up their development of these skills (albeit for different reasons, among them training teaching assistants, preparing students for the professoriat, reacting to current pedagogical research that privileges an active, democratic classroom and collaborative work), it is possible for us to state unequivocally that English PhDs will hold skills that are easily transferable to English education.

More important, graduate programs in English and foreign languages foster and produce sophisticated textual interpreters capable of engaging in nuanced readings and critical analyses of a wide range of texts. Though speaking of Australian English education, Bronwyn Mellor and Annette Patterson comment on the value of complex and culturally grounded literary instruction at the secondary level. They isolate the following key principles of such a pedagogy:

> the conception of texts and readings as "made" or constructed;
> the idea that a piece of literature emerges not from a timeless, placeless zone, but from a particular social context and that it is read in another context;
> the argument that texts and readings are never neutral (87).

Who better than English and foreign language doctoral students to engage in such practice and to teach these instructional principles to future secondary educators?

Theory has come to the secondary classroom in the United States, just as it has in Australia. Faculty members and administrators at primary and secondary levels of education actively revise curricula, incorporate texts representing different ways of knowing and different strata of society into classrooms, and critique limited definitions of literacy. With this exciting intellectual work taking place outside colleges and universities, new possibilities for engagement in the fields of primary and secondary English education present themselves routinely to astute students and faculty members in higher education. Look at the complexity of the questions posed by Mellor and Patterson:

> What has changed as a result of poststructural interventions in reading practices in English classrooms? It may be useful to begin with the changes in the kinds of questions we might ask about texts to signal the shifts in different "models" or approaches to teaching English. Rather than asking, for example, *What does this text mean?* or *What does this text mean to you?*, we now ask questions such as: What are possible readings of this text? Where could such different readings come from? How might such different readings be constructed? What values might such readings support or affirm, or oppose?
>
> (91)

The intellectual gap between secondary and tertiary education is narrowing, I believe. As such, graduate faculty members and students in English departments can participate in shaping the promise of English education.

———

If graduate students and recent PhD recipients think about making connections between their academic work and the work they choose to do or must do to survive, they may find synergistic, cumulative intersections that enhance their academic profiles. Cross-disciplinary thinking and interinstitutional consortia can help students in graduate school; when choosing jobs, internships, or areas of expertise; and after graduate school. The reality of the current job market indicates that one out of every two or three degree recipients will not land the full-time position he or she is seeking. After several years of fruitless job market experience, many frustrated PhDs tend to give up, resigning themselves to something else. Some of us find true career satisfaction this way and are not "resigned" at all, but many remain disaffected, depressed, and traumatized by the loss of their idealized conception of the profession and the professoriat.

I suggest, and I hope my career progress in the five years after receipt of my doctorate suggests, that some autonomous thinking might alter, and make more attractive, a candidate's curriculum vitae. Retooling, reshaping, and adding broader educational elements to one's experience might be helpful in crafting a new self to market a little later; it has been my experience (personal and, on the other side of the table now, during search committee work) that people who market themselves carefully and specifically some years from the degree receive favorable consideration from committees. Shelf life might not be as rigid and real as urban legend implies.

Graduate faculty members, in turn, can aid their doctoral students by teasing out additional features that will strengthen their job candidacy over a span of years. They can attend to cultural and personal distinctions that do not mirror the standard graduate career trajectory but may provide evidence of enhanced suitability for a professorship (e.g., a service orientation, skill in student guidance, outside experience, or cultural sensitivity). With a long view in mind, graduate mentors can provide recommendations for and encouragement to students seeking additional scholarly communities in which to belong at the global, national, and local levels. These communities might diverge somewhat from the student's main areas of focus, thereby augmenting the student's curriculum vitae and preparation to teach a variety of courses.

Finally, instead of letting the relationship with doctoral recipients who have not secured tenure-track positions become awkward, graduate faculty members could expect this situation to materialize for half their advisees, warn them in advance, and pledge their support regardless of the outcome of their job searches. Continued support could manifest itself as assistance in retooling, enhancing, or solidifying doctoral recipients' preparation for a successful post-PhD career (academic or otherwise). These strategies, if followed conscientiously for each advisee, could result in significantly improved mentorship at the graduate level, as well as increased job prospects for future students and better cross-cultural exchanges among practitioners from all sectors of higher education.

WORKS CITED

Bowen, William G., and Julie Ann Sosa. *Prospects for the Faculty in the Arts and Sciences: A Study of Factors Affecting Demand and Supply, 1987–2012.* Princeton: Princeton UP, 1989.

Mellor, Bronwyn, and Annette Patterson. "Poststructuralism in English Classrooms: Critical Literacy and After." *International Journal of Qualitative Studies in Education* 17.1 (2004): 83–98.

MLA Ad Hoc Committee on the Professionalization of PhDs. "Professionalization in Perspective." MLA. 8 July 2004 <http://www.mla.org/resources/documents/professionalization>.

Nerad, Maresi, and Joseph Cerny. "From Rumors to Facts: Career Outcomes of English Ph.D.'s." *Communicator* 32.7 (1999): 1–11.

Smith, Emily, et al. "On Learning to Teach English Teachers: A Textured Portrait of Mentoring." *English Education* 36.1 (2003): 6–34.

Wells, Kimberly Suedkemp, and Adam Fagen. "A Little Advice from 32,000 Graduate Students." *Chronicle of Higher Education* 14 Jan. 2002. 8 July 2004 <http://chronicle.com/job/2002/01/2002011401c.htm>.

HEIDI ESTREM

MAKING PEDAGOGY
OUR BUSINESS

*Strengthening the Ties between English
Education and Composition-Rhetoric*

THE RELATIONSHIP BETWEEN COMPOSITION-RHETORIC
AND ENGLISH EDUCATION

At its core, composition-rhetoric is a "teaching subject," as Joseph
Harris has named it.[1] Many scholars trace composition-rhetoric's modern roots to studies based on writers in classrooms: Janet Emig's work
with revision, for example, and Donald Graves's studies of elementary-
aged writers. Still, there remains some hesitance over embracing
composition-rhetoric's rich connections with pedagogy. During a discussion on the Writing Program Administrators' e-mail discussion list,
participants debated the relative merits of describing the field as
composition—with its explicitly pedagogical connections—versus
something like discourse studies, for example ("Western States"). The
reality remains, though, that the primary strength of composition-
rhetoric has been the willingness of its theorists and practitioners to
see teaching as a site for research and discovery rather than as an activity disassociated from research.

Compositionists well-trained in first-year writing pedagogy and
administration, and in composition-rhetoric scholarship more generally, leave their graduate programs to teach at a wide range of institutions. Whether explicitly acknowledged or not, teaching in many
English departments means teaching English education—and those
ties are even more explicit for writing specialists. As Robert Tremmel
notes, too often the faculty members who train teaching assistants and
those who prepare future public school teachers for their careers work

side-by-side without realizing that they both enact the enterprise of "writing teacher education." Further, while the work of educating teaching assistants to teach first-year writing falls on the composition-rhetoric faculty, it may not be as evident that educating preservice teachers (students intending to be K–12 teachers), whether in courses explicitly labeled methods courses or not, is, at many schools, also expected of English department faculty members of all kinds, including those with backgrounds in literature, journalism, and composition. With this in mind, we would do well to consider how a composition-rhetoric PhD can and should encompass K–12 writing pedagogy.

Practically speaking, a focus on working with public schools will broaden the options of job candidates as well as help them contribute to the important work done with preservice teachers in positions they may take. The strong job market for those with well-rounded backgrounds in either composition or literary theory as well as K–12 pedagogy and the growing demand for public school teachers bode well for broadly trained future faculty members.[2] Although it is always dangerous to generalize from the experiences of one, I do think my current position has features many composition-rhetoric teacher-scholars will recognize. Working from the skills and connections I need now, then, and pausing to consider briefly how key moments in disciplinary and institutional history have affected the fields of composition-rhetoric and English education, I will trace the kinds of experiences that can help enlarge graduate students' perspectives on K–12 teaching.

Spinning the Plates: Work at a Teaching-Intensive University

First, a brief explanation. Eastern Michigan University (EMU) is a regional comprehensive campus that prides itself on being "the largest producer of professional educators in the nation" (Polite). The student population is diverse in many ways—socioeconomically, ethnically, and regionally. While EMU offers a full range of majors, the university's strength lies in preparing students interested in K–12 education. In this large, vibrant campus, then, those who profess are also those who teach. I use "teaching" in this section's title because of EMU's focus on preparing future teachers and because professors here identify teaching as an important part of their careers and identities. Teaching loads are heavy, and, in addition to helping students in the classroom, service to the institution and research for the discipline are expected.

I teach first-year writing, coadminister our first-year writing program, and teach and develop methods courses for future K–12 teachers. I work closely with composition-rhetoric colleagues on various aspects of first-year writing, undergraduate writing courses, and MA writing degree options; I also work with colleagues who identify themselves more as English educators because we are heavily involved and invested in the methods and graduate courses that target preservice and practicing teachers. English education and written communications, as we call it here, are closely linked, and all the EMU English education faculty members participate on the Written Communications Committee, even though at least two of the English education faculty members' backgrounds are in education rather than writing. On any given day, I might teach a first-year writing class, talk to a graduate student about how to implement peer response into her pedagogical practice, teach a Writing for Writing Teachers class, and receive an e-mail from a student teacher struggling to work on revision with high school students. This is my dream job: I work with writers at many levels and discuss pedagogy extensively.

The Close Ties, and Tensions, between Composition-Rhetoric and Pedagogy

My kind of position is not unusual; I can immediately think of many teacher-scholars whose work I admire because they devote their careers to first-year writing pedagogy and administration as well as to K–12 pedagogy instruction. Patricia Lambert Stock at Michigan State University established and helped coordinate the Writing Center, worked as a high school teacher, and is a past president of the National Council of Teachers of English (NCTE). Lad Tobin, Susan Tchudi, and Stephen Tchudi represent a large contingent of composition scholars who have taught high school or secondary pedagogy for English teachers at some point in their careers or who continue to identify themselves as both compositionists and English educators. And there are many, many others who began as English educators of some kind and eventually specialized in composition theory and practice, or vice versa. Enough compositionists go on to have these kinds of mixed careers that it is important to keep their experience in mind and consider how those in graduate programs might best prepare their students to select a professional identity.

Acknowledging that the possibility of mixed careers exists for composition-rhetoric PhDs mitigates the homogenizing force specialization exerts in the discipline. As Dan Royer and Roger Gilles report:

> the first generation of writing theorists thought little of the distinction between "English ed" and "comp/rhet," [but] it seems unusual today for the two to meet. NCTE [the annual conference of the NCTE] and CCCC [the national conference for college-level writing educators, the Conference on College Composition and Communication] draw different groups of people, though this was not always so.   (106)

Indeed, those who identify as English educators have felt marginalized enough at CCCC to form a special interest group focused on English education's role in the composition community. For the past several years, this group has shared concerns about—and brainstormed possibilities to address—the perception that composition-rhetoric devalues English education work. As specializations increase in the field and as compositionists increasingly undertake a wide variety of positions in it (as writing program administrators, writing-across-the-curriculum or writing center directors, computers and writing specialists, and so on), reclaiming the vision of "English ed" and "comp/rhet" as having shared goals and interests will underscore the relevance of pedagogy to praxis.

Composition-rhetoric's pedagogical bent was readily highlighted in the 1960s in general and at the Dartmouth Conference in particular. The Dartmouth Conference in 1966, and the narratives that sprang from it, delineates a moment where

> two opposing ideas of English—one centered on loyalty to a certain kind of knowledge, the other rooted in a certain view of the classroom—met head on and found that they seemed to be talking about different subjects. The Americans tried to define the subject matter of English apart from the ways it was taught; the British saw the work of teachers and students as an intrinsic part of what that subject was.   (Harris 13)

Despite the divisions that remained after the conference and that continue today—an identification of theory with texts and ideas rather than with the classroom, which persists throughout English departments, even if to a lesser extent for compositionists—Harris identifies the importance of those at the conference (John Dixon, James Britton, and James Moffett, largely) who "proved that one can do serious work in English not only by studying literature or criticism but also by looking closely at the talk and writing of students" (17). For Harris, then, the conference's pedagogical focus makes it key to the history of composition-rhetoric.

Uncovering the roots of composition-rhetoric, Stephen North also identifies the significance of the Dartmouth Conference, naming it "part of the reform of English as a whole." Further, he writes, it marked the beginning of an effort to "find or create in Rhetoric a basis for Composition—not so much . . . to reclaim the classical tradition as a pedagogical system, but to invoke its voices as precursors in an age-less debate" (93). In North's conception of composition, the 1960s marks a time when compositionists turned to historical rhetoric rather than to educational traditions as a means of discovering a history and place for themselves. The early tension between pedagogical and historical or rhetorical perspectives on composition-rhetoric has an impact on current compositionists.

The significance of the Dartmouth Conference to composition-rhetoric and to pedagogical studies is two-fold: first, the conference participants who have most influenced writing instructional theory (Britton, Moffett, and Dixon) saw themselves as teachers and made practice their basis for theoretical speculation and discovery. Second, writing and writing instruction came into focus as a clear object of study. While the tension highlighted between the American subject-driven view and the British student-centered "growth model" view remains to this day, the important work of unabashedly regarding the classroom as a site of study, reflection, and theory was recognized, if not embraced, in composition-rhetoric.

COMPOSITION-RHETORIC, PEDAGOGY, AND THE COMPREHENSIVE UNIVERSITY'S NORMAL SCHOOL ROOTS

Like many other regional comprehensive state colleges and universities across the country, Eastern Michigan University began as a normal school. EMU's direct mission, in fact, was to be the first

"teacher- training institution west of the Alleghenies" ("Why EMU?").
Kathryn Fitzgerald's historical account of the role of composition and
pedagogy in nineteenth-century midwestern normal schools like EMU
demonstrates how the normal school ethic and mission both complicate and enrich composition-rhetoric's relation with English education.
Other histories of writing instruction at the collegiate level, however,
usually focus on its early roots in elite eastern institutions and some
midwestern and western land-grant universities and overlook the place
of the normal school (e.g., Berlin; Russell). A brief examination of the
role of the normal school helps place the state regional and comprehensive universities, the descendants of normal schools.

Fitzgerald argues that many current notions about writing pedagogies find their origins in earlier pedagogical theories and practices developed by faculty members from normal schools, including a recognition
of "the interrelation of theory and practice; the responsibility of the
discipline for teaching teachers to teach" (225). These stances were
possible at normal schools, she writes, because normal schools, unlike
the colleges to which composition's roots are traditionally traced,
"were intended to be inclusive, democratic institutions that focused
on professional rather than academic preparation" and drew on different "intellectual traditions. . . . [N]ormal school faculties had access to
European pedagogical theories as well as composition textbooks"
(244). These two factors created a "unique normal school ethos," one
that had as its "most notable feature . . . the active integration of theory and practice" (244).

Several researchers argue that the integration of normal schools
into state universities (for myriad reasons, including the desire to attract more male students and to increase degree options) "had the effect of destroying the status of pedagogy as a complex human endeavor
uniting theory, research, art, and method in a mutually constructive
conversation" (Fitzgerald 245 [paraphrase of Salvatori; Herbst]). While
composition-rhetoric's role as a discipline in contemporary higher education continues to be fraught with intellectual insecurity, those insecurities increase when faculty members expose or embrace its
pedagogical roots in a university system committed to traditional
scholarship. Composition-rhetoric's connections to K–12 teacher training and pedagogy, however, help professionals in the field as they teach
pedagogy, whether explicitly trained for it or not. Further, many grad-

uates will work for much, if not all, of their careers in teaching-oriented institutions, often state universities with historical roots as normal colleges or new agendas as teacher-preparation institutions, so composition-rhetoric is poised to direct conversations about research, scholarship, and the teacher-scholar's professional identity.

As I have grown into this position at EMU and my professional identity in higher education, I recognize the ways my graduate school experiences prepared me for the multiple facets of this job. (As a side note, while my graduate program in composition-rhetoric was not impervious to the tensions between pedagogy and theory, composition-rhetoric and English education were largely presented as integrated disciplines. In fact, until I took the position at EMU and began working in this large, diverse department, I did not realize how separately the two disciplines can be perceived.) Other experiences would also have been valuable preparation for a position like this one. At the risk of overusing a phrase that appears everywhere from textbooks to self-help tomes, there are several "habits of mind" extremely valuable for composition-rhetoric scholars who will work with preservice teachers. Graduate schools should begin to cultivate these ways of thinking about writing teacher education.

Habit of Mind 1: Literacy Education Is Theoretical

The popular imagination casts preservice teachers as wanting only what works in the classroom while hoping to skip over the theoretical implications of those practices. Yet I have found that when I am able to blend theoretical understandings with practical experiences (praxis), students embrace and even seek out theory. Further, they begin to see the classroom as an opportunity to understand and explore theory and to see theory as an intellectual product often born from the classroom.

To cultivate an understanding of K–12 (writing) pedagogy as theoretical, graduate seminars must engage students in theoretical, thoughtful material—writings by Donald Murray, as well as Mikhail Bakhtin, Thomas Newkirk, and Michel Foucault, and other recent, influential voices in K–12 writing pedagogy such as Tom Romano and Katie Wood Ray. Graduate students, especially those who have not considered K–12 education as part of their future career responsibilities, need to encounter texts that show them how to ground theory in practice.

HABIT OF MIND 2: LITERACY EDUCATION IS PRACTICAL

There's no denying that credibility factors into the relationships of future teachers and their current professors. Preservice teachers might think, "Well, all this writing process stuff is nice, but you haven't taught eighth graders or 125 students or remedial English." College and university faculty members need not have taught every grade that our students might teach to understand difficult K–12 working conditions and successful K–12 pedagogies, although the credibility that comes from firsthand classroom experiences is invaluable. Even though I have not taught as a licensed teacher, my students trust my ideas because I draw from the wide range of experiences I have had collaborating with public school teachers in public school classrooms. While actually having been certified as a public school teacher and working in a public school is an advantage, composition-rhetoric faculty members can gain public school experience in graduate school without going through the teacher certification process by proactively seeking partnerships with K–12 teachers.

To cultivate an appreciation of the day-to-day practice of K–12 teaching, graduate programs can encourage students to observe and listen (skills that we all need to practice continually). As part of a seminar experience or as an internship requirement for a degree, graduate students can participate in various projects that get them in public schools: working as reading buddies with children, helping in after-school programs, assisting teachers who request help, and becoming a regular presence in a particular school.

Of course, graduate students need to establish and nurture these kinds of relationships with public schools carefully. Many public school faculty members resist university engagement; too often in a university town, they have experienced research as subjects without the power to provide meaningful input. During my graduate years, I spent several semesters in the various sites that made up our school district's alternative education program, an experience that stands out as one of the most significant of my graduate career. Our English department had just formed a relationship with the alternative school as their "partner in education." To be perceived as a partner rather than as researchers swooping down to direct teachers, we explicitly set out to help teachers in any way we could. Sometimes this meant spending hours each week making copies; other times we became more involved in the classroom activities. For one year, I dedicated several hours each week in a classroom for pregnant teenagers correcting multiple-choice tests, participating in reading and writing units, discussing pedagogical ideas with the teacher, and comforting babies in the nursery next door. Other graduate students worked in various capacities for teachers in this school, which was made up of several sites scattered throughout the area, and everyone benefited from dialogue.

Habit of Mind 3: The Principles of Writing Instruction Are the Same, Regardless of Age or Grade Level

Teaching composition to eighteen-year-olds does not exactly mirror teaching writing to second graders, but the same principles underlie instruction at all levels: writers need to write about meaningful, engaging subjects; writers need time and space to develop their ideas; writers need to write for real audiences. When working with college-level writers, I draw from these concepts; when teaching a methods course, I make sure to bring those similarities to the surface and ask students to consider how they might work from these beliefs in various grade levels.

To develop a vision of writing instruction applicable across all grades and ages, graduate programs should avoid focusing so completely on first-year college writing that graduate students fail to identify similar and different aspects of teaching writing. Involvement with a local site of the National Writing Project facilitates an idea of writing instruction, inquiry, and theory as a cross-context enterprise. A model for K–16 teacher inquiry and an invaluable experience for those who will eventually teach future teachers, the National Writing Project also fosters friendships between K–12 and college teachers through its summer institutes, another valuable means to gain access to public schools.

Habit of Mind 4: Teaching Is an Act of Inquiry

Preservice teachers require the skills necessary to question what they see in classrooms and then to act on what they understand about teaching practices. Consequently, when instructing preservice teachers, I remain aware of my teaching as a site for research, thereby showing students the ways in which their classrooms can serve as sites of inquiry and change. In courses with preservice teachers, students should have opportunities to learn about the teacher-research questions we bring with us to their class and then monitor the evolution of those questions throughout the semester. In addition, students should read articles and books that draw explicitly from classroom-based research so they can trace teachers' intellectual trajectory from classroom work to the theoretical implications they draw from that work (by looking at the work of one author—Romano, say—and highlighting his moves between theory and practice).

To cultivate an understanding of teaching as inquiry, the pedagogy of graduate teaching, even in composition-rhetoric PhD programs, should highlight composition-rhetoric's teaching traditions, especially since such traditions attract little interest in our professional journals and at our conferences. While graduate pedagogy may not be explicitly discussed much, Louise Wetherbee Phelps argues that it should be "transparent to any compositionist [that doctoral] pedagogy—teaching methods, curriculum, use of technologies, mentoring practices, assessment—embodies a philosophy of education, including a conception of adult learning and adult development" (118). Many graduate seminars still operate under a model—read, discuss, write a seminar paper at the end—that differs dramatically from the engaged pedagogy we might offer to first-year writers. Graduate courses can reflect and enact a philosophy of education that guides our work with other kinds of writers. After all, graduate students, like first-year writers, encounter a new discipline and struggle with the new writing expectations of graduate school. As such, graduate seminars can become sites in which instructors model appropriate writing pedagogy and provide adequate support for developing writers. Seminars can include reflective writing throughout the course, and professors can reveal their pedagogy, showing graduate students how to develop teacher-research questions. What's more, professors can provide seminar time for writing workshops and feedback and give engaged, thoughtful responses to students' in-progress writing.

Graduate students should also pursue research projects in K–12 settings. Because the partnership with the local alternative school had been so carefully established during my graduate experience, two professors subsequently approached this school and gained permission to place graduate students with teachers as part of a Qualitative Research Seminar. Graduate faculty members gave a presentation to the school's teachers, who then filled out a form asking for a graduate researcher to help them resee a problem or think through a question they had. That semester, as a member of this seminar, I spent several hours each week in a classroom for recently paroled students. The teacher saw me as a partner, as someone who investigated literacy practices and had her own questions but who also discussed his questions with him. Interviewing students about their past literacy experiences gave me invaluable insights into the kinds of issues and problems that, say, a middle-school teacher might face.

EDUCATING FUTURE EDUCATORS

My colleague Cathy Fleischer added "Making Literacy Learning Everybody's Business" as the subtitle to her book. While her book focuses primarily on organizing to bring about change in schools, this subtitle has stayed with me as I continue to think about how, for so many English departments, literacy education is everybody's business. Adding a richer understanding of K–12 writing pedagogy to the graduate school experience in composition-rhetoric will endow graduate students with expertise that will best serve them as they work at colleges where teacher preparation is paramount. Despite ever-increasing specializations, a close study of writing teacher education, whether from the perspective of English education or composition-rhetoric, enriches scholars in both fields and models a professional identity for future K–12 and collegiate faculty members. Educating future educators is everybody's business, and composition-rhetoric scholars can take this reality into consideration as we theorize and promote the discipline. We have a debt to normal schools and a responsibility for preparing K–12 educators.

NOTES

1. Composition-rhetoric as a field is commonly called a variety of names, including composition studies, composition and rhetoric, rhetoric and composition, and Robert Connors's designation composition-rhetoric. For simplicity's sake, I use composition-rhetoric throughout this essay.

2. According to the National Center for Education Statistics, the demand for teachers will far exceed the supply through at least 2010 because of growing enrollments, high teacher attrition, and increasing teacher retirements (Henke and Zahn).

WORKS CITED

Berlin, James A. *Rhetoric and Reality: Writing Instruction in American Colleges, 1900–1985.* Carbondale: Southern Illinois UP, 1987.

Connors, Robert. *Composition-Rhetoric: Backgrounds, Theory, and Pedagogy.* Pittsburgh: U of Pittsburgh P, 1997.

Fitzgerald, Kathryn. "A Rediscovered Tradition: European Pedagogy and Composition in Nineteenth-Century Midwestern Normal Schools." *College Composition and Communication* 53 (2001): 224–45.

Fleischer, Cathy. *Teachers Organizing for Change: Making Literacy Learning Everybody's Business.* Urbana: Natl. Council of Teachers of English, 2000.

Harris, Joseph. *A Teaching Subject: Composition since 1966.* Upper Saddle River: Prentice, 1997.

Henke, Robin R., and Lisa Zahn. "Attrition of New Teachers among Recent College Graduates." *National Center for Education Statistics* 2 Apr. 2001. 31 Aug. 2007 <http://nces.ed.gov/das/epubs/2001189/>.

Herbst, Jurgen. *And Sadly Teach: Teacher Education and Professionalization in American Culture.* Madison: U of Wisconsin P, 1989.

North, Stephen M. *The Making of Knowledge in Composition: Portrait of an Emerging Field.* Portsmouth: Boynton, 1987.

Phelps, Louise Wetherbee. "Reproducing Composition and Rhetoric: The Intellectual Challenge of Doctoral Education." *Composition Studies* 23.2 (1995): 115–32.

Polite, Vernon C. "Welcome Message from the Dean." *College of Education.* Eastern Michigan U. 31 Aug. 2007 <http://www.emich.edu/coe/home/welcome.html>.

Royer, Dan, and Roger Gilles. "Combining History, Theory, and Practice in the Writing Methods Course." *Teaching Writing Teachers.* Ed. Robert Tremmel and William Broz. Portsmouth: Boynton, 2002.

Russell, David R. *Writing in the Academic Disciplines, 1870–1990: A Curricular History.* Carbondale: Southern Illinois UP, 1991.

Salvatori, Mariolina Rizzi, ed. *Pedagogy: Distrubing History, 1819–1929.* Pittsburgh: U of Pittsburgh P, 1996.

Tremmel, Robert. "Seeking a Balanced Discipline: Writing Teacher Education in First-Year Composition and English Education." *English Education* 34 (2001): 6–30.

"Western States Composition Conference." Online posting. 20–24 Jan. 2003. WPA-L. <http://lists.asu.edu/cgi-bin/wa?A1=ind0301&L=wpa-l>.

"Why EMU? Background." *College of Education.* Eastern Michigan U. 31 Aug. 2007 <http://www.emich.edu/coe/home/students/background.html>.

Notes on Contributors

DOUGLAS SCOTT BERMAN (former assistant professor of English, National Taiwan Normal University, 2000–04). The author of essays on theory and aesthetics in *Concentric: Studies in English Literature*, Berman is interested in discourses of professionalism and professionalization from areas as diverse as humanities and law. Fluent in Mandarin Chinese, he completed a PhD in literature from the University of Wisconsin, Milwaukee, in 1999 and earned a JD from Indiana University, Bloomington, in 2007. He now practices law at an international law firm in Hong Kong.

NANCY J. BROWN (associate professor of English, Lourdes College). Author of "A History of Lourdes College," which appears in *Cradles of Conscience* (2003), Brown is committed to academic life at a small college. After receiving her MA from the University of Toledo, she completed doctoral course work there in American Romanticism in 1992. She is a PhD candidate in community literacy at Wayne State University. Brown teaches composition, history of English, theoretical approaches to reading and writing, introduction to literature, and upper-division literature courses.

JO ANN BUCK (professor of English, department chair of English and humanities, Guilford Technical Community College). Buck earned her BA and MA in English at the State University of New York, Fredonia, and her PhD in curriculum and instruction at the University of North Carolina, Greensboro. She studies creative pedagogies and the influence of communication on effective leadership. Buck has been awarded the Board of Trustees Innovative Teaching Award and the SAMLA award for Excellence in Teaching.

GINNY CARNEY (vice president of academic and student affairs, Leech Lake Tribal College). Carney (Cherokee) holds a PhD in English from the University of Kentucky. She is past president of the Association for the

Study of American Indian Literatures and has published in anthologies and journals. She was the recipient of the 2001 Academic Writer of the Year Award from Wordcraft Circle of Native Writers for her book *Eastern Band Cherokee Women: Cultural Persistence in Their Letters and Speeches* (2005).

ROBERT CHIERICO (chair, Department of Foreign Languages and Literatures, Chicago State University). Chierico earned his BA and MA from Roosevelt University in Chicago and a PhD in Spanish literature from Northwestern University. He completed a certificate in Spanish business from Spain and taught business Spanish for many years. He teaches classes related to twentieth-century Spanish literature and Spanish culture. As director of the study-abroad program in Toledo, Spain, Chierico has traveled with students, guiding them in their research projects on Spanish culture. As director of the Hispanic Future Professionals Academy, Chierico has received funding from the state of Illinois since 2004 to support a high school–college transition program for Hispanic high school students.

ELLEN COHEN (professor of English as a second language, Arizona Western College). Involved in teacher training and TESOL in the United States and Mexico since 1979, Cohen holds an MA in teaching English as a second language from the University of Arizona. She is coauthor of *Spotlight* (1988) and *Prism* (1992). Cohen teaches ESL structure, reading and writing, and pronunciation courses and serves as the modern languages academic adviser. She has also been the director of the Center for Teaching Effectiveness and the South County ESL coordinator. The curricula she developed for Generation 1.5 students at Arizona Western College has been successfully integrated into the curriculum. She was named Arizona Western College 2002–2003 Teacher of the Year and is a recipient of the NISOD Excellence Award.

STEPHEN DA SILVA. After taking his PhD in English from Rice University, da Silva accepted a position at a private Catholic high school, where he teaches senior advanced-placement English, junior advanced-placement English, sophomore honors English, junior college preparation English, senior college preparation English, and an elective on creative writing. He has taught senior dual-credit composition classes with Houston Community College as well and has published five essays on topics in modernism, South Asian literature, and critical theory.

LYNNELL EDWARDS (adjunct professor of English, University of Louisville). For ten years, Edwards taught a variety of writing and literature classes and directed the Writing Center at Concordia University, Oregon. She is the author of two collections of poetry, *The Farmer's Daughter* (2003) and *The Highwayman's Wife* (2007). Her interests include poetry, women's literature, and rhetoric.

HEIDI ESTREM (assistant professor of English, Boise State University). For six years, Estrem taught writing, rhetoric, and pedagogy courses at Eastern Michigan University. She now directs the first-year writing program at Boise State and teaches courses ranging from first-year writing to graduate-level seminars. Her research addresses writing program sustainability and assessment.

FABIOLA FERNÁNDEZ SALEK (assistant professor and coordinator of women's studies, York College, City University of New York). Fernández Salek earned her MA in Spanish, with emphasis on colonial Spanish American literature, and her PhD in Spanish, with a concentration in cultural studies and film, at Arizona State University. Her research focuses on the construction of identity and gender in Latin America.

MACGREGOR FRANK (associate professor of English, Guilford Technical Community College). Frank earned his MA in composition-rhetoric from the University of Maine, Orono, and his PhD in twentieth-century literature in English from the University of North Carolina, Chapel Hill. He teaches composition classes and courses in American literature, in addition to his work with GTCC's Faculty-in-Training teaching associates. Frank's pedagogical and research interests include strategies for optimizing student success and methods of linking the mentoring relationship to professional development.

DEBORAH GILL (associate professor of Spanish, Pennsylvania State University, DuBois). Gill earned her MA and PhD in Spanish, with a specialization in Hispanic linguistics, from the University of Southern California. Her research interests include second language acquisition, languages in contact, and language variation and change. Gill teaches Spanish language courses as well as courses on women in developing countries and women in the arts and humanities. Her recent publications focus on the use of technology in the foreign language classroom. Gill has been awarded the Jack P. Royer Award for Active and Collaborative Learning, the Commonwealth College Excellence in Teaching Award, and the 2007 Alumni Teaching Fellow Award.

ANN E. GREEN (associate professor of English, Saint Joseph's University). A graduate of the University at Albany, State University of New York's program in writing, teaching, and criticism, Green's research and publishing focus on race, class, gender, writing, and service learning. She teaches courses in service learning and writing, including Literacy as Social Practice; Writing through Race, Class, and Gender; and Telling Stories: Men and Women Writing Their Lives. She founded the Saint Joseph's Writing Center and directed it from 1998 to 2004. Green currently directs the graduate program in writing studies.

AERON HAYNIE (associate professor of English, University of Wisconsin, Green Bay). Haynie received her PhD from the University of Florida. Coeditor of *Beyond Sensation: Mary Elizabeth Braddon in Context* (2000) as well as author of essays on Victorian literature, critical pedagogy, and cultural studies, Haynie is currently coediting a book on teaching.

JAMES W. JONES (professor of German and former chair of foreign languages, literatures, and cultures, Central Michigan University). Jones has published articles on German and American gay and lesbian literature and film, especially on the discourses of AIDS and the persecution of gays during the Third Reich. He is the author of *We of the Third Sex: Literary Representations of Homosexuality in Wilhelmine Germany* (1990) and is revising a book manuscript on gay and lesbian literature during the Weimar Republic.

MARK C. LONG (associate professor of English and American studies, Keene State College). Long received his PhD in English from the University of Washington. He teaches writing, American literature, poetry and poetics, American studies, and literature and the environment. Long has published essays and reviews on American poets, environmental writing, and the profession of English. He is coeditor of *Teaching North American Environmental Literature* (2008) and is currently associate editor for the journal *Pedagogy*.

ADRIELLE MITCHELL (associate professor of English, Nazareth College). Mitchell earned her PhD in literature from the University of California, Santa Cruz. She teaches courses in women's literature, composition and rhetoric, advanced grammar theory, English education, young adult literature, and gender studies. Mitchell's research interests include text-image relations, the graphic novel, modernism, world literatures, and English education. She has published articles on the poet Robinson Jeffers, school-university partnerships, and academic careers. Mitchell serves as the coordinator of English education at Nazareth College.

SEAN P. MURPHY (professor of English and humanities, College of Lake County, Illinois). Author of *James Joyce and Victims: Reading the Logic of*

Exclusion (2004) and articles about composition and literature, Murphy created the College of Lake County Graduate Student Internship Program and directed the college's New Faculty Institute for full-time faculty members. He holds an MA in English from the State University of New York, Brockport, and a PhD in literature, cultural theory, and social practice from Kent State University. Murphy teaches critical thinking, composition, surveys of British and Irish literature, and humanities courses.

EVELYNE NORRIS (associate professor of French, Chicago State University). Norris earned her MA in French at Roosevelt University and her PhD in French at Northwestern University, with a specialization in francophone African literature and film. Her primary interests include the integration of African studies in the French curriculum and global education. She teaches French and francophone studies as well as foreign language teacher education courses.

ANNE PASERO (associate professor of Spanish, Marquette University). Translator of the Spanish poet Clara Janés's *Roses of Fire* and author of articles on contemporary Spanish women's poetry and Spanish Renaissance literature, Pasero has taught all levels of Spanish language and literature. She has served as the Marquette in Madrid director on three occasions. Pasero was invited to serve as Vanderbilt University's and PRESHCO consortium's director in Spain. Her interests include Hispanic poetry criticism and translation, study abroad, and international curriculum issues.

CAROL RUTZ (director, Writing Program, Carleton College). Rutz directs the writing program and teaches a writing seminar for first-year students and a writing course for science students. She earned her MA at Hamline University and her PhD in English, with a specialization in composition-rhetoric, at the University of Minnesota. Her publications include three coedited collections: *Classroom Spaces and Writing Instruction* (with Ed Nagelhout, 2004), *Reflections on Learning as Teachers* (with Susan Singer, 2004), and *Building Intellectual Community through Collaboration* (with Mary Savina, 2007).

VICTORIA N. SALMON (affiliate faculty, Higher Education Program, George Mason University). Salmon earned an MA in English at Georgetown University and a DA (doctor of arts), with a concentration in community college education and composition theory, from George Mason University. She taught at Northern Virginia Community College for twenty years. At George Mason University, Salmon is director of graduate studies for the College of Visual and Performing Arts and teaches the scholarship of teaching and learning and theses and dissertations writing. She is vice chair of Georgetown University's Board of Regents.

VIRGINIA SHEN (professor of Spanish, Chicago State University). Author of essays on Latin American and Chinese literature, culture, and teaching methodologies, Shen earned her MA in Latin American literature at Instituto Caro y Cuervo, Bogota, and her PhD in Spanish at Arizona State University. She has been a committed professional in the research and teaching of Spanish and Chinese and has served as president of the Midwest Chinese Language School Association and president of the Mid-America Chinese American Professionals Association.

Teaching and Learning Bibliography

American Association of Community Colleges. *America's Community Colleges: A Century of Innovation*. Washington: Community Coll. P, 2001.

Bain, Ken. *What the Best College Teachers Do*. Cambridge: Harvard UP, 2004.

Bennett, John B. *Collegial Professionalism: The Academy, Individualism, and the Common Good*. Portsmouth: Greenwood; Amer. Council on Educ.–Oryx, 1997.

Boice, Robert. *Advice for New Faculty Members:* Nihil nimus. Needham Heights: Allyn, 2000.

Bowen, William G., et al. *Equity and Excellence in American Higher Education*. Charlottesville: U of Virginia P, 2005.

Boyer, Ernest L. *Scholarship Reconsidered: Priorities of the Professoriate*. San Francisco: Jossey-Bass, 1990.

Brookfield, Stephen D. *Becoming a Critically Reflective Teacher*. San Francisco: Jossey-Bass, 1995.

Brookfield, Stephen D., and Stephen Preskill. *Discussion as a Way of Teaching: Tools and Techniques for Democratic Classrooms*. San Francisco: Jossey-Bass, 1999.

Cohen, Arthur M. *The Shaping of American Higher Education: Emergence and Growth of the Contemporary System*. San Francisco: Jossey-Bass, 1998.

Dougherty, Kevin J. *The Contradictory College: The Conflicting Origins, Impacts, and Futures of the Community College*. Albany: State U of New York P, 1994.

Filene, Peter. *The Joy of Teaching: A Practical Guide for New College Instructors*. Chapel Hill: U of North Carolina P, 2005.

Flores, Stella, ed. *The Unfinished Business of Critical Thinking*. Issue of *New Directions for Community Colleges* 130 (2005).

Freire, Paulo. *Pedagogy of Freedom: Ethics, Democracy, and Civic Courage.* 1998. Trans. Patrick Clarke. Lanham: Rowman, 2001.

——. *Pedagogy of the Oppressed.* 1973. Trans. Myra Bergman Ramos. New York: Continuum, 1993.

Graff, Gerald. *Beyond the Culture Wars: How Teaching the Conflicts Can Revitalize American Education.* New York: Norton, 1992.

Hall, Donald E. *The Academic Self: An Owner's Manual.* Columbus: Ohio State UP, 2002.

Hall, John R., ed. *Reworking Class.* Ithaca: Cornell UP, 1997.

Kamm, Rebecca. *Cases for Community College Teachers: Thought-Provoking and Practical Solutions for Community College Educators.* Stillwater: New Forums, 2001.

Kennedy, Donald. *Academic Duty.* Cambridge: Harvard UP, 1997.

Kolodny, Annette. *Failing the Future: A Dean Looks at Higher Education in the Twenty-First Century.* Durham: Duke UP, 1998.

Laden, Berta Vigil, ed. *Serving Minority Populations.* Issue of *New Directions for Community Colleges* 127 (2004).

Linkon, Sherry Lee, ed. *Teaching Working Class.* Amherst: U of Massachusetts P, 1999.

Lucas, Christopher J., and John W. Murray, Jr. *New Faculty: A Practical Guide for Academic Beginners.* New York: Palgrave, 2002.

McGrath, Dennis, and Martin B. Spear. *The Academic Crisis of the Community College.* Albany: State U of New York P, 1991.

Nelson, Cary, and Stephen Watt. *Academic Keywords: A Devil's Dictionary for Higher Education.* New York: Routledge, 1999.

Nilson, Linda B. *Teaching at Its Best: A Research-Based Resource for College Instructors.* 2nd ed. Bolton: Anker, 2003.

Parini, Jay. *The Art of Teaching.* Oxford: Oxford UP, 2005.

Parks, Stephen. *Class Politics: The Movement for the Students' Right to Their Own Language.* Urbana: Natl. Council of Teachers of English, 2000.

Pickering, Sam. *Letters to a Teacher.* New York: Atlantic Monthly, 2004.

Prégent, Richard. *Charting Your Course: How to Prepare to Teach More Effectively.* Madison: Atwood, 2000.

Readings, Bill. *The University in Ruins.* Cambridge: Harvard UP, 1997.

Reynolds, Mark, and Sylvia Holladay-Hicks, eds. *The Profession of English in the Two-Year College.* Portsmouth: Boynton-Heinemann, 2005.

Rodriguez, Sandria. *Giants among Us: First-Generation College Graduates Who Lead Activist Lives.* Nashville: Vanderbilt UP, 2001.

Roueche, John E., Mark D. Milliron, and Suanne D. Roueche. *Practical Magic: On the Front Lines of Teaching Excellence.* Washington: Community Coll. P, 2003.

Shaw, Kathleen M., James R. Valdez, and Robert A. Rhoads, eds. *Community Colleges as Cultural Texts: Qualitative Explorations of Organizational and Student Culture.* Albany: State U of New York P, 1999.

Shulman, Lee S. *Teaching as Community Property: Essays on Higher Education.* San Francisco: Jossey-Bass, 2004.

———. *The Wisdom of Practice: Essays on Teaching, Learning, and Learning to Teach.* San Francisco: Jossey-Bass, 2004.

Stewart, Deborah A. *Effective Teaching: A Guide for Community College Instructors.* Washington: Community Coll. P, 2004.

Thelin, John R. *A History of American Higher Education.* Baltimore: Johns Hopkins UP, 2004.

Toth, Emily. *Ms. Mentor's Impeccable Advice for Women in Academia.* Philadelphia: U of Pennsylvania P, 1997.

Vaughan, George B. *The Community College Story.* 2nd ed. Washington: Community Coll. P, 2000.

Wolff, Janice M. *Professing in the Contact Zone: Bringing Theory and Practice Together.* Urbana: Natl. Council of Teachers of English, 2002.

Index